The Brawn Story

An American once said that nice guys finish second.

These ones didn't.

The Brawn Story

CHRISTOPHER HILTON

The man and the team that turned Formula 1 upside-down

SECOND EDITION

Haynes Publishing

First hardback edition published in December 2009
This paperback edition, with additional material,
published in May 2010

A catalogue record for this book is available from the
British Library

ISBN 978 1 84425 999 1

Library of Congress catalog card no 2010924916

Published by Haynes Publishing,
Sparkford, Yeovil, Somerset BA22 7JJ, UK
Tel: 01963 442030 Fax: 01963 440001
Int.tel: +44 1963 442030 Int.fax: +44 1963 440001
E-mail: sales@haynes.co.uk
Website: www.haynes.co.uk

Haynes North America Inc.,
861 Lawrence Drive, Newbury Park, California 91320, USA

Designed and typeset by Dominic Stickland
Printed and bound in the USA

CONTENTS

INTRODUCTION

On Friday 28 November 2008 Ross Brawn went to a Heathrow hotel and when he emerged he was facing unemployment. On Wednesday 10 March 2010 he went to Buckingham Palace – up the Grand Staircase, through the Picture Gallery to the Green Drawing Room – and when he emerged he had been decorated by The Queen for his achievements since that Friday in November.

This is a big story about a big man.

It is a compound of adventure, opportunism and terrifying risk, all distilled into those 14 months. It is simultaneously an example of mechanical excellence to beat the world, of many human strengths and some human weaknesses. There are pages with tears running down them; gentle, happy tears, it is true, but tears all the same.

Ross Brawn did what you and I have always dreamed of doing. Your company faces liquidation and in response you buy it. During the life of Brawn Grand Prix, his name would become famous far beyond the confines of Formula 1, the sport he was turning upside down, and when the two championships he contested had been won he took the next big decision. He sold the company.

He'd lost Jenson Button, who took a World Championship with him to McLaren, and gained Michael Schumacher, who brought seven World Championships with him.

A big story? They don't get any bigger.

It reached its natural climax – perhaps summit would be a better word – after the second last race of 2009. Jenson Button was crying in the cockpit if his father John is to be believed. John might not be the most reliable witness because he was crying himself and, he insists, so was everybody around him.

Button sent triumphal whooping noises echoing down the in-car radio and, as he circled slowly round the bowl of a track in the suburbs of São Paulo, he was coming to understand something else. He had joined Mike Hawthorn, Graham Hill, Jim Clark, John Surtees, Jackie Stewart, James Hunt, Nigel Mansell, Damon Hill and Lewis Hamilton, and in a very real sense had touched immortality.

Ross Brawn, who'd spent the Brazilian Grand Prix as he spent every other Grand Prix – impassively watching screens – seemed as composed as ever. He never made whooping noises and spoke so softly it was almost a whisper. While Button was winning so was he: Brawn Grand Prix took the Constructors' Championship. His heritage was to join Enzo Ferrari, John Cooper, Jack Brabham, Ken Tyrrell, Bruce McLaren (posthumously) and Frank Williams as the only men whose cars had won that title carrying their own name. In a very real sense Ross Brawn had touched immortality too.

There was a private moment as Button circled, the race finished. His team-mate Rubens Barrichello, who'd gone into the race looking for the championship himself, drew level and gestured his congratulations. Barrichello subsequently explained that he wanted this privacy because if he'd had to barge through a crowd of well-wishers it would have looked all wrong. Perhaps that caught the essence of the adventure and the tone Ross Brawn had set. In this most frenetic human activity, constantly drawn in extremes, Brawn would proceed with a quiet dignity.

When Jenson got back to the pits John went to embrace him – a long, profound, masculine embrace, a 'big squeeze'. John wore dark glasses. They'd mask his tears.

A television camera loomed at Brawn and he was asked a most innocent question, so innocent nobody would ever remember what it was. He began to answer almost reflexively, the way he had answered so many questions in so many places across the long year, but his voice suddenly changed and faltered. He looked away, something he never did. Tears welled in his eyes and for a long, profound, masculine moment he was visibly struggling to regain control of himself. Nobody had ever seen this before.

The natural climax – the summit – was too much for even strong men to take.

The big story began when Ross Brawn, arch Ferrari strategist in *their* conquests, joined Honda after a sabbatical – he'd been happily fishing – but the global financial credit crunch crunched the Honda team. The story moved from the bidders who didn't bid to the one who did, Brawn himself, although he'd never imagined or sought having his own team. It deepened from an anonymous test session at Silverstone to, within weeks, the beginnings of the conquest. It finished when Mercedes-Benz bought the team at the end of 2009, Button and Barrichello left for new challenges and Schumacher and Nico Rosberg came. Brawn continued to run the team so that, in the best F1 tradition, the end became a beginning again.

Formula 1 is by its nature not only extreme but a jigsaw puzzle of endless moving pieces, and a season is a compilation of endless pieces too. I have tried to reflect that through the medium of the Brawn team in 2009 – their only season – wherever possible quoting what the drivers said when they said it. Often enough they say the same sort of things because they are talking about the same sort of things: practice, qualifying and the race in Australia on 29 March were arranged in exactly the same format as in Abu Dhabi on 1 November. The repetition is the authentic sound of Formula 1.

I am indebted to many good people and true for their insights and memories, particularly Team Principal Ross Brawn and Chief Executive Officer Nick Fry – for making time and telling it exactly as it was – as well as Communications Manager Nicola Armstrong, Brawn's PA Nicole Beame and Fry's PA Denise Hazell.

I pay tribute to the others in no particular order: Russell Sheldon, Senior Vice President of Network Passenger Sales Development at Emirates Airline, Gary Anderson, Eddie Jordan, Frank Dernie, Alastair Macqueen, Louise Goodman, Trevor Steggles, Derek Warwick, Tom Walkinshaw, Jackie Oliver, Rory Byrne, Neil Oatley, Paul Stewart, Steve Matchett, Derek Cooper, McLaren Team Principal Martin Whitmarsh and their Group Head of Communications and Public Relations Matt Bishop.

Clive Gee, Director of Development & Alumni Relations at Brunel University, and Andrew Kershaw of their Media department provided active assistance. Gee sent photographs of Brawn being made an Honorary Graduate.

Actually, of course, there was another summit – the one at Buckingham Palace when Brawn, accompanied by wife Jean and daughters Helen Young and Amy Smith, was given the Order of the British Empire.

Just before he flew out to Bahrain for the start of the 2010 season, Ross Brawn summed up the adventure. 'At the end of my Ferrari career you sat there and thought "it doesn't get any better. Now I can look back and enjoy what we have achieved." Well, it did get better – and it is still getting better. You just keep pinching yourself.'

CHAPTER 1

THE PERFECT STORM

On Monday, 12 November 2007, the Honda Racing F1 Team announced that Ross Brawn, late of Ferrari and on a sabbatical fishing his way round the world, was joining them as Team Principal. He would begin work on 26 November.

At one level the announcement surprised nobody, because Brawn had spent his whole adult life in motor racing and his tactical ability compelled people to gaze at him in awe. Within motorsport that was only part of his reputation. He was known as a planner, a designer and an organiser who had served a hands-on apprenticeship and knew exactly what he was talking about. He played chess, which few knew, and approached any job in motorsport having worked out the combinations several moves ahead.

At another level the Honda team were delighted. Nick Fry, the Chief Executive Officer, said that for six months he'd been attracting new talent to the team in design, engineering, aerodynamics and marketing. Brawn's arrival represented a 'satisfying conclusion [to] the process of refreshing and revitalising a strong and determined team'.

As a multi-national, Honda were particularly serious about their racing – the workforce numbered over 700, for example, and they deployed the largest budget. They bought out the BAR team at the end of 2005. This was a new beginning to an old story. Ken Tyrrell founded and ran his own team from 1970 to 1998 when he sold it to Craig Pollock, driver-manager and entrepreneur, who created British American Racing (BAR) with American tobacco money. In its seven seasons BAR contested 117 races and took 227 points.

Across 2006, Honda's first season as owners, the team scored 86 points to be fourth in the Constructors' Championship.

Jenson Button contributed 56 of them and Rubens Barrichello the other 30. In 2007 the team scored only 6 points, Brawn was available, and it all made perfect sense if they were, in Fry's phrase, to get Honda 'back into championship contention'.

Button was among the delighted. He happened to be testing at Barcelona and said, 'I have spoken to the guy and I cannot wait to meet up with him.' Button hoped the meeting would be soon and they could 'run through a few things. I think everyone is excited about the new appointment. One man does not turn round the whole team but I think his input, his guidance and his direction are going to make a big difference. He has done it all before and I am really looking forward to working with him.'

In turn, Brawn expressed his own excitement and said all the right things, something he was accomplished at. 'Honda has a proud heritage in Formula 1 and the opportunity to help the team to realise its potential represents a fantastic new challenge for me in the sport. The team has already done a great job of giving due consideration to its future and has spent a good deal of time putting in place both people and first-class engineering resources to achieve its ambitions. I look forward to working alongside what I know to be some very talented people and helping Honda to rediscover its winning ways.'

There is an inescapable irony in these words, but remember, Brawn was talking in November 2007 when the full consequences of the credit crunch were unclear, however potentially terrifying. Banks across the western world had lent too much, a lot of it to people who couldn't pay it back, and governments were having to support them. For ordinary people, money tightened, and it would devastate car sales. The Honda Motor Company were as vulnerable as anyone else and, as the crunch deepened across 2008, Brawn himself would explain that in some places Honda's sales were down by 40%.

The racing team, however, had a three-year plan, and so, as it happened, did Brawn. 'I'd had the year's sabbatical and then came back and thought I'll undertake a three-year programme with Honda. If, at the end of it, things haven't worked out well so be it.

'When I joined it was accepted that in 2008 we would compromise to focus on 2009. There's a new set of regulations for 2009 and we started work on the car at the end of 2007, in fact. We said, "Let's leave things as they are for 2008, let's focus on 2009."' Interestingly Brawn had done exactly this once before, with Jaguar in sports cars, and the result was a car which is still regarded as a classic. It was so succcessful that, as Tom Walkinshaw – who hired Brawn – says, they had to change the rules.

'We had the opportunity to put all our resources into the new car and to have more time to put into it,' Brawn says. 'We had 15 months with the full effort of 700 people in the UK, plus more in Japan. McLaren and Ferrari were in a nightmare situation where neither could give up their fight for the title [in 2008] but they were doing that at a time when the regulations were going to change for 2009, so all the development they were still doing right to the end of the season took time and could not be rolled into a new car. Everything they did at the end had to be thrown into the bin.'

Brawn anticipated that when 2009 came around the Honda would be far ahead of the competition, as the Jaguar had been.

On Friday 21 November 2008, Honda made a very different kind of announcement. The company intended to reduce its capacity by 61,000 vehicles in Japan and Europe, including 21,000 at Swindon on top of the 32,000 announced earlier in the year. The factory there would close for 50 days, although no redundancies were planned.

The following Friday, Brawn and Fry attended a meeting with senior Honda executives at an hotel at Heathrow Airport.

Entering the meeting, Brawn felt 'we were going to be able to make changes without affecting our competitive situation'. In short, save money. That caught the general mood because Formula 1 was facing that, too. The Formula One Teams Association (FOTA, Honda a member) were discussing it urgently with the governing body, the FIA.

The Honda management in Tokyo had moved far beyond that. After what seems to have been a period of private agonising – no word of it seeped out – they had decided to leave Formula 1 unilaterally, disbanding the team and closing the factory at Brackley, Northamptonshire.

'We had had no pressure whatsoever from Honda to reduce our budget and we had had no guidance whatsoever on what they wanted, which was a bit mysterious,' Fry says, 'but we had voluntarily taken it upon ourselves to draw up a budget for 2009 which was substantially lower than the amount of money spent in 2008. The meeting was in two parts. The first was three of us, Ross, myself and Mr Hiroshi Oshima, who was head of motorsport. He informed Ross and I that, for reasons of the Lehman Brothers recently having gone down,[1] American dealers were refusing to take stock of new cars, Honda were obviously going to have to make cutbacks at Swindon – and that they would have to withdraw from Formula 1.

'My immediate reaction was surprise but not shock. I have to say we went to the meeting feeling that draconian budget cuts were more likely than them pulling out, but clearly it was in our minds that that might be the outcome. Mr Oshima was obviously very distressed and he was borderline tears when he told us. It was then suggested we go to a bigger conference room.'

In it were three more executives, including the second-in-command of motorsport and the Japanese head of industrial relations.

'Honda were taking it very seriously indeed to produce these people,' Fry says. 'They were all sat round and there seemed to be an expectation that we were going to go back to the factory, tell the staff and turn out the lights. My response was, "Have you ever thought about selling the team?" Someone said, "We haven't had time to think about it."

'There was a subtle difference in that, under Honda ownership, Ross was never a director of the company. The directors were myself and the finance director, Nigel Kerr, so it was appropriate for me to point out that as directors we had a responsibility to our employees but also the suppliers and the wider community. We were duty bound to come up with the best solution. To do otherwise would have been against the rules regarding the directorship of a company. They agreed that this should be the case.

'I must be fair to Honda. They had done a lot of good as well as being a little bit naïve in some respects. The reality was, I think, that at that point the easiest solution for them would have been: Ross turns out the lights, they write a big cheque [to cover redundancies] and that would have been the end of it – but life is not like that and Honda have a history of doing the right thing...'

Honda's agonising is easily understood. Soichiro Honda, who founded the company, adored racing and felt it was a good thing to be doing. As a manufacturer of motorbikes they formed a team and ventured to the Isle of Man TT races in 1959, where they were regarded as a curiosity, nothing more. By 1961 they were winning *everything* and began to turn their gaze to racing cars. They entered Formula 1 in 1964 and won two races before withdrawing in 1968. They missed the racing and returned, as engine suppliers, in 1983. They'd supply Williams, Lotus and McLaren, reaching an astonishing climax in 1988 when McLaren won 15 of the 16 rounds (and would have won all 16 if Ayrton Senna hadn't crashed at Monza). They withdrew at the end of 1992, returned with the BAR team in 2000 and bought them out at the end of 2005 to become a manufacturer again. They had a successful season before declining in 2007 and 2008.

The credit crunch changed everything.

Honda would continue to fund the team until March, although on a more modest scale, and that would get them to Melbourne and the first Grand Prix. It would not, however, get them to the pre-Christmas testing at Jerez, although of itself that was not crucial: the new car was not due to run until the end of January.

Brawn reiterates what Fry has said. 'When Honda told us they were going to stop, I asked our financial director to look at the numbers for us to take the team over. Because we didn't know enough about what was going on, it didn't look that feasible, so we set about trying to find a buyer.'

Rather than face the redundancy bill for the 700 employees, Honda agreed to accept a modest amount of money from a buyer. It looked an attractive proposition: a going concern with a state-of-the-art factory, carefully selected workforce, Brawn and Fry, two experienced drivers in Button and Barrichello, and a car which they'd been working on for a full year. Brawn described it as 'a fantastic opportunity because this is a great team with probably some of the best facilities in Formula 1, and I think we have a race-winning car next year so it is an opportunity for somebody'.

One immediate problem, however, was that Honda would no longer be supplying engines. It meant if anybody bought the team they'd have to source a new engine *and* fit it into a car specifically designed for Hondas – within a few weeks.

Brawn and Fry remained silent until deep into the following week while a plan was developed. On the Thursday evening – 4 December – they'd tell the team. As Fry recounts, 'we did keep it secret for a week. The people who knew were me, Ross, the finance director Nigel Kerr, the HR director John Marsden and the legal director Caroline McGrory – the people who would turn out to be shareholders. None said a word. We are a fairly tight ship here.'

Barrichello was on holiday in Brazil and 'there were two days where I didn't get any feedback so I called Ross direct and he could not inform me what was going on'.

Button had been on a week's training at Lanzarote and felt particularly fit. He'd just landed 'and then I got the call from Richard [Goddard], my manager. The phone just dropped out of my hand. Everyone was staring at me thinking *what's the matter with him?* He's just got off a Ryanair flight.' Button would subsequently describe this as giving him an inkling but he wasn't '100% sure' .

You might describe 4 September as the longest day.

FOTA were meeting in London. 'Ross and I had breakfast with Luca di Montezemolo,' Fry says, 'and Luca offered on the spot to provide a Ferrari engine. He was incredibly generous, offering the Ferrari engine at cost without hesitation. At the FOTA meeting later we informed the rest of the teams that Honda were planning to pull out and Mercedes – or to be specific McLaren – said they would also help us out.'

Martin Whitmarsh of McLaren gives the background. During

the FOTA meeting 'I offered to facilitate a possible engine supply from Mercedes-Benz, should it be required to prevent the team from closing.'

Negotiations would begin the following day.

After the meeting, Brawn and Fry travelled to the factory to tell the team. That was at six o'clock. Brawn felt it was a 'tragedy' – his own word – compounded by the fact that Christmas was so close, the worst possible time to be told that you might be facing redundancy. A secondary tragedy would be any interruption to work on the car. After the staff had been told, some of them went downstairs to have a look at the car and try to gauge what they'd have to do to get a new engine into it. Someone described this as 'a huge positive vibe'.

Barrichello was 'away with my family. It was the only vacation we'd had after the last race, with five days out of São Paulo. The team called me there, and it was shocking. I couldn't believe it. It was more shocking than if they had called me to tell me they had chosen a driver different to myself' – Honda had been showing an interest in Bruno Senna, Ayrton's nephew. 'You could never have imagined that Honda would have these problems. I never heard anything about money but perhaps the budget was too much, with too many things to do. It was very strange.'

The team would continue to function as before because, as Brawn explained, 'it's difficult for a Formula 1 team just to stop work. We have schedules to meet, we have races to go to, so unlike a car factory – which you can perhaps turn off for a couple of months – you can't do that with a race team. There's a certain inertia in the system that takes time to work through.'

The day after the announcement, and as the Mercedes engine negotiations began, Button was at the factory meeting the workforce in an attempt to raise morale.

Button would say that Honda's withdrawal 'made me train harder, in a way. I couldn't do anything about the decision. I just had to train as I would coming into a new season, thinking I was racing. For sure, I wasn't as smiley as I usually would be over a winter.'

Because of the time gap, when the workforce were told at the factory it was already the early hours in Japan. That day Honda Chairman Takeo Fukui gave a news conference in Tokyo and announced – evidently to the consternation and anger of the Japanese media – that the company wanted to sell the team and would withdraw from the 2009 World Championship if nobody bought it by the end of December.

'This difficult decision has been made in light of the quickly deteriorating operating environment facing the global auto industry, brought on by the sub-prime[2] problem in the United States, the deepening credit crisis and the sudden contraction of the world economies. Honda must protect its core business activities and secure the long term as widespread uncertainties in the economies around the globe continue to mount. A recovery is expected to take some time.'

One commentator said: 'Honda has publicly declared that "racing is our DNA" and behaved as if it was a company symbolising motorsport. For being that way, it is socially responsible as a member of the racing world ... that responsibility is something that cannot be abandoned in such a selfish manner.'

Just as pertinently, former Japanese Grand Prix driver Aguri Suzuki, whose own team went broke earlier in the year – when Honda decided it could no longer offer backing – said: 'Formula 1 is a great goal for children in karting. With Honda's withdrawal, that goal may seem to be crumbling down. They may possibly feel that the "world of dreams" is disappearing.'

Fukui clarified the situation with Button. 'We had a deal with Button and we are going to restart the talks to undo that contract.' They intended to do the decent thing and make him free to drive for another team. Brawn, naturally, would not stand in Button's way but anticipated that, if Button did contemplate leaving, they'd talk it through and was confident Button wouldn't leave without doing that. Brawn foresaw 'open dialogue' and said he wanted, if possible, to keep him – Brawn understood that an engineer could take a sabbatical, as he had done, but for a driver to do that was more difficult.

At least, Mercedes felt that keeping the team, and all the other FOTA teams, alive was paramount. This alone was encouraging in what Brawn would describe as 'dark days'.

Whitmarsh says that when the engine offer was 'gratefully accepted by Ross Brawn and Nick Fry' – and the reason why they picked the Mercedes offer rather than the one from Ferrari will be fully explored later – 'I flew to Stuttgart to secure the agreement of Dieter Zetsche [Chairman, Daimler] and Norbert Haug [Motorsport Vice President, Mercedes-Benz]. So it wasn't a case of McLaren supplying a reaction to a Mercedes-Benz request. On the contrary, McLaren was very much involved in the negotiations that led to the agreement for Mercedes-Benz to supply engines to Brawn, as was FOTA.

'I suppose you could say that the decision to supply Brawn with engines was taken jointly by McLaren and Mercedes-Benz, and supported by FOTA in the context of finding a solution that would ensure the survival of the team formerly known as Honda – protecting hundreds of jobs that would otherwise have been lost. It was successful. As such, too, it was a fine example of the positive effects of the teams banding together in a co-operative association whose remit and aims were – and still are – to improve the sport in any way it can.'

Barrichello, who had no contract, flew over and went to the factory but found it a strange experience. He was saying 'Merry Christmas' to the people he met and who didn't know if they'd still be there after Christmas. He felt mixed emotions from him to them and them to him.

He talked with Brawn and said he'd lost weight, he was fit to race and he wanted to race. Far from being too old, the fires all burnt as they had always done. He'd even won some kart races in Brazil. He added that he felt his experience could be a valuable asset for the team.

He said that even on New Year's Eve, when he'd be splashing about in the sea, he'd have his mobile phone switched on.

To own the Honda team had immediate appeal and the ubiquitous David Richards of Prodrive, a very experienced operator in the world of motorsport with hands-on experience of Formula 1 with BAR, was conducting a business evaluation for what was described as two interested parties. Formula 1 can leak like any British government's cabinet or be more secretive than MI5: when money is in play, secrecy is everything, and when people are sniffing round Grand Prix teams with a view to a purchase, secrecy is everything too. From here on, much of what did and did not happen around Honda would be rumours – and that was only the bits we did hear about...

(One of the interested parties was reported to be Kuwait-based Dar Investment, but frankly I don't know and in retrospect it seems curiously unimportant.)

Button wasn't his usual chirpy self over Christmas and 'the family noticed'.

Barrichello explained that it wasn't as if he knew about the various takeover attempts 'before the rest of the world did. I was up one day, down the next. It was very tough mentally.'

A prime example of the rumours came a few days after Christmas when Brawn and Carlos Slim, a very rich Mexican in telecommunications, both denied they were talking. (The rumour evidently began in the Italian press.) Brawn said he wished the rumour was true but it wasn't. Slim's company, Telmex, sponsored Bruno Senna, which gave the rumour a particular credibility: Barrichello had still not re-signed and if Slim wanted Honda *and* Senna nobody was going to stop him.

A statement killed it. 'Escuderia Telmex informs you that Carlos Slim Helú did not buy and did not close any negotiations with the Honda team. All the information and assumptions on the matter have been completely false.'

There was talk of a Greek shipping magnate and a Swiss consortium, while the Force India team were said to be eyeing the facilities and assets.

Fry said he hoped to have a sale in place by the end of January. Brawn said: 'There has been a huge amount of interest. It's now got to the stage where we need to filter out the serious from the not so serious. We're all hopeful that something will happen and we're anxious to turn up the wick again in the New Year.'

In mid-January, Mercedes announced it could supply the team with customer engines but naturally sought financial guarantees that the team was going to survive (and thus pay its bills).

The rumours expanded to include, for the first time, a possible management buy-out with Fry prominent. Fry strongly refuted suggestions that this involved a conflict of interests: him trying to buy and sell the team at the same time. More properly, in a desperate situation and with the first race – Australia, 29 March – looming ever closer, he was doing what anybody sensible would have done: keeping every option open.

Meanwhile, the Emirates Airline had already come close to signing a sponsorship deal with Honda, but Honda's withdrawal inevitably changed that. Brawn and Fry approached them, saying there was a good chance they might acquire the team. Would Emirates be interested in title sponsorship? However sympathetic Emirates might be, there was no way round the uncertainty over the engine situation, the team's overall funding or that the cars might trundle round at the back of the field. Emirates understandably couldn't take the risk, although they said they'd try and help in other ways.

Reportedly there were *twelve* bidders – or even, at the very margins of credibility, *thirty*, which had been reduced to the twelve, one evidently serious. Fry was keeping Honda in Tokyo in touch but, overall, the team took a policy decision to ignore the rumours, particularly those that appeared in print. The limit was reached when a very respectable British broadsheet daily carried a story on its *front page* that the team was to receive government aid – an unfounded absurdity.

By the end of February, Mercedes had shipped an engine to the factory. Brawn estimated that the team would need six weeks to marry the car and its new engine. Others suggested it could be done quicker, although with the risk of gaining time but losing reliability.

In the background, Bernie Ecclestone was using his influence and persuasive powers to find a way of keeping the team alive. As Formula 1's commercial rights holder he had a direct interest, not least because a grid with 20 cars on it was infinitely preferable to a grid with only 18 and, if the credit crunch claimed further teams, a depopulated grid – say, 14 cars – would provide a bleak spectacle on the world's television screens. Ecclestone was considering making an advance payment of 40m Euros from the television money to help keep 'Honda' alive. 'We've been talking to them and whatever happens we'd like to see them stay in business,' he said. At one point after mid-February Ecclestone offered to help financially with a buy-out.

Rumours hardened that the potential management buy-out included Brawn, but also that a 'hostile' bid was being prepared from an unnamed bidder. This bidder was (reportedly) a solid, global name that could bring financial stability.

The Honda management in Tokyo found themselves in a very delicate position. They had their shareholders to consider and felt that in the present climate they could not justify the team's annual budget of $300m – hence the decision to withdraw in the first place – *but* had a moral obligation to the huge Brackley workforce. If they allowed a management buy-out and it failed, would Honda be deemed negligent? If they did not allow a management buy-out and the 'hostile' bid melted, as so many other bids had melted, would Honda – again – be deemed negligent?

Honda's stipulation to prospective bidders was that they protected the workforce and had adequate resources to make the team competitive.

Rumours suggested that Sir Richard Branson's Virgin group might want to buy, but four days later Branson refined that, saying he was interested in Formula 1 but not until its costs were curbed and it became more environmentally friendly. In time – when Virgin decided to sponsor the team – Ecclestone would say, 'I've been pushing, pushing, pushing and pushing.'

On 23 February, Chief Executive Fukui said publicly that there were no *serious* bidders and the company was finding the 'sale process difficult'. The team, however, were preparing for the pre-season testing at Barcelona, beginning on 9 March, and the word was that a deal might be close.

It was.

Brawn and Fry had seen an opening. Some of the bidders wanted Honda to make substantial contributions – reportedly over $100m in some cases – to cover possible redundancies and other commitments. 'Given that the parties that were coming in with an interest in taking over the team were making fairly large demands on Honda for the liabilities that came from taking on the redundancies,' Brawn says, 'then an approach that we could adopt became more attractive to Honda: allowing the team to carry on.'

The opening was, in the end, simplicity itself: armed with some help from Honda, the prize money from FOM and some sponsorship, Brawn and Fry would have enough to run the team themselves.

'As the situation developed,' Brawn says, 'it became clear what the costs involved in closing the team in the UK environment – the redundancies – would be and *then* it started to become a little bit clearer that we ought to look seriously at running it ourselves. It happened by happy accident. Being a team owner just evolved as the only solution to the Honda problem.'

The alternative was to turn off the lights.

Brawn had been able to persuade Honda to 'hand over fixed assets that included buildings, factory equipment and machinery that had no other use, as well as some money that the motor manufacturer would otherwise have spent on closing the company'.

'It was at the Honda offices in Slough when I signed the papers,' Brawn says. 'That was it. I felt surreal when I came out of the room, because it was never an ambition to own a Formula 1 team. I can say that genuinely. It became a need because that really was the only way out. I was never [as Fry has pointed out] a director of Honda GB and in fact my current contract with Honda had terminated by the time this all happened. My employment contract had certain conditions which Honda informed me they couldn't maintain. So I wasn't a Honda employee at the precise moment when I bought the team. It *was* a very strange and surreal experience.'

How did Fry react to the moment? 'I felt completely confident that we would be successful because when we put together the business plan at the end of December, beginning of January, it was based on some very good assumptions and it was very good timing.'

Fry expands on that, a fascinating what-might-not-have-been. 'Would I have joined Ross in taking over the team a year earlier? I doubt it, because even though the economic circumstances of the year before were certainly better, you were "fighting" other teams who at that time had vast resources. There was no sight of any resource restrictions in Formula 1. The budgets were clearly well beyond what a private team could possibly raise, but the beginning of 2009 was really the perfect storm – in a positive sense. It was a confluence of circumstances: the economic situation was bad so the big companies couldn't afford to spend so much, FOTA was already talking about resource restrictions that were going to bring down the costs of competing in Formula 1, you'd got the engine restrictions and no testing. The circumstances were very favourable. You'd have been much more nervous a year or two earlier.'

There remained a problem: what to call the team? They played around with names but, as Brawn explained, none seemed to be right. Then Caroline McGrory, the legal director, said, 'Why not call it after you, Ross?' She pointed out that Brawn had a reputation within Formula 1 and Brawn pointed out that they hadn't had a better idea. At that instant the Brawn GP Formula One Team was born.

He understood that he needed experience in the cockpit and that meant retaining Button and Barrichello. Button took a pay cut, which helped.

'I had a big smile on my face when I heard about the team being saved,' Button said. 'I found out the same time as the team did. There was no preferential treatment.'

Brawn rated Bruno Senna highly, in terms of his approach and his attitude, but explained that the team was in a position where it had a low budget (as Formula 1 budgets go – they'd be taking 45 people to a race rather than the usual hundred), testing was tightly restricted (denying Senna the chance to know the car and the circuits), and, literally, they couldn't afford damage to the cars. Barrichello was an old head, Brawn knew him well from their days together at Ferrari and he was a good team member.

At midnight on 5 March the buy-out – involving Brawn, Fry, Kerr, McGrory and HR director John Marsden – was formally announced.

Brawn said: 'The past few months have been extremely challenging for the team but today's announcement is the very pleasing conclusion to the strenuous efforts that have been made to secure its future.

'Firstly, it is a great shame that having worked with Honda Motor Company for so long we can no longer continue together. I would like to thank Honda for the fantastic co-operation and support we have received throughout this process – particularly those members of the senior management who were closely involved with concluding our agreement – and for the faith they have demonstrated in myself and our team.

'I would also like to take this opportunity to pay due credit to our staff at Brackley. The levels of motivation and commitment that I have witnessed at the factory deserve the highest praise.

'It would be impossible to mention all of the people without whom today's announcement may not have been possible. However I would like to express particular appreciation for the support we have received from Mercedes-Benz Motorsport, the FIA, FOM [Ecclestone's Formula One Management], FOTA, BERR [the UK's Department for Business, Enterprise and Regulatory Reform], Bridgestone, our other team partners and our many fans the world over.

'The journey ahead will be challenging but exciting and we know we can count on their continued enthusiasm for our team and its ambitions.'

Brawn said that Fry would remain as Chief Executive Officer and paid tribute to the part he had played in the negotiations.

(At a subsequent FOTA Press Conference, Fry would very publicly thank not only Mercedes-Benz but also McLaren.)

Oshima, Honda's head of motor sport, said: 'Since announcing our withdrawal from Formula 1 racing on December 5 of last year we have conducted various studies and discussions so that the team can continue its activities as a new team. We are very pleased that we could sell the team to Ross Brawn, with whom we have been partaking in the challenges of Formula 1 competition, and are grateful for his decision. We offer our sincerest wishes for the new team which will be led by Ross.'

Barrichello felt he and Button formed one of the best combinations. He stressed how well they worked together and added this: 'With a competitive car we could score a lot of points next year, and that is what is going to make the team survive. It is the impact we can make in the first year that will keep it alive. I believe that we can jump straight into a top ten contender in qualifying, and then race to the points or even better. The only problem with the first race could be reliability because we might not have many tests beforehand.'

The day after the buy-out announcement, the Brawn ran for the first time – behind closed door at Silverstone – with Button at the wheel. Discussions between Mercedes personnel and the Brawn team about fitting the engine had been going on through Christmas, the New Year and up to the car's official launch.

Nick Fry explains the engine situation, and uses as his starting point 'the fact that we were generously given the option of a Ferrari or a Mercedes. Frankly, from a performance point of view there was probably not much in it. The thing that really swung the balance in favour of the Mercedes engine was it simply fitted rather better. By that I mean the mounting points to the chassis and the mounting points to the gearbox were in a more similar position to the Honda engine. That's what enabled it to happen.

'In some cases, the engine mounting points of the Ferrari went into fresh air, whereas the Mercedes actually went in to places where there was already some structure, like a bit of carbon on the back of the chassis that it could be bolted on to. Obviously we had to redo the back of the chassis to have more substance and structure in the areas where the bolts were going into, but at least there was structure for them to go into. With the Ferrari engine, in many cases there was nothing except air.

'I don't want to underestimate the size of the job, regardless of the fact it fitted rather better. It was a vast amount of work, however – and not only that, it was done by the engineering and manufacturing team with, basically, no or very little supervision. Enormous credit has to be given to the people who did it because, as you can imagine, from the beginning of December right through until, really, the beginning of March, Ross and myself were principally engaged in trying to put together the deal with Honda. The engineering and manufacturing guys basically did the work by themselves.

'One thing is very interesting and, although people quickly forget, it was the reality of the situation. The installation was and would remain significantly compromised. We wanted to use the gearbox we'd designed, and it was unlikely that McLaren could have supplied us with their gearbox anyway. In fact, because of the famous diffuser [more on this later] we were determined to use our gearbox – which, of course, had been designed for the back of the car – *but*, because we wanted to do that, we ended up with a gearbox in the region of 20mm higher than it should be. That may not seem a lot but, in Formula 1, raising the centre of gravity of the back of the car by nearly an inch is a significant amount.

'The size of the radiators and the cooling package overall is very specifically designed for a certain engine, because you design the cooling pack to work with an engine which has a certain heat rejection at certain revs and so on. So you need a certain water flow, a certain size of water radiator and a certain size of oil radiator. None of those things we could change.

'We did the best we could, but in some areas it was definitely compromised. The car would be generally over-cooled for what is required, meaning the radiators are bigger than they need to be and consequently the aerodynamics suffer as a result.'

This was another aspect of one of the most remarkable Grand Prix stories, perhaps the most remarkable. A few weeks before, the story might well have ended with a formalised obituary when the lights had been turned off for the last time and the factory fell silent.

After the traumatic winter and the pressurised timetable, and with the 2009 season now upon them, they were tired but discreetly, prudently, quietly confident.

They had no idea they were poised to breathe a great gale of life right through Formula 1.

Notes

1. The Lehman Brothers investment bank went bankrupt in September 2008, ushering in the 'credit crunch'.

2. Sub-prime – a term unknown to the general public before the credit crunch – involved making the most risk-laden property loans, specifically in the United States, to people with little chance of repaying them.

CHAPTER 2

BIG BEAR

The voices echo from many different people who were in many different places at many different times, but they are so similar they become a chorus. Listen.

'I said "Look, you know, if we are going to get on, if we are going to work together, I'll make a proposal about how we should do it because I think I know what I can do and I know the areas that I am not good at." I made some suggestions and Ross just sat there. He thought about it for 30 seconds. He got up, he came over and we shook hands. That was it.' – Rory Byrne.

'When he tells people what he wants he's got the knowledge and he's very clear in his instructions. He knows what it takes to get the best out of people.' – Neil Oatley.

'It was just the way he went about it, very methodical, very unflappable, very quietly spoken and pleasant.' – Derek Warwick.

'Well, he's a normal guy who's a born engineer, who's a chess player and fisherman. You have to think of him in terms of long-term car planning and he's very quietly determined, I would say. He plans everything he does a long time ahead.' – Frank Dernie.

'Ross stepped back and said "I'm not doing it like that. We are going to use *this* much money, we are going to do it *this* way and it is going to take me *this* long. If you don't want to come on board, fair enough." I would never have had the balls to do that. I was always part of the project rather than coming in to lead a brand new project. For me, that was something that Ross did brilliantly and I'd never seen it done before: that a technical person would take that control.' – Alastair Macqueen.

'When Ross came on board there weren't really a lot of

tactics in Formula 1. They didn't figure out about changing tactics in the middle of a race. He could see the possibilities from sports cars: you could influence it and change it if you watched what everyone else was doing. You could always beat Williams because they'd start off and never change their strategy no matter what was happening. We'd change ours. Ross mastered that and now he's probably the best in the business at it.' – Tom Walkinshaw.

'Ross is probably the calmest person I have ever known. His cars will be leading a Grand Prix and there's a wry smile, no jubilation, no gesticulation.' – Russell Sheldon.

These quotations are set down in no particular order and, interestingly, if you rearrange the order in any way you want, the overall impression is precisely the same.

Normally, when you ask the many different people from the many different places and times about a human being they have all known, you'll get slightly disconcerting, sometimes discordant, voices. Each of them is likely to be authentic and the discordance is no surprise because they reflect the human being evolving and maturing through different situations and, inevitably, each sees a different facet. The real human being is a composite.

Ross Brawn seems to contradict that absolutely, which is why you've just been listening to the chorus. If you wanted someone to turn Formula 1 over – do it quietly, undemonstratively, with the wry smile spreading above his latest version of a mini-beard – Brawn would do nicely. You see him striding the pit lane, bestriding the pit wall and, confronted by a microphone, talking the greatest common sense couched in sardonic irony. He doesn't stride the pit lane as if it was theatre and he must have the leading role. He strides it because he's a big feller and his natural presence takes care of the rest. Listen again:

'He had a lot of respect from everyone he was involved with. He was never one of these people that had to spell out that he was the boss. You knew he was the boss, even though he didn't ever have to specifically say it. He had the respect of the people beneath him and the people above him.' This is the view of Rory Byrne, who worked closely with him at Benetton and then at Ferrari so that they formed arguably *the* most successful partnership in Grand Prix history (seven driver's World Championships, nine Constructors' Championships), unless you include Michael Schumacher and make it a triumvirate.

Ross Brawn was born in Manchester on 23 November 1954 and 'lived in a house which was very much like you see on Coronation Street: a two-up, two-down terraced house where the doors were always open and there was very little crime. Everyone looked after each other. I lived there until I was eleven,' he says.

'My dad' – Ernie – 'worked for the Firestone Tyre and Rubber Company. I don't know if it's a bug I got from that but it's where the association comes from. What started at a very early stage was that my dad used to do all sorts of things like go-kart racing and stock car racing. We became very keen on slot car racing and we raced at a club in Manchester. It started off as slot rail and then became proper slot racing circuit. That was affordable and I was actually making cars by the time I was ten or eleven. So I'd got this interest in slot car racing and making bits and pieces. I had been introduced to it and encouraged into it by my dad.'

Models cars compete on specially built tracks. The British Slot Car Racing Association says: 'Organised slot car racing has come a long way since the humble beginnings using home set equipment in the 'sixties. Modern cars can lap a typical 30-metre club track in five seconds. In those five seconds the driver has to brake and drive round six or more corners. The faster cars are capable of 60mph on the straights (that's actual speed, not scale speed) and have covered over 400 miles in 24 hours.'

Russell Sheldon, a slot car expert, explains that it 'was absolutely huge in the 1960s. It was a global fad. People say it was a bit like the yoyo and the hula hoop but there were a lot of very serious people as well, which gave birth to organised clubs and associations and so on.

'Although the origins can be traced back to before World War Two the hobby only became popular at the 1957 Harrogate toy fair, where a small British company, Minimodels Ltd, unveiled a commercially available slot car home-racing system under the product name Scalextric (scale – electric).'

The hobby expanded and 'within a short space of time there was a multitude of British, American, European and Japanese companies manufacturing their own slot racing systems. By 1963/64, slot car racing had become so popular that it represented big business. To promote their products, Scalextric used Jim Clark in their advertising, while French company Jouef had actor Alain Delon, and the American Aurora company featured Stirling Moss. During this period, Aurora, for example, sold some two million slot car racing sets and over twelve million cars.

'The popularity was fuelled by the amazing growth of commercial raceway centres where the public could race on huge custom-built circuits. One was founded and run by Peter Warr, who went on to manage several Formula 1 teams – Lotus, Fittipaldi and Wolf.' As we shall see, Wolf took over the Williams team when Brawn was there.

'In the early 1960s his dad Ernie was a member of the Ashton-under-Lyne slot car club in Lancashire, where he introduced Ross to the hobby,' Sheldon says. 'At the age of nine his engineering skills were already apparent and a picture of his beautifully built 1/32nd scale Cooper Oldsmobile sports racing car featured in a 1964 issue of *Model Cars* magazine.'

When he was 11 the family moved to Reading.

Ernie Brawn, in Ross's words, 'became boss of the Firestone Racing Division – not the overall boss but he ran all the logistics and the transportation. He was the manager of that and he looked after getting the tyres to the race, getting them fitted – in fact, looked after everything. He didn't do engineering – that was a different department. He travelled a lot and he used to bring back Super 8 – or whatever the home movies were shot in – of where he'd been, places like Daytona or Sebring. For periods Firestone were in Grand Prix racing and I went to the races in the UK. I remember going to Brands Hatch when I was 11 or in my early teens, and my brother playing with Damon Hill in the paddock. They were the same age and they played in the gravel of the paddock. I got to races quite often.'

He joined the Reading slot car club.

'I was lucky enough to attend Reading Grammar School, which, of course, is a very good school,' Brawn says. 'I got there on the strength of my academic qualifications whilst I was in Manchester. I never really settled, if I am honest. I loved sport, I loved some of the subjects, but culturally it was quite different for me. I had come from a poor but honest northern upbringing, where a spade is a spade, to an environment which was a bit different for me, and I never truly settled at Reading School. I definitely didn't make best use of it, I didn't engage as well as I should have done, and while I came out with a number of O-levels I didn't do academically as well as I should have done. My headmaster gave me some advice. He said he didn't think I was the right sort of candidate to continue an academic career and I should go out and earn a living as soon as I could.'

When Brawn joined the Reading club, Russell Sheldon says, 'that's when he became serious about it. After the boom, going into the early 1970s slot racing lost its popularity so some of the more active associations, such as the British Association, decided to introduce a beginner's class – a bit like Formula Ford. You had to use an over-the-counter chassis which had to be built within certain parameters, very much like Formula Ford. Ross and his then partner decided to get into this business. They were called Formula 32 chassis. The scale that was – and is – the most popular, and which Ross competed in, was the 1:32nd scale.

'He continued to pursue the hobby with passion into his early working career, contributing technical articles to *Model Cars* magazine and at the same time developing his business skills, when in 1970 he partnered with Tony Hough, a colleague at the Atomic Energy Research Establishment in Harwell, to manufacture and sell slot car racing components in 1970. Their part-time cottage industry was called HB Products – Hough and Brawn – with Ross mainly designing and building the slot car chassis.

'In the late 1960s, to attract more people, the governing body introduced a low-cost class of racing, Formula 32. These cars used stock components and a very basic low-cost chassis with stringent design limitations. From 1970 to 1975, Ross made Formula 32 chassis under the HB Products brand, which were hurriedly built and rather crude. As Ross says, they were built down to a price, not up to a quality. In fact all were dogs to drive and needed loads of lead weight to keep them on the track – no matter who designed and made them.

'Ross continued to compete in open meetings, where his chassis were well designed and considered to be innovative. Although not quite up to national championship standards as a driver, Ross was a competitive racer who some remember as being a somewhat hirsute young man. Derek Cooper, British National Slot Car Champion in the 1972 Grand Prix class, recalls racing against Ross with great enthusiasm. HB Products also sponsored some slot racers, the most notable being Ian Jenson and Pete Hore, who both went on to win multiple British National Championships.'

Cooper remembers 'we used to go drinking together when slot car meetings were up here in this area. He was just another driver. He was getting towards the top end of performance levels, probably helped by the fact that his cars were so good. He'd reach semi-finals and the odd final. We'd talk about cars. He was taking the slot car racing very seriously. We didn't talk a lot about other things and I didn't know much at all about his private life.'

There were a few stories, of course, and here's one, sanitised. A racer lived in a student's house and he decided to take all the other racers back for a party. One of the other students had arranged a fancy dress party. Brawn emerged from the toilet at the top of the stairs just as a pantomime horse came through the door with two people in it. Brawn said 'I can ride that!' stepped off the top step and went down on to it, collapsing the horse.

'He always seems such a serious character now,' Cooper says, 'but in those days he could be a bit wild. It was just normal 20s tomfoolery. It was quite usual for competitors to shout at marshals in the heat of the moment – you'd go and apologise to them afterwards – but I don't remember him ever shouting at marshals.'

Brawn insists that 'I never set out to have a career in motor racing. I liked the engineering and I liked my slot car racing, which continued until I was in my very late teens, early twenties. In fact I started a business called HB Model products with a friend of mine' – Hough. 'We used to make these slot cars and sell them to people.'

Sheldon became friends with Pete Hore, who 'Ross went on to sponsor – because Ross never really achieved anything other than keeping the track marshals very busy. He was too big – physically too awkward and too heavy – to be a competitive kart racer, either.'

In fact, his strong physique would militate against any form of single-seater racing even if he'd had ambitions to do it – but, as we've just heard, he nursed no ambitions to have a career in motor racing at all. The slot cars were purest pleasure and rewarding in different ways but they weren't *life*.

'What he did,' Sheldon says, 'was bring great engineer skills to it and he was exceptionally good at that side. I have a photograph of a model McLaren that Ross built and entered in one of the big slot car races. He actually won a prize for it, so I think his skills were already coming through then.

'He took the product he'd built and gave it to one of the top drivers, Pete Hore. That's how I got to know Ross in the very early 1970s. He was a very likeable sort of a person. He wasn't chasing girls, because slot car racing consumes a lot of time if you are competitive, like any sport.'

Brawn followed his headmaster's advice. 'Because I was interested in engineering I applied for an apprenticeship at Harwell [the Atomic Energy Research Establishment]. It was the time of one of the postal strikes and my application was lost or delayed. I got a letter saying "Sorry, the application's too late." I appealed, along with two or three other people, they reconsidered and I managed to get it. I did a four-year apprenticeship and I started my further education. I was becoming a bit more serious then. I did mechanical engineering and, whilst I was in the middle of that, the view was to finish an HNC [Higher National Certificate] and maybe even go to university.'

He also studied instrumentation.

'Then' – it was 1976 – 'I saw an advertisement in the local paper in Reading for a job at Frank Williams' Grand Prix team as a machinist. I acted under pure speculation. I went along and met Patrick Head, who interviewed me and showed me lots of things. He said "Can you make this? Can you do that?" And of course everything was in the affirmative. You have the confidence to say "Yes, I can do that no problem." I didn't hear anything for about six weeks and eventually got a call from Frank's PA, Lizzie, who said "We'd like you to come and work for us." It turned out they had offered it to somebody else who after some time declined, and I was the second choice. That was a little twist of fate.'

Brawn's immediate thought was to accept the job almost as his gap-year, and then 'get back to what I should be doing,' which was civil engineering.

There'd be another twist of fate, because 'I then had my years with Frank, during which we won two World Championships. That really was the period when Frank Williams Engineering was fully established. I was employee number 11 when I joined and there were 220 when I left: impressive growth.'

In fact the chronology would be interrupted in 1977. 'I joined and did a year then Frank lost control of the company to Walter Wolf.'

The eyes of the Slovenian-Austrian-Canadian Wolf had long been upon Williams. In 1976 he financed the team and subsequently bought a majority share, keeping Frank Williams as team manager. The team was not a success and Wolf removed Williams, replacing him with the experienced Peter Warr. Williams, Head and some other team members departed to form Williams Grand Prix Engineering, which it remains to this day.

Brawn remembers doing 'all sorts of jobs' (in *Frank Williams* by Maurice Hamilton) before Wolf took over. 'There was nothing wrong with Peter Warr but he wasn't who I had gone to work for. Peter got up at a meeting and said, if anyone didn't feel like supporting the team in the future, they should say so and leave.

A short while afterwards, I said I really wanted to try something else. It was all fairly amicable.'

Brawn adds: 'I'd got the bug by then and decided that what in fact I was going to do was go off and become a mechanic. I applied to March'[1] – initially as a milling operator before he worked on their Formula 3 team. That involved doing 'everything: engineer the car, mechanic it, drive the truck. I had a great time and thoroughly enjoyed myself with a Brazilian called Aryon Cornelsen-Filho. He didn't make a big impact.'

No, he didn't. He finished joint 19th in the BARC BP Super Visco British F3 Championship, along with Stefan Johansson. For your interest, Derek Daly of Ireland won, Derek Warwick fifth, Didier Pironi tenth, Tiff Needell 11th and Elio de Angelis 12th. All would adorn Formula 1 in their various ways (albeit Needell only on two occasions).

Sheldon points out that 'Ross left slot racing behind when he got into full-size motorsport with March, no doubt entirely due to a lack of spare time rather than loss of interest.'

The season was also invaluable experience 'for a lad who had hardly travelled,' Brawn said.

Then 'towards the end of the year Frank rang me to say that he had got back on his feet and was building the team up at Didcot, Oxfordshire. Would I consider going back? [This was 'the famous carpet factory'.] I joined at the end of that year for the second time, which was to be a seven-year period. I was there a year or two before Frank Dernie joined. I did some mechanic-ing and other things for the first year, just to help get the thing off the ground. It wasn't what I was really wanting to do and as the team started to establish itself I became the kind of R&D person.'

In a very real sense, because the Williams team was so small, Brawn was continuing his Formula 3 life, 'machining pieces, fitting them to the car, driving them in a truck to the tests, being a mechanic at the track. When you only have a limited number of people you have to be pretty flexible.'

It gave him the sort of scope, openings and versatility completely unknown in today's specialist age and, inevitably, it gave him a wealth of practical experience which would prove invaluable later. When he asked people to do things, he had the advantage of knowing how to do them himself. He feels 'it's just a great help if you are designing or doing something if you have done it yourself. Maybe the ways of doing it now [2009] are different but, if you understand it, that helps a great deal.'

The car was the FW06, a good one to work on. Williams had extensive and crucial backing from Saudi Arabian Airlines, who were now title sponsors. Williams had sounded out several drivers to put in the FW06 and some didn't even return his call. He settled on the rugged, ambitious Australian Alan Jones who'd spent 1975 with the Hesketh team, then Surtees, then Shadow.

Jones remembers that at the time 'Frank was still one of the game's all-time least successful constructors. Everyone told me I was crazy and taking a big step backwards in my career.'[2] Jones, however, had been to the factory, had a long talk with Patrick Head and seen the plans for the FW06. He liked what he saw in every direction and signed. The Williams team had always been serious, and now what they were doing had become serious too. Jones seems to have been serious from the moment he was born.

Brawn and Neil Oatley 'both started at Williams very close together, late 1977,' recalls Neil. 'I started in the September and Ross appeared in November–December time. I was Patrick's junior, really. Patrick had been the only engineer and I joined to help draw up what became the FW06 car, the first of the modern Williamses. Ross started as a machinist. I didn't know him at all. In fact, the first time I met him was when he turned up at Didcot. I thought he was a reasonable bloke. He lived fairly locally and I got to know him socially. I think he got married either just before or just after he arrived.

'It was a small team then. There were only about 15 of us so everyone tended to socialise and it was a nice atmosphere – there was a pub just up on the corner from where the old factory was! He was a pretty interesting bloke. He's about the same age as me so he was in his early 20s. He'd had a good education. I'm not sure he got up to degree standard but he did get to the level below that, giving him a good technical background. As well as that, he went through an apprenticeship as a machinist so he's one of these people who can turn his hand to almost anything, and certainly working in a Formula 3 team, where you have to improvise somewhat, would add to those skills. Obviously the team expanded fairly rapidly over the following couple of years.'

As we have seen, Frank Dernie joined after Brawn. Brawn, don't forget, was employee number 11 and Dernie became employee number 23.

Brawn remembers (in Hamilton's *Frank Williams*) that 'Frank had tremendous drive; so did Patrick. But it continued to be tight financially. They were pretty strung out and there were a few times when it looked a bit shaky. Even when they had started to do well, Frank would extend himself as far as possible. There were a few times when we had the meter man come round to cut us off, but we managed to persuade him not to.'

Dernie says that 'in simple terms' Brawn was 'a front-end mechanic on Alan Jones's FW06.' He'd now married Jean and 'when their eldest daughter was born Jean didn't want him to travel any more – he was hardly ever home – so he came and worked for me in R&D. It was a very small team then. I think he was almost one of the first people to move from Frank Williams Racing Cars to Williams Grand Prix Engineering,' via March, of course.

'He was a spectacularly good craftsman and a good, good guy. He had great long hair but I mean everyone did in the late 1970s. We were young. I'm a little bit older than Ross but basically we were having fun.

'Eventually we had two more technicians who reported directly to Ross. Then we had the wind tunnel. He and I did all of that! I did everything electrical, he did everything mechanical and we bolted and soldered it together, just the two of us. This was at Didcot in the Station Road industrial estate (yes, the former carpet factory). We got a double unit to build it in. It was my idea to get a wind tunnel because I thought *Christ, every time I go to the wind tunnel at Imperial College we come back with a massive step. If we had our own we*

38

could do it more often and it would be brilliant – but it all had to be done on a shoestring so we built it ourselves. We got the bits and pieces and had them shipped in. I wrote the software, Ross built the moving ground and we dragged a few mechanics over to help us when it was too difficult. I ran all the cabling, soldered all the connectors in, designed all the connection boxes. Those were different days...'

Brawn says Dernie 'did all the control stuff and I did the building blocks – the Lego bit!'

'He is a very calm person,' Dernie says, 'and that's one of his great strengths and one of the things I most admire him for. He does get frustrated with people but he doesn't over-react and he keeps control of things among his close colleagues and friends. He is very in control of himself. I feel great admiration for that because I don't have it.'

Neil Oatley 'certainly wouldn't have predicted where he'd end up. Although he came on as a machinist I think that only lasted a fairly short time and then we bought a wind tunnel off Specialised Mouldings up in Huntingdon and that was installed in another factory unit next door to our race shop. Ross took on the project of installing that. I think Ross did the lion's share of all that work. [Dernie might not agree.] That showed how versatile he was and how good at adapting to new situations, planning the project through. That all went smoothly, worked very well, did the team proud until the technology moved on.

'What we were getting was a glimpse of what would happen at Brawn on a much bigger scale – getting the job done, dealing with people, getting the best out of them. When he tells people what he wants he's got the knowledge and he's very clear in his instructions. He knows what it takes to get the best out of people.'

Brawn describes the Williams years as 'a great education'.

It was. In 1979 the team won their first Grand Prix, the British at Silverstone, and by now were fielding two cars and drivers, Jones and Clay Regazzoni – who won the British. Jones became World Champion in 1980, Carlos Reutemann might have become champion in 1981, Keke Rosberg did become champion in 1982. The 1983 and 1984 seasons were disappointing although the team now had Honda engines, which, very soon, would usher in another whole era.

Dernie remembers Brawn leaving after working on the FW09, the 'first Honda car' – the first Williams specifically designed to take the Honda.

He went to the newly formed Beatrice team. Beatrice were an American consumer conglomerate who'd been sponsoring Carl Haas in IndyCars and now wanted to expand to Formula 1. Haas eventually set up a factory at Colnbrook not far from Heathrow, moving from Woking, and recruited Teddy Mayer and Tyler Alexander – both men with extensive experience at McLaren – to run it. Oatley, John Baldwin and Brawn were the designers.

'We both left Williams almost at the same time and went to work for Teddy and Tyler at the Beatrice team,' Oatley says. 'That would have been right at the end of '84. It wasn't intended that we'd leave together, it was just the way things happened. They were recruiting and it looked serious for a year or so. Initially I was a design engineer but my responsibilities were shared between myself, John Baldwin and Ross. I became the chief designer so I was in charge of the detail of building the cars, and Ross ran the wind tunnel programme. That's how the work was divided. At the time Beatrice started it was in Woking just behind the McLaren factory. We were both still living in Oxfordshire and we rented a room in Woking – a bedsit we used during the week – and we went home at the weekends.'

For a time the Beatrice-Lola (as it was known) seemed poised to become a significant player because of the backing and the expertise of the personnel. The car made its debut at Monza in September 1985, Alan Jones driving it, but lacked reliability. It didn't finish any of the final three Grands Prix – Europe at Brands Hatch, South Africa and Australia.

Jones stayed for 1986 and was joined by Patrick Tambay. Between them they scored six points and the Beatrice-Lola team faded from view.

'There was a boardroom coup at Beatrice and the new incumbents thought it was a waste of time and stopped it,' recalls Oatley. 'I don't think Carl Haas was that bothered about the Formula 1 side of his operation and didn't really put much effort into keeping it going, which was a shame. If we could have sustained it there were a lot of good people there who went on to much better things. It's a pity it couldn't have gelled at that time.

'The end of Beatrice was the end of 1986. We were both out of work and looking for a job, looking around to see what was available. One possibility was that we were both going to go to Arrows but then I got the offer of a job at McLaren and that to me looked like a better option. I took it.'

The man running Arrows, Jackie Oliver, sets out the background. 'I was trying to get Neil Oatley, the designer, and I was talking to him. I suspect that other teams were talking to him because he was of the higher order then as a name than perhaps he is now, when he's more of a backroom guy. At that time Neil Oatley was a name on people's lips as a potential top designer along with Adrian Newey and people like that.

'These negotiations go on during a racing season, where everybody is jostling for positions, and of course a number of teams, including myself, were looking at the Beatrice organisation as a potential failure. They had good people and the idea was to go and get them.'

Oliver's PA, Rosemary Wright, received a call.

Wright: 'I've got a Ross Brawn on the phone and he wants to talk to you.'

Oliver: 'What about?'

Wright: 'He wouldn't say.'

Oliver: 'I don't know him. Does anybody know him? Well, stick him through.'

(As Oliver says, 'I'll talk to anybody about anything, I'll turn over all the stones – you never know. So he came on the phone and…')

Oliver: 'Yes, Mr Brawn, how can I help you?'

Brawn: 'I've been talking to Neil Oatley and he says you've got a position as a technical director available at your team.'

Oliver: 'Ah, right, that means that Neil's not going to take up my offer and he's suggested that you call me.'

Oliver, chuckling at the memory of it, says, 'So that's how it happened. I said "It would have been nice for Neil to have called me and said 'Thank you for the offer but I'm going somewhere else,' but of course nobody does, because as soon as they do you know where he's going – so they always play it close to their chests. I met up with Ross, looked at his CV and signed him on a five-year contract with an escalating fee on performance.'

Oatley says that 'Ross was very interested in Arrows and obviously that worked out very well for him. I think he took quite a few of the designers to Arrows from Beatrice [some reports say seven] and they more or less designed what would have been the next Beatrice car.

'It was unusual for me at McLaren – not working with him after all that time. It had been nearly ten years and it had been a good period. I never fell out with him. I think we are both fairly easy-going characters and I can't recall seeing him lose his temper at all.

'He has a gift for handling human being, drivers, the people who design the cars. I think he's very astute. He knows the right thing to say, and not the wrong thing to say, and he has a very good feeling for getting the best out of people. He knows that just bawling somebody out is never an answer: it's working to improve people's weaknesses and trying to boost their confidence. He's good at understanding where people's plusses and minuses are, and working on the bits that need working on.'

Oliver, as he says, didn't know him but 'I was impressed with his interview. The proof of the pudding, however, is in the eating. I liked his approach. He was ambitious, aggressively ambitious, but he does it in a very quiet, smooth way. He managed to expand my organisation – because we didn't have a lot of money – but he expanded into areas like, particularly, carbon fibre production, by persuading me to rent more factories across the road, and we did it on a shoestring. He did it very well. But as I went along with Ross his strategic thinking technically and his ability to manage a technical staff – and enthuse them, and include them – is his strength. That was a natural ability. He had a style of technical management which got the results from everybody underneath him and that is something that he had at Arrows – and he would carry it to great effect at Ferrari, which must have been a much more difficult political environment.'

Brawn would be chief designer at Arrows and the 1987 car was his creation. Derek Warwick and Eddie Cheever drove it.

Warwick remembers meeting him during the course of the season before when the Arrows 'wasn't brilliant, to be honest. The engine wasn't good and it just wasn't really working. Then Ross came along. It was an instant impression. You knew that all of a sudden you had a chance. It was just the way he went about it, very methodical, very unflappable, very quietly spoken and pleasant. He wasn't a prima donna, he wasn't someone that believed his own hype, he was just somebody that was trying to make the best of what he had. He changed a lot of the dynamics of the team in terms of the personnel, the work ethics, how we worked, who was responsible for what, and really built this.'

Arrows scored 11 points in 1987.

Alastair Macqueen of the Jaguar sports car team remembers: 'My very first contact was at the end of '87 when Ross phoned me and said "Have you got plans for '88? The Formula 1 Arrows team might be interested." I can only imagine this was because of my mate Eddie Cheever. Ross and I shared drivers, not knowing one another – we shared Eddie Cheever and Mr Warwick during the 1986 and 1987 seasons [the drivers drove for Jaguar and Arrows – 'It was the era when drivers did both,' Macqueen points out]. I suspect it was Mr Cheever who put my name forward. I guess Eddie said "Well, why not get this bloke, because he worked fine with me over at Jaguar?" I still had things to do at Jaguar because we'd yet to win Le Mans. We'd we'd won races in 1986 and won the championship in 1987 but I still had work in progress to win Le Mans, which happened in 1988. Le Mans is the big one and that's what we were all aiming at. I said "Thanks very much but I need to be winning Le Mans for Jaguar. That's what I set out to do and that's what I've got to do."'

They'd meet, Brawn and Macqueen, and in a most unlikely place – Macqueen's place.

Arrows scored 23 points in 1988 and 13 in 1989.

That 1989 car, Warwick insists, 'was a Grand Prix winner. It had the V8 Ford engine and it was a very small car. Eddie Cheever was again my team-mate for the third year running and it was a fantastic little car. We led Grands Prix with it' – Warwick from laps 35 to 38 in Canada, no mean feat when Ayrton Senna and Alain Prost in the McLaren between them led virtually every lap everywhere.

'Unfortunately,' Warwick says, 'it was under-financed and we had a few mechanical problems that weren't Ross's fault. It was really a matter of the finances of the team. It was a difficult process for him at Arrows.'

Brawn left Arrows at the end of 1989 to join Jaguar in the world sports car championship – Macqueen's place, in fact – and Warwick left Arrows, too, joining Lotus. 'We lost him at the end of the year. It was enough for me to go and find another team,' Warwick says.

Brawn would explain his own reasoning. 'I'd worked at Arrows for three years. Arrows was a great little team in those days but it had no money. There's nothing more frustrating in Formula 1 than not having the resources. We did quite good cars over the winter, but as soon as we started to run them there were no funds to develop them, so you'd see the car show some promise but then have a frustrating year trying to keep up with it while everyone else was moving forward.'

Jackie Oliver concedes the lack of funds. 'We got on very well but the expectation of Ross was beyond my capabilities. I wasn't able to give Ross what he wanted so he went somewhere else. He went with Tom [Walkinshaw] – went to someone else who was capable of doing it. I am a great admirer of Ross. It's a shame he broke his contract because he did it at the time I got Footwork, and I think that their connection with Arrows, with Ross at the helm, would have produced a lot more success for Arrows and for Porsche. Unfortunately he walked away just at the wrong time. Life is timing.

'It would have been useful if Ross had said "I'm thinking of going, and I'm going for this reason. What's your prospects?" But unfortunately in life people don't do that. Three months after Ross walked I got millions of pounds from Footwork which would have solved his problem, and he may have been able to persuade us not to go with Porsche.'

Brawn says that at Arrows 'we had Eddie Cheever and Derek Warwick at the time, who were also driving for Tom Walkinshaw. They were full of praise for Tom, who was a very determined and ambitious guy.

'He approached me and said he wanted to do Formula 1 racing, but before he could do that he wanted me to support the sports car programme. It was like opening a candy shop with no one there. I was used to a regime of very strict regulations in Formula 1 where everything was covered and was so restrictive. Suddenly I opened this rulebook and there were about half a dozen regulations. It was such a great opportunity. So we built a Formula 1 car and clothed it in sports car bodywork. There were some objections, but we were careful with our interpretation...'[3]

Tom Walkinshaw signed Brawn from Arrows: 'I wasn't involved in Arrows at that stage, it was Jackie Oliver and Alan Rees. I knew Ross wasn't very happy there. We were already doing the sports cars and we'd been doing a good job but I was aware that the rules were going to change to three and a half litres Formula 1 engines, so I spoke to Ross and I said "You'd better come over and design our new sports car." He'd not done a sports car before. I had no doubts because the rules were very similar to Formula 1 in terms of ground effect cars and engines so there were lots and lots of similarities. The challenge was something that interested him in terms of doing something completely different. He came on board. He was given free rein and he was with a good group of engineers and designers already working with Jaguar. I felt we ought to move on in terms of Formula 1 thinking, and that's why I offered him the job. We always got on very well and we still do. We can discuss things and tell each other what we want to tell each other.'

Walkinshaw says that 'Ross sat down in the beginning and drew up a list of requirements,' and that these were met without 'restraint in terms of cost or time. I put him in charge of the TWR [Tom Walkinshaw Racing] Design Centre. We needed to make a step up because we knew that Toyota and Peugeot were already working on that type of car, and with huge resources, so to do the car properly he had to be in charge of all our engineers and design staff and all the facilities and resources we had. He was made Technical Director of all of that. I gave him total leeway.

'Obviously we discussed the ideas he was having and so forth. We satisfied ourselves that whatever we were doing was the right interpretation – or a possible interpretation! – of the rules. Then we came up with something that was pretty radical. I don't think you can interfere. You put your trust in the people and if you can't you shouldn't have them there. When he needed to come and talk he did.'

Macqueen says 'Ross came at the beginning of 1990 and this was the first time I'd physically met him. We shared a desk for about three months because there was nowhere to put him while they built his new drawing office above the workshop at TWR. Obviously a lot of things passed between us, although we were both mostly working on separate projects. As ever with these things, where he'd come from one discipline and I'd come from another, there was a lot of useful information that the other person has. I think that the best visualisation of that was when looking at his new car, which was going to be the 750 kilo Group C car. My attitude was: "How on earth am I am going to lose 150 kilos from this 900 Group C car to make one of those?" Ross was coming from a completely different direction: "How on earth am I going to add 150 kilos of kit to my Grand Prix car to make one of those – all this extra weight I've got to find from somewhere?"

'In the two years he was with Jaguar the *modus operandi* was very similar to what you'll find at Honda and now Brawn. He came in and demanded a huge amount of what was required, took a year to conceive the whole thing and then was massively successful with what he'd got – but he didn't jump straight in and do it. In fact in 1990, when he came, he said, "Well, look, you carry on with the Le Mans thing because you've got that under control and frankly I'm not that interested because you are using the V12 cars. I'll have a look at the turbo cars for Group C racing" – and after a couple of races he left that to me and I continued to run the whole thing while he concentrated on the design and build of his new car.

'I think that's rather similar to what happened at Honda last year [2008], almost a rerun, and it doesn't come as a great surprise to me. That's the way Ross does his best work. Later he went into Benetton and Ferrari in a similar manner and took a year to fully understand. I think that's what set him apart from anybody I'd ever met in a technical capacity before. He called the shots.

'With a rolling project that I moved into at the end of 1985 with Jaguar we had already set out our stall of what was going to happen, the budgets were defined and the car was essentially in the design process then. I just had to guide them to completion, whereas Ross stepped back and said "I'm not doing it like that. We are going to use *this* much money, we are going to do it *this* way, and it is going to take me *this* long. If you don't want to come on board, fair enough."

'I would never have had the balls to do that. I was always part of the project rather than coming in to lead a brand new project. For me, that was something that Ross did brilliantly and I'd never seen that done before – that a technical person would take that control, as opposed to the team principal or the marketing guys or whoever, who were already running something. That was a complete turnaround. Ross was expensive but he did it properly. I had never seen anyone from the technical side who would go to Tom and demand "You're going to have to find *this* much more money or I'm not doing it." I'd got a salary, I was told what I had and told to go and get on with it. What Ross did was a novelty for me.' Macqueen repeats it: 'I had never seen a technical person who had that much clout or demanded that much clout.'

Frank Dernie says 'Ross is good at that sort of thing. It was quite funny. When he was working for me he used always to be hassling me for more people, more budget, more kit or what have you.'

In 1990 Jaguar found themselves competing against Sauber-Mercedes, Nissan, Toyota and Porsche. Jaguar used two pairings: Martin Brundle and Alain Ferté, Jan Lammers and Andy Wallace. They finished second to Sauber-Mercedes with 30 points (Sauber had 67.5). However, Brundle – now paired with John Nielsen and Price Cobb – did win Le Mans from the second Jaguar (Lammers/Wallace/Franz Konrad). Even this was no preparation for what was to come. Brawn, of course, was concentrating on the 1991 car, although evidently he did some 'tidying-up' work on the 1990 car before the Silverstone round in May. The Jaguars finished 1-2.

'It was fortuitous for Ross that it was the start of a brand new breed of car, and nobody thought it through as well as he did,' Macqueen says. 'His car was very good and wiped the floor with anything else in '91, but Toyota and Peugeot came up with cars which were far superior the following year. If I can liken it to Grand Prix cars his car was the original Lotus 78 and following that principle.

'Ross didn't actually increase the downforce of a car that we'd already invented. The turbo car was creating a similar L over D, similar downforce levels to the car that Ross invented; but what Ross's had was 150 kilos less – and 150 in 900 is quite a big percentage. You increase the cornering capability by exactly that percentage, so the G forces went up by a big chunk.

'In the 1970s I was a sound engineer so I was used to taking control of large events and technically running them. I've been at the back of quite a few rock concerts and run the show from the desk. Group C racing to me was absolutely brilliant because I could take control of a technical event in exactly the same way as I did sound engineering. The disciplines are very, very similar: you have a whole bunch of high tech equipment which you've got to get working to its optimum. You take it to a venue, put on a show, pull it down again and move on. That is exactly the same as sports car racing, or racing generally. The fact that in Group C, as the technical controller, you actually had a physical part to play in the race was like bliss to me – it was where I was, what I could do.'

Brawn would subsequently say that he learnt a great deal about race tactics from Macqueen.

'Yes. Once he had learnt the tactics he realised that you could apply it to Formula 1. That's why I think Ross was interested in what I did, because Grand Prix racing was basically this: you waved goodbye to the driver at the start and you saw him at the end of the race, but once they began putting tyre stops and fuels stop in then strategy obviously came into it. I'd been practising this for a few years. We'd won the championship in 1987 and 1988, had a disasterous year in 1989, but I was reasonably good at it by the time Ross came along. It was one of the things I had specialised and our paths crossed at that point. We learned a great deal from each other. I went on to specialise in long-distance sports car racing and he went on to specialise in Grand Prix racing.'

To which Brawn says: 'I was lucky because I walked into Jaguar and there was a whole team of guys there who were used to strategic racing. Alastair Macqueen was the strategy guy at Jaguar, a very clever guy who had years of experience of the strategies involved in motor racing. I was able to pick it up from Alastair very quickly and that really was my first exposure to it.'

Macqueen explains that Brawn is 'a very slow burner. He's got a lot of tolerance generally, he's pretty laid back. That's the persona which is very, very useful in that [racing] environment and I tend to be the same way, Mr Stress-free, not getting upset about anything because, in technical operations, it doesn't benefit anybody. Certainly as a team manager and a team principal, occasionally *venting* – letting off steam – is probably good in order that people can respect what you are doing, but in the technical operation it can be counter-productive. I think both Ross and I recognised that. By nature we are similar people in terms of being fairly calm and calculating rather than in the [Flavio] Briatore mould.'

Brawn, Warwick says, 'was instrumental in me going to Jaguar. He made Tom sign me, basically. I'd driven for Lotus in 1990 and, as we all know, the team folded at the end of that season. I was left without a Formula 1 drive. I then had a phone call from Ross saying that the new Jaguar for the 1991 season was pretty spectacular and "Do you fancy coming to look at it?" I wasn't really sure whether I wanted to do that because I was thinking of doing IndyCars.

'Then Tom Walkinshaw sent a plane over to Jersey, where I live, for me. I went to the factory and was met by Ross. He gave me a big sales pitch on the new car, how much aerodynamics it had, how quick it was going to be and, as it turned out, the car was even better than that. It was obviously a compliment for me because he insisted that I was to drive the car. That was good for me and it worked, because I ended up signing the contract for the season.'

'We always ran strong drivers when we went sports car racing,' Walkinshaw says. 'I believe there were certain compromises we had with the Jaguar – the V12 was a fantastic engine but it was pretty heavy – so that was when I decided I wanted to have a carbon car. So we did the first carbon sports car. I decided you needed Formula 1 drivers to drive it to get the best out of it. We always had the best drivers we could possibly get. We had Derek Warwick and Cheever and Brundle.'

The 1991 Jaguar, the XJR14, was launched at Silverstone in March and provoked something of a sensation. *Autosport* magazine described it as 'dramatic looking' and designed to take on the challenge of the Peugeot 905 and Mercedes C291.

Warwick took it out in the wet for its initial runs. 'I remember the first time I drove the car it was *phenomenal*, a Formula 1 car with bodywork for sure. Every time you came in touch with Ross he gave you that confidence that you were getting the best car out there.'

Next day Teo Fabi, in the dry, started to do *Grand Prix* times, and found the car had so much downforce that handling it was giving him a sore neck. Walkinshaw pointed out that Fabi had been in IndyCar racing where, at Indianapolis, you just turn left so his neck was no longer accustomed to turning right as well. Walkinshaw added that Warwick had complained of a sore neck too, and this 'impressed' him.

Alastair Macqueen remembers 'Teo getting out of the car

and saying "I can't drive it any more, my head's falling off my neck." At that point we knew it was going to work...'

Walkinshaw, a very pragmatic Scotsman, said yes, the car was *phenomenal*, and they were all delighted, but the real test was yet to come, and that was winning races.

The first of them would be Suzuka, Japan, on 14 April.

The Sauber-Mercedes comprised the Mercedes 'youth' team – Michael Schumacher and Karl Wendlinger in one car, Jean-Louis Schlesser and Jochen Mass in the other. Peugeot fielded Keke Rosberg and Yannick Dalmas, Mauro Baldi and Philippe Alliot. Against them Jaguar had Warwick and Brundle, Fabi and Brundle (yes, Brundle driving both: this is sports car racing, *not* Formula 1).

At Suzuka the Jaguar team indulged in Formula 1 psychology, however, keeping their garage doors firmly locked against prying eyes and positioning green plastic covers over the front and rear wings when the car was in the pit lane. Warwick (1m 48.0s) took pole from Rosberg (1m 50.5s) and Wendlinger (1m 51.8s), Brundle sixth (2m 03.4s).

Warwick took the lead immediately from Rosberg, Brundle fifth – but he went only to lap 4, when an electrical fault halted him. Warwick commanded the race but needed a new starter motor – which inevitably took a long time to fit – and he finished ten laps behind the winning Peugeot of Baldi/Alliot.

The worst was over. Three weeks later at Monza the Warwick/Brundle car beat the Fabi/Brundle car by a lap and the leading Mercedes by two.

Frank Dernie says that during the period when Brawn was sports car racing 'he and I were not competing, if you know what I mean, so I had many a chat about wind-tunnel tests and philosophies and stuff like that. I was reasonably up to speed with how he was getting on with his sports cars – brilliant job.'

'In the races the car was fan-tastic,' Warwick says. 'It was running against Schumacher and Wendlinger and Frentzen, who were driving for Sauber, and I have to say it was the best car out there by far. It was difficult to drive because the steering was heavy, the gearchange was on the left-hand side and in motor racing it's always on the right-hand side. It was on the left because of the way the car was designed: remember, in a sports car you do sit to the right of the car' – so, like any British saloon, the room is on the left.

'Because Ross was so clever with his suspension and with his aerodynamics, the most difficult thing was room to get in and out. Obviously you had to get out the door, but it wasn't really a door, more like a bloody window! The most difficult thing for me was driver changes, because to get my big lump out of a window was not easy. One of Tom's favourites was John Nielsen, the big Dane, but he couldn't fit in the car either. It was ideal for Fabi, of course, because he was only little – three foot six or something.'

At Silverstone, two weeks after Monza, the Warwick/Fabi car beat the Wendlinger/Schumacher Mercedes by a lap, Brundle third. Warwick got nothing for this drive, however, because he hadn't been officially entered for it.

'That was a bit of a controversy,' Warwick says, 'because I won the race and later in the year got penalised and had the points taken away. With that I lost the World Championship (Fabi 86, Warwick 79). Tom wanted to swap me from one car to the other, and I said "Tom, I haven't been nominated for this car." I remember Tom's exact words. He said "You worry about driving that [expletive] thing and I'll worry about the registration."

At Le Mans, Jaguar took one XJR14 for, as someone noted, a cheeky assault on pole (cheeky because pole has no meaning in a 24-hour race), but would run three XJR12s in the race. Mazda won it, the Jaguars second, third, and fourth.

That was June. In July Walkinshaw bought heavily into the Benetton Formula 1 team, which had lost its designer, John Barnard, shortly before. Walkinshaw had control of all aspects of the team except sponsorship and marketing: these remained the province of Flavio Briatore. The TWR operation would be kept separate.

Autosport wrote: 'No major changes are expected in the short term, although the TWR staff includes many ex-F1 personnel, among them Ross Brawn and Roger Silman.' Walkinshaw was quoted as saying 'there will be a crossover of information and technology' between Brawn and Gordon Kimball, who replaced Barnard. 'Hopefully all the guys can work well together.'

This did not happen in isolation. Brawn said a year later that both he and Walkinshaw 'had ambitions to be in Formula 1'. Before Walkinshaw bought into Benetton he and Brawn had had many discussions, because 'Benetton, we thought, was the best route to get us involved'. The commercial side, Brawn concluded, was strong but the engineering weak.

He now found his time divided between concluding the sports car championship – in still had four rounds to run – and, as he phrased it, 'putting the technical side of Benetton together.'

Benetton, the fashion chain, had been sponsors in Formula 1 since they began with the Tyrrell team in 1983. They bought the Toleman team in 1985, inheriting designer Rory Byrne as well as Pat Symonds, an unorthodox and highly effective thinker about motor racing. It ran as Toleman through 1985 and became Benetton in 1986. It seemed forever on the edge of joining the big teams: 19 points in 1986 but then 28, 39, 38 and 71 in 1990, falling to 38.5 in 1991. The distance they were away is easily expressed. Williams won the Constructors' Championship in 1986 with 141 points, Williams again (137) in 1987 then McLaren 199, 141, 121 and, in 1991, 139.

Byrne left to join the Reynard team, but it ran into severe financial difficulties and was bought by Benetton. By August, Byrne and others were working on a new car, the B192, for 1992 because, although they could – as Brawn points out – have run the B191 through into 1992, 'we decided we wanted our own car for fairly major technical reasons, but also because it would bring the team together'.

Byrne 'knew who he [Brawn] was because he'd been at Williams, but I had never met him until 1991. He'd done the Jaguar sports car for Tom Walkinshaw. Flavio had got rid of John Barnard and he'd brought Tom on board to try and steady the ship. I remember the first time. We had a meeting at Tom's place – myself, Roger Silman and Ross. My first impression was that he didn't talk a lot, he listened, and what he had to say was sensible. What impressed me was that – obviously – we were discussing how we would work together. I was coming from a position where I'd been the chief designer, he'd been a chief designer, so how *are* we going to work together? You don't know each other, it can easily get political and difficult and everything else.

'I said "Look, if we are going to get on, you know, if we are going to work together, I'll make a proposal about how I think we should do it – because I think I know what I can do and I know the areas that I am not good at. I made some suggestions and Ross just sat there. He thought about it for 30 seconds. He got up, he came over and we shook hands. That was it. We worked well together ever since.'

Walkinshaw remembers 'I completely restructured Benetton and that's when I brought Ross in, I brought Rory Byrne in, Patrick Symonds. I put them all together and persuaded them all to work together and then we created the first proper Benetton, which of course had the active suspension and everything else. In those circumstances, Ross was good. He was in charge of the technical department, Rory was in charge of all the aero and design, Pat was in charge of all the suspension and all that sort of stuff. He did all the active suspension work. It was as good as I could put together.'

Macqueen, ruminating on Walkinshaw taking Brawn to Benetton, says that Walkinshaw had 'seen what Ross had down with the XJR14. It wasn't entirely reliable but it was a breath of fresh air in terms of the sports car world.'

Frank Dernie, however, feels for an undercurrent. 'When Tom bought into Benetton, Ross went there as Technical Director. As far as they were concerned, his previous history had been an ex-mechanic, failed Formula 1 designer and sports car guy, so the people at Benetton – who were at that time an arrogant bunch of bastards – were giving him a bit of a hard time. A sports car, even if it was a good one, was beneath their contempt. They didn't really want him and were being very difficult. I ended up being asked by Ross to come as chief engineer so at least he'd have one ally that he knew and trusted. So I worked again with him in 1992 through 1994 but, that time, roles reversed. Instead of him working for me I was working for him.'

In August at the Nürburgring, David Brabham and Warwick won from the second Jaguar. Schumacher in the Mercedes had an engine failure after ten laps. Leaving the Nürburgring, Fabi led the championship with 62 points from Warwick (50), Schumacher joint 11th (23).

Walkinshaw had noticed Schumacher. 'I rated him and he was always cocky. I can remember when Warwick came in doing his pieces because Schumacher had pushed him out of the road on a qualifying lap. He was only a kid and Derek was an established Formula 1 driver. So we watched him closely.'

Brawn judges that Schumacher was 'the only guy who gave us a hard time in sports cars', despite being paired with two young drivers of the calibre of Frentzen and Wendlinger. 'He was outstanding because he was smooth, he used less fuel than the other guys, he was quicker. What I couldn't believe is that they didn't keep him in the car. There was some democratic process in the team where he only got one of the three stints in a race. We were relieved he didn't drive that much, but it did make us aware of Michael Schumacher.'[4]

The story is folklore by now. Bertrand Gachot was convicted of assault in a London court and Eddie Jordan needed a driver to replace him at the Belgian Grand Prix, which happened to be a week after the Nürburgring. Schumacher had never driven a Formula 1 car and never driven Spa, but that didn't deter Jordan. Schumacher impressed everyone, and although inexperience punished him at the start of the race – he burnt the clutch – he became a very desirable commodity.

'It was obvious immediately that the kid was going to be quick,' Walkinshaw says. 'The following week I contacted Jochen Neerpasch [of Mercedes] to see what the deal was in his contract. There were a lot of rumours around that Mercedes had the option to take him back if anybody signed him. I wouldn't sign him under those terms. Eddie wanted paying from Mercedes for him to drive. I said I'd pay him to drive but I wanted Mercedes to waive their option on his contract. Mercedes came back and said if we were going to sign him properly then they wouldn't stand in his way. I hired him the week after Spa and he drove at Monza.'

That was the Italian Grand Prix where Schumacher finished fifth, launching his career in earnest.

The sports car season tailed away. The Jaguars were third and fifth at Magny-Cours, sixth in Mexico City and second and third at Autopolis.

Warwick guards precious memories ... of Alastair Macqueen 'because he was a super guy and he was engineering my car at times. I got on really well with him [...] What I really remember is how quick Schumacher was in the Mercedes and how good Ross Brawn was for me. They really stand out. At Le Mans things change all the time and that was Ross's strength, of course: his ability to think on his feet and his ability to stay calm through the pressure of a race was second to none.'

Brawn describes the XJR14 as a 'very pretty little car. It started the season three and a half seconds quicker than the opposition', but this decreased because Walkinshaw – yes, a canny Scot – saw how much of an advantage it held and 'wouldn't spend any money on it'.

Notes

1. March was a racing team founded in 1969 by Max Mosley, Alan Rees, Graham Coaker and Robin Herd – hence the name. They contested Formula 1 and made customer cars across the single-seater spectrum.
2. *Driving Ambition,* by Alan Jones and Keith Botsford (Stanley Paul, London, 1981).
3. www2.ferrariromania.ro/formula1/159/lung-dar-interesant-interviu-cu-ross-brawn.html.
4. Ibid.

CHAPTER 3

GONE FISHIN'

Ross Brawn was now in a position to deploy strategy during the Grands Prix, drawing on what he had learnt at Jaguar. He points out that sports car racing then resembled Grand Prix racing now, with fuel stops and tyre stops. Grand Prix racing *then* involved pit stops to change tyres and that was it. 'I was a little bit shocked because, quite frankly, we were applying quite straightforward strategies to races and other people didn't seem to be following a very logical path. This kind of reputation of black magic appeared that was not correct, because it was relatively straightforward, logical strategies.'

He 'really enjoyed the period at Jaguar. Alastair Macqueen, a very nice guy, was fascinated by, and really into, the strategy side, and of course in sports car racing it is a vital element. Alastair opened my eyes to what strategy was in sports car racing. I suddenly saw a facet: you could get involved in the pit wall rather than just watching the cars go round. It all fitted perfectly because, when refuelling was permitted again in Formula 1, there I was with the experience of a couple of years of sports car racing where this type of thing was the norm and vital to success. In Formula 1 they were very slow to pick it up and not everyone really engaged in it, so it was great fun and for a couple of years, for sure, people treated it as an unfortunate distraction rather than an opportunity.'

Of course, something you haven't thought of and which proves extremely effective may appear as black magic – a bit like conjuring tricks until you have them explained to you – but Brawn was simply applying common sense. It worked like this: refuelling was a slow process, and if you could carry extra fuel in the car you'd spend less time at the re-fuelling rig because you'd need less fuel put in. Under the laws of gravity, the car was inescapably heavier and slower hauling round the extra fuel *but* a long pit stop was even slower. Benetton deployed this for two years and Brawn was astonished that nobody else 'cottoned on'.

Walkinshaw says that 'when Ross came on board there wasn't really a lot of tactics in Formula 1. They didn't figure out about changing tactics in the middle of a race. He could see the possibilities from sports cars: you could influence it and change it if you watched what everyone else was doing. You could always beat Williams because they'd start off and never change their strategy no matter what was happening. We'd change ours. Ross mastered that and now he's probably the best in the business at it.

'He always said he learned a lot from the sports car team and how you had to change during a race. You had to *live* a race like Le Mans and interpret it as you went along. That was taken into Formula 1, and we won a lot of races people would have thought normally we'd never win, just because we did change tactics in the middle. Williams always got respect but they were very predictable. We'd change the pit stop strategy – and all sorts…'

Brawn settled in at Benetton and would become, in Byrne's judgement, 'the key. He was the Technical Director and he did all the strategy calls on the pit wall apart from technically managing the company.'

Byrne remembers the fourth race of 1992, the first time he and Brawn had gone to the Spanish Grand Prix as part of the same team. 'Michael finished second behind Nigel Mansell and it was fairly obvious from there that Ross had a pretty good control of the pit wall. It wasn't an easy race, it was wet but you could see he knew what he was doing.'

This was a great deal more than a second place. Benetton were based at Witney, Oxfordshire. When John Barnard was with the team he set up the technical group at Godalming, near his own base at Guildford. Brawn insisted they had to return to Witney and some didn't fancy a third move, some simply lost belief – but Witney it was.

Benetton had taken the previous year's B191 to the first

three rounds but now, in Spain, had the B192, which Schumacher put on the front row, an enormous psychological step forward after all the uncertainty. The second place reinforced that: Brawn saw that the team saw they were going in the right direction.

I put it to Byrne: *Somebody said you were slightly suspicious of somebody coming in because he might trample all over your bit of the domain, but he ended up doing all the admin, which suited you perfectly.*

'No, I don't think it's fair to say he did the admin. He had a lot to contribute technically, but how it actually worked, at Benetton and later at Ferrari, was that Ross looked after the overall technical aspects of the company. It included the budgets, it included all the racing and it included the general technical aspects of the company – the technical management of the company. He left me to get on with, specifically, the car design and the research that supported the design. This is what I wanted to do, anyway.

'If I look back at my days at Toleman and Benetton, and up until when Ross arrived, to be honest I was too focused on the car design and I wasn't building up the technical infrastructure of the company – so the company was nowhere near what it should have been technically. I hadn't built up the tools to be able to allow me to do a better car, so yes, it suited me perfectly when Ross came.

'He had a lot of respect from everyone he was involved with. He was never one of these people that had to spell out that he was the boss. You knew he was the boss, even though he didn't ever have to specifically say it. He had the respect of the people beneath him and the people above him. He also knew what he was talking about, was astute technically and, of course, brilliant on the pit wall.

'He did comment on my designs. I never designed in isolation. We did some pretty radical things from time to time and I never set sail on my own and did it – we always had an office next door to each other. I'd knock on his door and say, "Ross, you got five minutes? I want to run this idea past you." That's how we worked. We never had a cross word. In fact, I don't think we ever had a fundamental disagreement – we might have had some detailed disagreements but at the end of the day we'd have a discussion and we'd resolve it. In all the time I worked with him, I never heard him shout in any meeting or anything. You did know when he wasn't happy. I've seen times when he was like that, but the fact that he wasn't happy didn't mean he lost his temper. He was *always* under control.'

Derek Warwick says that 'you've got to remember Ross Brawn is not really a designer, he's more the concept man. He understands what's needed within a team for the team to work and to get the right people around him. And he knew that Rory Byrne was the right person. It's not so much leaving Rory to get on with it – because Ross understood as much as he did – but he also knew that he couldn't do all the jobs, so therefore he filled in the areas that were weak to make them stronger until they got stronger, then he moved on to a different area. He was a master at it. You've got two people there that haven't got egos. Neither Ross nor Rory has an ego. It was a partnership in heaven, it really was. They wouldn't have wrong word because you've got two characters that live, eat, sleep and drink motor racing. They are passionate about it and if they see people around them giving 110% they love you. They are very similar characters.'

Race mechanic Steve Matchett joined Benetton in January 1990. 'Ross arrived over the winter of 1991-1992. Flavio Briatore got involved with Walkinshaw and it was on the strength of that that Ross arrived.'

Briatore and the designer, John Barnard, fell out and Barnard left.

'I didn't know Ross at all until he arrived,' Matchett says. 'They hired a chap called Gordon Kimball and he lasted until they got Ross signed up then he disappeared out of the door. And off we went with the 1992 car.'

Matchett explains the difference between Byrne and the aerodynamicists ('I am sure they see things differently to everybody else') and Brawn the pragmatist. 'Rory's designs were completely impractical but good in the wind tunnel! For example, the rear brake ducts on those early Rory cars. He had made it in one piece. If you wanted to change it because it was getting too hot, too cold or whatever you had to take the rear corner off the car, the upright, the suspension, the driveshaft, then you put the new brake duct on and reassemble.

'Even on a good day that was 15 minutes' work, and that's 15 minutes' track time gone [at a test]. He'd designed it like that because he didn't want to have the button head of a screw in his airflow, that he'd have to have if he'd split the brake duct. Ross came along and said "This is crazy. You've got to be able to work on the car! You've got to get the car on track!" So for the 1992 car he said "Just split it and we'll bolt it together round the driveshaft." You could take it on and off in about 30 seconds. From that point on, that's how it was designed. If the car failed on the grid we needed to make the change in 30 seconds, not 15 minutes...

'That's the difference, I think, between Rory as an aerodynamicist and Ross as a mechanical engineer. You put the two together and you've quite something. I think Ross did a tremendous job of controlling Rory's way of looking at it – that light in which aerodynamicists see everything. I've never worked with Adrian Newey but I've looked at some of his cars and I think he's the same way. The practicalities of life don't cross their field of vision.

'If Ross and Rory had both been mechanical engineers or if they had both been aerodynamicists – I always think of Ross as a mechanical engineeer – I think there would have been a great clash, but because you've got a man each side of the fence, as it were, there was no clash at all. Ross was able to say "Yeah, but we need to be able to do this. The radiator ducts need to be big enough, Rory, that they will cool the car and not make the engine burst into flames at Hockenheim."'

This is how you win championships, and how Benetton then Ferrari did.

'I have a great deal of respect for Ross and I always have had,' Matchett says. 'I think the reason for that is he's a bit like Frank Dernie: very normal, very approachable and it doesn't matter who he's talking to – whether it's the guy driving the truck, the mechanics, the engineers, the designers. He'll have a chat one-on-one. He would listen to anything anybody had to say. People say "The office door is always open and if you have a problem, come in and talk to me," and of course you know full well that the office door may be open but it is completely shut off. There was nothing like that with Ross. I think that stems from the fact that he learnt everything from the ground up, starting as a machinist. That gave him a very good grounding in how things work – the fact that you do have to listen to every department. And he was not afraid to delegate.'

In 1992 Schumacher came an astonishing third in the World Championship. Astonishing? Going into the season his whole Grand Prix career comprised six races at the tail end of 1991. Now he finished above Senna and Gerhard Berger in the McLarens.

Ross Brawn was a big man physically and was about to cast his shadow over the Williams team, Damon Hill, McLaren, Ayrton Senna – and anybody else who went near Benetton. This was but a prelude. With Schumacher, Byrne and small, sharp, arch-organiser Jean Todt, he'd cast his shadow over the whole *history* of the World Championship.

Benetton ascended in direct proportion to Michael Schumacher's career gathering a terrible strength. Schumacher was the point of delivery. Byrne could design the car, Symonds could see what others couldn't see – and, incidentally, could understand how Schumacher's mind worked – and Brawn could see through the shifting patterns and sudden dramas of a race to what lay beyond. Each of these good men and true – pensive, quietly spoken and *all three* minus egos – needed Schumacher to translate their efforts into something tangible: to deliver, in fact.

Frank Dernie remembers that 'by the time Ross got to the level he was at with Benetton his involvement in the design of the car was much less than it had been previously. Very much less. Without Rory, the Benetton success in terms of having a competitive car wouldn't have been possible. Ross's arrival in the beginning meant Rory had someone ahead of him – above him. He very quickly realised that Ross made his life easier. Ross wasn't being competitive with him, Ross was making sure that everything Rory needed to get the job done the way he wanted was provided to him. Ross would take care of that.

'If you needed more money, if you needed more people, Ross went to the boss and fought for it. Rory came to the conclusion that with Ross there, all the things that he personally hated to do, but had to do, were going to be dealt with by Ross, and Ross wasn't going to interfere hideously with all the things Rory liked doing – Rory realised early on that he was in great shape. He was left to design the car.'

This stands as confirmation of what Byrne has already said and bears repetition because an entirely new, astonishing and historic *era* was beginning which would, in its fullness, redefine the possibilities of Grand Prix racing, no less.

Schumacher's strength truly was terrible because it was constructed on more than great physical fitness, complete dedication and unearthly car control. He wanted *it* and he wanted it very badly. He would go to war with Damon Hill and across two tumultuous seasons leave a lot of wreckage on a lot of different tracks, not least Adelaide in 1994 when he won his first World Championship and Walkinshaw helped lift him clean off the ground. Schumacher retained the championship with some ease but there was, perhaps only in retrospect, something temporal about all this.

He'd answer a bigger calling, from Maranello.

The Benetton years *were* tumultuous. 'Ross coped with that very calmly,' continues Dernie. 'He never really let anything faze him publicly. You never saw him stressed. I'll tell you one of the things that always struck me, and now to all of us it seems so obvious – the French Grand Prix of 1994 where there was all that talk of launch control on the Benetton. At the end of that race I remember Damon saying "The pace of the Benetton is unbelievable. It's not possible for it to be this fast etc etc. They must be doing something underhand."

'Of course, we were just getting into the idea of fuel in the car: we were running a three-stop strategy and Damon was running a two. In hindsight, now we have all got used to fuel loads – and how important the weight of the fuel is to the performance of the car – it's so obvious why we were fast:

because we were running lighter. We were probably 25 kilos lighter. When 25 kilos is a second a lap that's the performance difference and also the acceleration difference, because you're not hauling it off the line. Now it all seems so obvious.

'Ross, from his sports car days, had all this knowledge of fuel loads and the differences they made. Remember that 1994 was the first year back with refuelling after a ten-year break, and the likes of Williams were completely on the back foot trying to figure out what the hell to do with it to make it work. That was Ross's great strength. In 1994 he knew how to make it work – and if you follow him through the Ferrari years, look at Magny-Cours again when he asked Michael Schumacher to do a four-stop strategy against Alonso, and Pat Symonds was scratching his head thinking "How the hell did they do that?" So when Damon said the Benetton's speed was unbelievable it confused a lot of people.

'What really upset Ross was the fact that he knew how he was making it work, but of course he didn't want to give the secrets away. He had to take it on the chin and say "We are doing nothing wrong." He even had a press conference to explain as much as he could without giving the game away why the car was so fast. From the first race of 1994 he knew how to make the car fast and it took the other guys a long, long while to catch up.'

Trevor Steggles 'was the managing director of a company based in Essex that manufactured electronic components. In the mid-1990s my design manager and I were invited to attend a presentation about computer-aided design and manufacture, organised by Hewlett Packard. Ross Brawn was the keynote speaker and he described how the design process within the world of Formula 1 had changed dramatically during his career. Using a number of examples, he explained to the audience how the time from the drawing board to the grid had reduced from months to weeks and to days.

'I recall that as a speaker Ross was a little slow to start, but as he warmed to the topic he kept the audience interested. His observations about the world of Formula 1 and how engineering had changed over the years was fascinating. I particularly remember the way he used some examples of how problems were resolved quickly through the benefits of having the design office linked directly with the manufacturing machines.

'He also detailed how the CAD/CAM systems [computer-aided design and computer-aided manufacturing] allowed him to free up the time of the production team, making the whole company more efficient and more effective on track.

'His explanation of the way that parts could be machined directly from the design data demonstrated to us the power of good computer technology linked with design management expertise. It was clear that Ross was a confident engineer but at that time he wasn't the greatest public speaker, although his hesitations and his desire to present things accurately held our attention.

'Following his speech Ross took questions from the floor, most of which – to the best of my memory – he answered fully. He only avoided any queries which might have compromised the Benetton Formula 1 team.

'Ross Brawn sticks in my mind as being almost a slightly diffident character, who was not entirely comfortable with a public speaking event but who had a very deep understanding of his subject. He was clearly a person used to design and manufacturing in a much-pressured environment. He also struck me as being a warm character, the sort who'd be good but quiet company down the pub for a beer.'

Benetton was a good place to be but not *the* place. To reach that you had to take the autobahn past Bologna into the charming, rolling hillsides of central Italy, following the road signs for Modena – or, as in the case of Schumacher, take a small plane.

Michael Schumacher did that, became the highest paid Formula 1 driver of all time, and prepared to measure himself against the ultimate challenge: to revive Ferrari after almost two decades of failure. John Barnard had been designing the car from Guildford and very soon realised that his ideas and Schumacher's were different – and Schumacher wasn't about to change. Barnard left and in December 1996 Brawn came in as Technical Director.

Before we leave Benetton, Steve Matchett has a revealing

anecdote. 'The importance of the weight of the car was everything and Ross knew this. We were testing the B195 car at Silverstone for, I think, three days. We were trying different suspensions, different uprights and everything else. On the last day we had worked through the programme and we had something like half the day left. I was putting the car together for another run and Ross came over to me. He said, "Steve, I want you to take a little bodywork screw out of one of the panels of the rear bodywork – around the rear suspension. It was held on by five little screws that collectively weighed, I suppose, an ounce [28gm].'

Brawn: 'I want you to take this screw out here [points to a particular screw] because I don't think we need it on the car.'

Matchett: 'I can do that, of course, Ross, but what difference is it going to make?'

Brawn: 'That's what we're here to do. Let's try it and if we don't need it on the car it ain't gonna be on the car.'

The Benetton went out and did a five-lap run – it was testing other things apart from the screw. 'We had a look at the panel,' Matchett says, 'and it was safe, it hadn't moved at all because there was a screw missing, so the drawing was modified after the test. If you take a little bit here and a little bit there, in the end you take enough to make a difference. That was always his philosophy: make it as light as possible.

'The other thing which has really transformed Formula 1 – and I think Ross had a huge amount to do with it – is reliability above all else. You've got to finish the race. It's pointless to have a really fast car that breaks down on the last lap. From day one, Ross was on top of this. I saw him instil it absolutely at Benetton: *you've got to finish the race, you've got to finish the race.*'

He had all the obvious attributes we have come to know and one very small, private one. Rory Byrne had retired from motor racing and was in the process of setting up a scuba diving business off a remote island in the south of Thailand.

Virtually nobody had the phone number of the house where he was staying.

Brawn did.

Byrne was on the beach when he saw his landlady waving, indicating that he had a phone call. Because so few people 'knew where to get hold of me I was really worried. I thought *is there a problem with the family*? But no, no, this was Jean Todt, so the person that made the approach was him. Obviously I knew that Michael was at Ferrari and I knew Ross had gone to Ferrari but it was Todt who phoned me up and said, "How would you like to be chief designer at Ferrari?"'

He would.

As Dernie says, 'Rory was as big a part of what Michael wanted at Ferrari, and also what Ross wanted there too. They dovetailed perfectly: Schumacher wanted Ross and Rory.'

Brawn made an immediate impression, but not in the way you'd imagine. Maurizio Ferrari (no relation) was a talented technical man who we'll be meeting again. He recalls: 'The thing that – how to say? – defined him to me was the moment he walked into Ferrari he started to use the loo that all the members of the team were using. You understand what I mean? Not an executive toilet, the same loo.'

Paradoxically, Maurizio 'didn't meet him until I had my goodbye interview with him.' He wanted to go off and build a slot car business.

Brawn would have to move quickly to (as he would describe it) 'stabilise the situation' at Ferrari. 'When we went there we had to make quite a few rapid introductions to try and stabilise the situation. There were a lot of areas where the team was not strong enough and we had to draw on the UK's motorsport valley. So we brought quite a number of people in. But after a period we were able to start to grow internally, which was very pleasing because the standard of people coming through was very good. To be frank it gave a more harmonious structure. We were able to build a culture. People knew they had an opportunity if they showed ability and application, and they could move through the organisation. There had been a fractious period within the English group before I arrived under John Barnard. There was a lot of anxiety and mistrust when I arrived, but that soon started to build. I would think now there is a small percentage of specialist engineers and technicians on the racing side, but the vast majority of staff are of Italian origin.[1]

'The job was huge and pretty tough,' Byrne says. 'John Barnard had done all the car design and most of the research from England. Here at Maranello there was no real design office. There was a small wind tunnel with minimal staff and not much else in terms of R&D. It was all fairly small and more of a support to Barnard in Guildford. I'm sure that's how John Barnard set it up. So you imagine that not only did we have to race the 1997 car – which we didn't know at all – but we had to build up the infrastructure and then get on and do the 1998 car. A huge job. Because Ross and I knew each other from Benetton days we really approached the thing in the same way: up sleeves and at it. Our split of responsibilities was pretty well the same. We assembled all the necessary personnel and so on. We were busy, I can tell you. Ross reacted to that fine, the same as ever.

'We had an extraordinary run and we did have a number of people who failed to understand exactly why we did it. We strung together winning championships continuously and we did work well together as a team, Jean Todt, Ross, myself, Michael – we all worked well. We built up a number of strategic advantages that Ferrari had relative to our competitors and you saw the result.'

Ferrari were a team that lived on emotion until you got there.

'To be honest, I found the people very hard-working. Yes, the Italians in general are different to Anglo-Saxons, they do behave differently, but everyone works very well as a team. I found less politics here than at Benetton. You ask Ross and I think he'd probably tell you the same thing – at our level, anyway. Maybe there's stuff that goes on above us. I don't know. All I know is at our level I found fewer issues like that at Ferrari than there were at Benetton.'

There was obviously a bond between him and Michael, almost a brotherly thing.

'Occasionally there'd be a few hiccoughs but in general, yes, they had a very good relationship.'

One race came to epitomise that and I propose to recreate it in great detail, because it also epitomises Brawn's tactical abilities in the heat of battle – something that would be important, and sometimes crucial, during Schumacher's astonishing run of championships between 2000 and 2004. Brawn could *think* Ferrari out of nasty corners and, having thought, imparted it to Schumacher who *drove* out of them.

Michael Schumacher qualified third for the Hungarian Grand Prix in August 1998, behind the McLarens of Mika Häkkinen and David Coulthard. Häkkinen led Schumacher in the World Championship by 16 points.

Because the Hungaroring resembled, as someone observed, Monaco without the houses overtaking was rationed to turn 1 at the end of the start-finish straight. Each year the race established its own rhythm lasting an hour and a quarter: dart at that first corner, circle for 2.4 miles, dart if you could, circle for 2.4 miles, dart if you could, circle for 2.4 miles…

Third was altogether the wrong place to be, but Ferrari's hopes and tactics came together in the simplest way. On the grid Schumacher would line up in the left-hand column behind Häkkinen, Coulthard on the right where the track was dusty because cars rarely strayed there to clean it. They were always over on the left, preparing for the dart into turn 1, a right-hander. Schumacher could expect to get in front of Coulthard during the rush to turn 1 and settle behind Häkkinen. They'd all be on two-stop strategies, allowing Schumacher to follow Häkkinen and then, when Häkkinen made his first pit stop, stay out a lap or two, do thunderously fast times so that he'd gain enough time to pit and retain the lead. It had worked often enough before and it would prise open the Hungaroring.

In the matter of fast laps, nobody on the planet could live with Schumacher and it gave Brawn options no other strategist enjoyed.

As the five red lights blinked off the McLarens accelerated fast and in tandem, the Jordan of Hill veering across towards Schumacher, who drew in front of it – but the McLarens were gone. Irvine had a semi-dart at Schumacher into turn 1 and so did Hill, before they all formed the traditional crocodile and circled. Distances didn't mean anything, only positions, and that of course was Schumacher's problem.

Our strategy, Brawn mused, *is not necessarily going to work.* Habitually, the night before a race, Brawn and Schumacher would go through permutations until they felt they'd covered them all, enabling them in theory to respond to any situation that might arise. The trick – the art, the touch of mastery – was selecting the right permutation and the right instant to switch to it.

They crossed the line to complete the opening lap with Häkkinen 0.8 of a second in front of Coulthard and 1.9 in front of Schumacher. The McLarens were fast and Häkkinen might have motored away but Coulthard pushed him and Schumacher held on, so that after the third lap Coulthard was a second away and Schumacher the same 1.9. By ten laps Häkkinen had forced it out to three seconds, Schumacher a second further away.

Brawn brought Schumacher in on lap 25 – before the McLarens and hopefully giving him clear air when he emerged for fast laps. Coulthard, however, pitted the following lap and Häkkinen two laps after that. Far from reversing the race order the pit stops solidified it, except that Schumacher emerged behind Jacques Villeneuve in the Williams who was *visibly* holding him up. Television commentator Murray Walker summed it up in a plain sentence: 'It's looking black for Michael Schumacher.'

Brawn decided on lap 26, and said: 'Michael, we are moving to a three-stop strategy.'

Schumacher had to endure following Villeneuve for five long laps, trying to dart, circling, trying to dart, circling and while he did this he kept thinking *there's a long way to go, keep pushing.* He also worried that the three-stop might be 'the wrong choice' now that he had to follow Villeneuve.

Villeneuve finally pitted on lap 31, freeing Schumacher who immediately set a new fastest lap at 1m 19.9s – the first under 1m 20s – and within three laps had caught Coulthard again. Schumacher was travelling so fast he locked brakes into one corner and drew smoke from the tyres. By then he could see Coulthard just ahead.

On lap 32 Schumacher was 6.1 seconds behind Häkkinen, Coulthard still in between of course. A couple of laps later that had become three seconds. Schumacher was now attacking

Coulthard, travelling so fast he put wheels on to the grass, digging dust.

Brawn brought him in for his second stop on lap 43 and he was stationary for only 6.8s. Walker, commentating, said 'and it looks now as if Michael Schumacher's race in terms of potentially finishing in second or third position is going to be a very, very hard one indeed'. Walker was echoing a general sentiment. Schumacher looked trapped and lost and had to factor in a further pit stop.

McLaren responded by bringing Coulthard in next lap – a mistake, because Schumacher's Ferrari was faster, meaning that Coulthard would emerge behind. If McLaren had brought Häkkinen in, however, he had enough of a lead to emerge in front.

It was too late.

Coulthard was stationary for 8.0 seconds, Schumacher coming round the Hungaroring like a missile. As Coulthard moved down the pit lane Schumacher went past at such speed that, side-on, he appeared a sort of blur.

That was lap 44. The following lap Häkkinen did 1m 21.5s, Schumacher 1m 19.9s. Häkkinen, some 23 seconds in front of Schumacher, pitted next lap and was stationary for 8.4 seconds. It was just like Coulthard: as Häkkinen moved down the pit lane the red blur went by. Schumacher finally had the Hungaroring to himself. On the radio he heard the flat, calm, almost gentle voice of Brawn saying something which would pass into history: 'Michael, you have 19 laps to build a 25-second lead. Go ahead.'

Schumacher thought *thank you very much. I will try my best*, but replied, with masterly understatement, 'OK.' Brawn had in effect committed Schumacher to what the latter would describe as a sustained qualifying run (asterisks indicate laps when Schumacher was not quickest)[2]:

	Schumacher	Next fastest	
Lap 46	1m 19.5s	Coulthard	1m 20.8s
Lap 47	1m 20.6s	Frentzen	1m 21.2s
Lap 48	1m 19.8s	Fisichella	1m 21.0s

Lap 49	1m 20.6s	Frentzen	1m 20.7s
Lap 50	1m 21.2s	Frentzen	1m 20.7s*
Lap 51	1m 20.3s	Frentzen	1m 20.9s

Schumacher was pushing so hard on lap 52, as he confessed himself afterwards, that at the last corner he speared off onto the dry grass – the car slithering as if it had a mind of its own – and by the time he'd returned he'd lost five seconds. Häkkinen had chronic understeer and Coulthard went past him into second place. Schumacher was fourteen seconds up the road.

| Lap 53 | 1m 20.6s | Frentzen | 1m 20.8s |
| Lap 54 | 1m 19.8s | Villeneuve | 1m 20.1s |

During this lap Schumacher took 3.0 seconds out of Coulthard and 3.7 out of Häkkinen.

Lap 55	1m 21.0s	Hill	1m 21.1s
Lap 56	1m 20.1s	Frentzen	1m 20.8s
Lap 57	1m 20.1s	Villeneuve	1m 20.0s*

At this point, Schumacher led Coulthard by 17.0 seconds.

Lap 58	1m 19.6s	Villeneuve	1m 20.3s
Lap 59	1m 19.9s	Frentzen	1m 21.0s
Lap 60	1m 19.2s	Frentzen	1m 21.0s

The lap was actually 1m 19.286s, the fastest of the race and so fast that it would remain so. Schumacher now led Coulthard by 24.9 seconds.

| Lap 61 | 1m 19.5s | Villeneuve | 1m 21.4s |

The ITV roving reporter James Allen approached Ferrari to try and unravel what was going on. He was met by a wall of the politest smiles you could see – and silence. 'The people at Ferrari are relaxed and cheerful. They don't look under pressure.'

Brawn never does.

A gap flicked up during this lap 61: 26.9 seconds, ample for the third pit stop. Schumacher brought the Ferrari in and was stationary for 7.7 seconds. As he emerged, crossing the broken white line and reaching the track, the McLaren of Coulthard loomed into view far back down the start-finish straight. The race was over and, frankly, spectators at the circuit and on television round the world had almost no idea how it had been done.

From this moment the perception of Brawn changed from master strategist to conjuror. Typically, Brawn was circumspect and gently ironic, all at the same time. 'When I told him what he had to do,' Brawn said, 'I'm sure he took a deep breath. He just said, "OK," which is what he normally says.' Brawn added that only Schumacher could have done this. 'That drive by Michael in the middle of the race was just stunning. He's done it again.'

Three stops was a brave strategy and McLaren didn't seem to be able to respond to you.

'No. I mean, it was a pretty aggressive strategy and it's one we went to once we realised we were behind Coulthard and Häkkinen, because Coulthard was obviously protecting Häkkinen. We thought we had nothing to lose, quite frankly, so we went for it.'

Schumacher set the *nine* fastest laps of the race, Villeneuve the tenth with 1m 20.0s on that ill-fated lap 52.

Alastair Macqueen says that he and Brawn 'kept in touch to some degree when he was at Ferrari, we sent a few e-mails backwards and forwards about how he was doing. He was quite intriguing about Schumacher on occasions: you know, was he just teasing us when he won by only just enough to do the job? We bounced e-mails backwards and forwards because Ross kept getting asked about the XJR14 and he couldn't remember anything about it – so anything to do with sports cars, "Ask Alastair".'

One thing is certain. On the hot, cloudy afternoon of 16 August 1998 Michael Schumacher wasn't teasing anybody, including himself and Ross Brawn.

Much later Brawn would explain his philosophy. 'Everybody in the team knows that there is one person who has the last word on making strategy changes during a race and that person is me. I have a network of people who supply me with quality information. It is not at all sure that I will make the right choice but it is at least a choice. I like the challenge because I like to be on the pit wall.'

Byrne feels that 'it was a combination of Ross and Michael working very well together. Ross would work out the strategy and that strategy would require Michael to drive in a certain way at certain periods in the race. Michael was very good at that. Ross would get on the radio and say, "Michael, the next ten laps are the most critical point in the race." Michael would put the hammer down for ten laps, do what he had to do and after the pit stops everyone would be saying, "Oh, how did he do that?" Ross was brilliant at working out how you could do it – because you couldn't plan it all beforehand and things happen in the race that you've no control over. You've got to be able to think on your feet.'

The Todt-Brawn-Byrne-Schumacher axis was not just a fusion of different talents but acquired a terrible strength of its own, dominating Formula 1 so completely that – after the barren and bitter years – it threatened to make it, literally, a turn-off. Millions of televiewers found a new way of watching the races. They'd see Schumacher safely into the lead in turn 1, then watch something else and return at the end to see how much Schumacher had won by.

Derek Warwick 'wasn't surprised at what Ross did at Ferrari because you've got to remember I come from '89 when I had the best Arrows ever built, I come from '91 when I had arguably the best sports car ever built – and I'm including Mercedes and Porsche and all those. He went to Benetton and with Schumacher turned that into a championship-winning team. Then he was taken to Ferrari with Rory Byrne – when you think of Ferrari you have to think of Rory Byrne, Ross Brawn *and* Jean Todt. Those three changed the fortunes of Ferrari.'

And changed Grand Prix history.

By 2006 Brawn had become such a presence that in January

he was awarded an honorary degree of Doctor of Engineering at Brunel University for services to motor sport. The award was made 'at a fund-raising dinner in central London [...] where Sir Frank Williams (Williams Grand Prix Racing) gave the welcome speech. The dinner at the Institute of Civil Engineers saw over 240 guests gather to celebrate the University's successes in engineering, and to raise money for our award-winning Formula Student teams.'[3]

That October, Ferrari announced that Brawn was leaving – it was time, after all that had gone before, to let a new generation come through and, anyway, he'd earned a rest.

He'd conquered the world (you know what I mean).

Maurizio Ferrari puts it with touching simplicity. 'He was very deeply respected – and he is missed.'

Thereby hangs one of Russell Sheldon's tales. 'Ferrari used to conduct all their meetings in English, for Ross's benefit. Six or seven months after he had left Ferrari, he bumped into one of his ex-colleagues, and they said, "A funny thing happened the other day. We suddenly realised that we no longer had to conduct our meetings in English."'

Brawn fully intended to fish his way round the world before, as he says, he got too old. Fishing was a lifelong passion and woven into that was a lifelong ambition to catch a Permit, which is a saltwater fish that feeds on shrimps, has a pug nose and splayed tail – which make it look faintly sinister – and can weigh 56lb (25kg). One report says: 'Permit fish swim in schools of fish and never bump into each other. They have sensors running in a line down the length of their bodies, a little like radar in a way that helps them with physical position in the water and hunting food.'[4]

Brawn finally caught up with, and caught, one in the Seychelles.

His world tour took him to Russia, where he found, as so many others have, that the country may be immense and beautiful but Russian bureaucracy is something else. 'The authorities decided to confiscate our provisions, so for a while we just lived off the salmon we caught, and beetroot!' He'd been having 'great adventures' flying round in a military helicopter, too. As I say, this is Russia...

He was also to spend six weeks in New Zealand, during which period the first race of 2007, the Australian Grand Prix at Melbourne, was to be run. That was March, and understandably enough he was undecided whether he should watch it. Understandably? He *was* on a sabbatical trying to get – and stay – away from it, allied to the fact that watching a race on television, rather than have it flood past him on the pit wall, would be an entirely new experience. The dilemma seemed to have solved itself, because he was staying in a lodge which didn't have a television and didn't have access to the Internet. There was, however, a pub about five miles down the road, and his daughter asked if they'd be showing the race. They would. Brawn went and discovered that the pub had been bought by an Englishman a few months before who just happened to be an avid Formula 1 follower. He recognised Brawn immediately, of course, and said these immortal words to him: 'I'd have been less surprised if Elvis Presley had walked in.'

Brawn and the owner sat together and watched Kimi Räikkönen, from pole, lead every lap except his two pit stops and win it comfortably enough from Alonso (McLaren). Räikkönen was in a Ferrari, of course…

Even the tour did not 'satiate' Brawn's appetite for fishing, but any more would have to wait for another day because in the autumn rumours began to circulate that Red Bull were hunting him and if they got him that might help lure Alonso. Red Bull were a serious team with serious funding and there'd be a deep irony throughout the 2009 season about Brawn *not* going there.

In November, Honda announced that he was joining them as Team Principal.

It was, Nick Fry says, the end of a long journey 'which really started in 2002–2003, and the truth is the only reason Ross could be persuaded to come to our team was because by the stage we approached him we had built the appropriate facilities and we had the right engineering structure and processes in place, such that he felt we had a chance. During one of my first meetings with Ross, when I was trying to persuade him to come to the team, he only had three questions. One: "Tell me about the facilities." Second: "Tell me about the staff." Third: "Tell me about the budget." Without those things I am pretty certain Ross wouldn't have come. In many ways Ross was the final piece, the catalyst that brought the engineering side together.'

Honda, too, were a serious team with serious funding, and one of the largest workforces in Formula 1 at over 7009. Brawn began work with them on the understanding that there would be a three-year plan, which essentially meant holding station in 2008 and working immediately on the 2009 car, which would race under new Formula 1 regulations.

Frank Dernie – watching so closely – claims that in fact, and despite something approaching mythology surrounding the subject, the team did work on the 2008 car. 'I don't know, being honest, to what extent they *didn't* do much last year. My information is that they made some pretty big developments, it's just that they didn't make any difference. I got from one of the test and development team a report that they had actually been working quite hard on the 2008 car – it was just that none of the updates really made any difference. This story that they didn't do anything is to an extent a convenient thing to say because, you could argue, if everyone thought you were doing lots of development last year and it wasn't working, you're a bit lost. I can't imagine Ross, knowing what a competitive bugger he was, being there as boss and being happy for them not to do anything, although he may not have got deeply involved in it personally.

'He'd be pretty damned disappointed with where things were and he'd be doing what could be done. I think it would be fair to say, however, that this year's car [2009] wouldn't have been compromised in any way, especially with such a big rule change coming.'

Then, all at once, from nowhere and in a few weeks he owned the team.

Eddie Jordan – watching so closely – first encountered Brawn at March in 1974 when 'he was a young engineer there, just one of a lot of young engineers out of college. It was controlled by Robin Herd, who was the key man. I bought a car from March and went racing. When I came to live in England in the late 1970s I had the Formula 3 car, although during those times Ross had left so I didn't really come across too much of him.

'He has a couple of brilliant, brilliant qualities and there's a couple of things that need to be looked at. As a team principal, which he now is, his engineering skills and his design skills are well known. He has been a bit lucky in the sense that he did benefit greatly by the demise of Honda. I'm not saying it's all, not by any means, but some of the basic concepts within the team he has been a little bit fortunate to inherit.

'He is a hugely skilful tactician and I wouldn't put anyone above him. He is a very resilient man – taking Jaguar into a new era, winning twice at Benetton with Michael Schumacher then five times at Ferrari.'

Brawn was asked during 2009, as a Manchester United supporter, if there were similarities between Alex Ferguson, running that team, and a Formula 1 team principal. He replied: 'There is a common objective, which is to obtain the maximum from a group, but in Formula 1 the two drivers are rivals. The players in the same football team are not. For this reason the first objective in a Formula 1 team is to avoid the environment of confrontation, and psychology is important.

'There are circumstances where I had to take tough decisions for the greater good. When there is a collective interest it is clear that individuals may have to suffer but it is no pleasure to act like this.'

He was asked if he was tougher than Jean Todt. He replied: 'I am different. Jean was more devoted than I am to team organisation and to economic aspects. I live the same challenge but from the point of view of an engineer, and that's different, but the lessons I have learnt are all valid.' He gave one specifically. 'Loyalty towards people.'

He'd also underscore his philosophy, or rather his perspective, which was that team owners and team principals should use everything they legitimately could to beat each other on the track then sit down together afterwards over a beer and have a laugh about it – but, he'd add, 'you need to separate those things' and not everyone could. That created problems when these top people were discussing the overall well-being of Grand Prix racing.

Brawn ruminates on not losing his temper. 'It's a rare event. I worked with Joan Villadelprat at Benetton and he took great pleasure in being one of the few people who made me lose my temper. Joan almost announced it on the PA that I had lost my temper and it was a fascinating event. He could make you lose your temper because he was a lovely guy but he did push you to the boundaries. Especially as I have grown older, it's not something I like to do and inevitably you find things more frustrating with your family than you find with your business!

'In the position I am in now I can't afford to radiate that. That was one of my principles at Ferrari. If I lost control why should I expect the people around me to maintain theirs? You make it worse. Maybe it's my nature, but it's something that I've tried not to do. I find that if you don't lose your temper a stern word is often more effective than screaming and shouting because, in comparison to the norm, a stern word can mean everything. So that's how I like to operate. That's the Japanese way. One of the interesting things working with the Japanese – with Bridgestone and Honda – is they'd never lose their control but the quiet, stern word is very significant.

'Ferrari was portrayed as being a volatile environment but in fact it very rarely was…'

Before we move on, I want to include a tribute from one of Ross Brawn's friends, Richard Boughton. It was intended as an interview but in fact became a tribute and, because it sums up several themes that have run through the last chapter and this, I quote it verbatim.

Boughton and Brawn found themselves neighbours in their Oxfordshire village. 'I have known Ross for nigh on the last 20 years. I am a motor racing fanatic and I do some racing myself (I've done a little bit of rallying at the amateur-enthusiast level). I wasn't when I first met him, although it has been my passion since I was about five – I've maintained the passion all the time, although I had two boys growing up when I met Ross and I was on the touchline instead.

'He lived directly opposite me. My wife and I moved out of our house for six months while we had it redeveloped. We let him know that the house would be effectively a bit of a shell and would he keep an eye on it? He did the dutiful thing, patrolling round a bit at night with his dog. He was working at Benetton at the time and we chatted and he gathered from that I was an enthusiast. The next thing I was invited to go along to one of the Benetton events.

'We had some common ground because I am a bit of an expert on beer – I'm a brewmaster by profession – and I think Ross found this quite interesting because he has developed an increasing interest in wine over the years. He realised that I had a reasonably good take on the whole wine world: I have studied wine a fair bit. I'm keen on food and drink, and he is too. We also had our own areas of interest which did not overlap. For example, he is a very keen fisherman and I'm not.

'I'm fairly gregarious by comparison to him and I think he finds that contrast interesting. In some senses I am very laid-back, but on the other hand I can be a bit of a tease. He probably enjoys that – because I don't stand on ceremony for him, if you know what I mean. He would be the last person to actually want that anyway.

'He is an incredibly good listener. He is very precise. The way in which he approaches everything he does is with a level of thoroughness that produces a result which is very, very, very good. For example, when I had the makeover on my house, he thought it was fantastic. From that, the builder who did my house then did his, although obviously to his specification and in an entirely different way. *He* appreciated the thoroughness of it. He will make sure things are done right and that's the way he approaches everything – *everything* – he does. He will research something much better than I will, and I admire that.

'He appreciates that people work best in a stable environment, so whether instability is created by huge success or huge failure, Ross will level it. There are a lot of people quite good at levelling out *in*stability which has been caused by something not going right – they say, "Come on chaps, let's pick ourselves up and move on." Ross could win the World

Championship and still have the same post-race revue as though it was any other race meeting. That would be quite extraordinary for some people because they can't wait to open the beer cans or the champagne or whatever. Ross will just sit down and follow his usual agenda.

'He's great company. If he's in the pub and strangers come up, he'll talk to them. He is the easiest-going guy, very nice, very engaging. Even when he's had a very long day he'll still take the time to talk with the person who comes up and says something.'

This is the man who inherited a strong team from Honda, not least of whom was Nick Fry as Chief Executive Officer. Born in Epsom in 1956, Fry had an impressive CV, leaving the University of Wales with an economics degree. He began with Ford, rising to become Service Director then Product Planning and Business Director of their European operation. He became Managing Director of the BAR team in 2002 and continued quite naturally into the Honda years.

Fry describes himself professionally as a 'senior automotive manager in that I have worked in the car industry since 1978 in all sorts of guises but tended to be in senior positions, fairly broad based. I've done everything from running engineering programmes to Managing Director of Aston Martin to customer service director to project director, so I've got, if you like, the broad wheelbase that you need to run a Formula 1 team overall, which is obviously a combination of commercial, technical, and personnel plus many other aspects. The words I would use: always optimistic and proactive, so very much a can-do type of person, one that tends to lead from the front and get involved where necessary – not afraid to get my hands dirty.

'I'd also say in the main I'm tiresome in that I am relentlessly enthusiastic. You need to be in the Grand Prix world.'

Loïc Bigois, born in Aix-en-Provence, was Head of Aerodynamics (he lists his hobby as 'wind tunnel testing', which seems to confirm Matchett's view that aerodynamicists *do* have a different view of life). He came to Honda in 2007 from, respectively, Ligier, Sauber, Ligier again, Prost, Minardi and Williams.

John Owen was the Principal Aerodynamicist and 'always

wanted to work as an engineer in Formula 1 or the aircraft industry, so at school I took mainly scientific subjects such as maths, physics and chemistry with a view to doing an engineering course at university.' He joined Sauber in 2001 and learnt a great deal because their aero department was small. He joined Honda in 2007.

Ron Meadows from Liverpool was Sporting Director. He'd started as a mechanic with TWR in 1980, been a chief mechanic in Formula 3000, been a team manager in IndyCars, and joined BAR in 1997 as project leader for buildings and new facilities. He became Race Team Manager in 2000, continuing into the Honda years.

Andrew Shovlin, Jenson Button's Senior Race Engineer, had been working with him since 2003. Shovlin, also from Liverpool, studied mechanical engineering at Leeds University and had a PhD in Vehicle Dynamics and Control. He joined the BAR Research & Development department in 1998.

Shovlin on Button: 'If I tell him [on the radio] to push, I get away with it one time or twice, but by the third time he gets a bit hacked off. He doesn't like to be told to go quicker. Jenson and I talk on the radio most laps but I tend to talk a lot more than him. Normally he just listens – well at least, I hope he does! You need to give him an idea of how the race is panning out, what the gaps are to other cars and how the tyres are performing.

'We also advise him if we see anything on the data that might allow him to find some more pace, or ask him to change various engine settings if we need to save fuel. Jenson might be telling me how the car is handling so that we can make an adjustment to the tyre pressures at the next stop or he might have a particular question such as what lap another car is likely to come into the pits. We don't normally disagree but sometimes we'll have different opinions on which tyre to use or what to do with the strategy, so you can end up having a bit of a debate.'

Peter Bonnington was Assistant Race Engineer to Button. From Cheshunt in Hertfordshire, he studied mechanical engineering at the University of Hertfordshire and began in

British Touring Cars as a design engineer in 1999. He joined Jordan in 2002, had a season at Minardi and then joined Honda to work with Button.

Jock Clear, Barrichello's Senior Race Engineer, was one of the most experienced men in Formula 1. From Portsmouth, and a self-confessed rugby follower, he started with the Lola team as a design draftsman in 1988 and was doing composite design at Benetton a year later. He moved to Lotus as Race Engineer for Johnny Herbert, then Williams with successively David Coulthard, Jacques Villeneuve and Takuma Sato – the last at BAR. When the team became Honda and Barrichello joined he worked with him. That was 2006.

Ricardo Musconi, Barrichello's Assistant Race Engineer, came from Imola and studied mechanical engineering at the University of Bologna. Later he studied vehicle engineering and joined the Dallara team in 2003. He joined Honda in 2006, working with Barrichello.

Matt Deane, from Northampton, was Chief Mechanic. He went to Northampton Technical College and served as an apprentice mechanic with the Alan Docking team before joining Jordan in 1997. He worked with Heinz-Harald Frentzen, Jean Alesi, Sato, Ralf Firman and Giorgio Pantano before he joined BAR in 2005. And if you've ever wondered about the pit stops, here it is: 'Pit stops always look busy and stressful but every move is carefully practised and needs to be extremely precise. When a car comes into the pits to refuel and change tyres, 30 people are in action for those eight to ten seconds. I'm in charge of the lollipop and directing the driver into the box and telling him when to leave. At the front of the car is the front jack man, one mechanic ready to take the nose off if needed and another guy to put the new nose on. One mechanic will be in charge of adjusting the front wing if the driver has asked for a change on the radio before coming into the pits.

'Moving to the sides of the car, three mechanics are in charge of each wheel so that's one to take the old tyre off, one to put the new tyre in place and the wheel gun man. Seven people are in charge of setting the fuel delivery and operating the fuel hoses plus the spare hose and rig if we need to make a quick change. At the back of the car are the rear jack man and two people who are in charge of rear wing adjustments. Finally we always have someone carrying a fire extinguisher, one person cleaning the driver mirrors and someone ready to change the steering wheel.'

By definition these men were spearheading a very capable team, but in a sense they could only be the spearhead of the team of 450 employees. Consequently it may seem slightly unfair to highlight them so, to redress that balance, a full list of the Brawn GP team personnel is given at the end of the book.

The team had, of course, another spearhead: the two drivers.

Notes

1. www2.ferrariromania.ro/formula1/159/lung-dar-interesant-interviu-cu-ross-brawn.html.
2. Bira in forums.autosport.com/showthread.php?s=&threadid.
3. www.brunel.ac.uk/about/hongrads/2006/brawn.
4. outdoors.webshots.com/.../1004286296014636972FWoCfLMbBP.

CHAPTER 4

MEN IN WAITING

You can sift through the words. They have an additional power because Jenson Button talks with fluency in an English middle-class way and invariably to the point. Rubens Barrichello, who has been known to surrender to tears but only in circumstances of extreme emotion (like winning Grands Prix), has learnt the knack of wrestling the English language until you know exactly what he means. These are some of the words, sometimes partially repeating themselves.

Button: 'tough times' ... 'a dark time' ... 'stressful' ... 'very tough' ... 'a beast' ... 'dark moments' ... 'traumatic few months' ... 'up one day, down the next' ... 'very tough mentally' ... 'horrible person to live with.'

Barrichello: 'critical three or four months back home waiting' ... 'horrible to just sit there' ... 'been horrible driving a bad car.'

One of the words from Button – 'traumatic' – encompasses all the others and covers the close season when both men had to confront the fact that they may not have drives and, by extension, that their Grand Prix careers might be over. Button, who made his debut in 2000, was born in 1980 and so was on the verge of his 30s. Barrichello, who made his debut in 1993, was born in 1972 and so was a lot nearer 40 than 30. Approaching 2009, he faced being replaced at Honda by Bruno Senna, nephew of Ayrton, and would not, perhaps, have been surprised if it had happened.

By a great irony, Barrichello in his callow youth had been a protégé of Ayrton's. When he – Barrichello – crashed at Imola in 1994, Ayrton came to the Medical Centre to see him and, although Barrichello was fine, it seemed to cast a *mental* shadow over him. The irony now, of course, would be the nephew taking the drive from Barrichello. That's not all. Barrichello had been scheduled to do the second Jerez test and, with young Senna there, direct and inescapable comparisons could and would have been made. Barrichello insisted he was relishing this but, of course, it never happened. When Honda went all the testing went with them.

Neither Button nor Barrichello could really complain if it was the end. Barrichello had driven 268 races for four teams – Jordan, Stewart, Ferrari and Honda – and won nine. Button had driven 153 for five – Williams, Benetton, Renault, BAR and Honda – and won one. Cumulatively, they'd had their chances and as a duet seemed ideally suited to adorn a touring car championship. It was a well-trodden path from Formula 1 for drivers of a certain age and, evidently, good fun as well as continuing to pay the bills. It also postponed the day when a driver had to decide what to do with the rest of his life.

Certainly, Barrichello stated publicly that when Honda announced their decision his telephone began to ring with inquiries about whether he'd be available for the World Touring Car Championship and the 24 Hours of Daytona, while he would have been prepared to go to the Indy Racing League (IRL). He needed speed in his life and would go to whoever was offering it.

Neither he nor Button had really fulfilled themselves in Formula 1 or, as Barrichello put it in a telling phrase, he still had 'unfinished business' there.

It wasn't just that they'd had their chances, they'd had a *lot* of chances: between them, 421. Ten wins was a meagre total from that. Michael Schumacher won more in a single season – twice (2002 and 2004). Schumacher represented, of course, the reason Barrichello's total was so meagre in the six seasons they were team-mates at Ferrari, because Schumacher had priority; but, putting it starkly, for most of that time Barrichello had a winning car and didn't win in it.

The contract situation, Barrichello would subsequently claim, stopped short of Schumacher getting special engines or indeed anything special on the car but did give him control of race strategy, a crucial aspect which meant that, to win, Barrichello would have to be lucky. This somehow became a dominant factor in Barrichello's thinking rather than concentrating on maximising what *he* had, and never mind Schumacher. Easier said than done, of course, especially against Schumacher.

Barrichello said plaintively that he was not ready to leave Formula 1 and he explained why, citing David Coulthard (born 1971, 246 races, 13 wins) who was leaving because he felt he had done enough. Barrichello didn't feel like that at all. He did feel that if you have experience but your speed's gone, you're gone – experience won't bring it back – but believed strongly that he still had the speed. He loved Brazil, always had, and would return there when he had had enough. That definitely wasn't yet, not least because he felt he still had a World Championship inside him. It was exactly the opposite of Coulthard, in fact.

Button reached far too much far too soon, and anyone can understand why. He was handsome and he could express himself in coherent sentences – the fluency. He was personable and, as a driver, he was just plain good. The British media, easily the most powerful and numerous in the sport, roam the circuits hungry for British heroes – good for circulation, good for column inches and good for aeroplane tickets to the next race – and here, suddenly, was one. He was a sort of James Hunt without the sharpened edges and was duly accorded the Hunt treatment by the media.

It is a dangerous place to be, especially when young: you haven't had a chance to fully understand that Grand Prix racing is quite unlike any other formula. This is not just a question of scale – by definition Grand Prix racing is bigger – but that the scale brings you to somewhere harder, to what someone has called The Piranha Club, where ruthlessness is considered entirely normal and acceptable behaviour.

He'd imagined that Grand Prix racing would be, literally, a passport to many different cultures as you travelled the world, but found, as all young drivers do, a great merging into airports, hotels and circuits to the point that, soon enough, you only distinguished the difference between *this* place and the last place you were by the temperature change.

The young man needs a mentor and in the case of Barrichello he found one in Eddie Jordan, who nurtured and protected his drivers like a mother hen (they were among his great assets, after all).

It is what Button needed just as it is arguable that every driver just approaching or crossing the threshold needs it. Button almost got it.

'I tried to sign him,' Eddie Jordan says. 'Trevor Foster, who worked for me, was his biggest fan. We used to have confrontations in the board meetings about drivers for the following year and I'd say "Trevor, are you putting up Button again? OK, well that's Trevor's thing." I'd say to Gary Anderson "What do you say?" and he'd be off on his own tangent and I'd wind up signing somebody else. We were very familiar with Button, we had several discussions and talks but it just never really quite came to it. He was my kind of bloke, a top man, got a great style: very natural.'

Jackie Stewart, no less, felt that early in his Formula 1 career Button had managers who overplayed him when he simply wasn't ready. Button, in fact, acquired a reputation for the good life – Monaco, yacht and so forth – before the career justified that in terms of achievement. Formula 1 drivers are paid a lot of money and what they do with it is, literally, their business. The criticism was that achievement ought to lead to the yacht but the yacht would never lead to the achievement.

He matured out of that (a Renault fitness expert, who worked drivers hard, reacted with indignation to the suggestion that Button didn't train properly, and riposted that he'd just had him running up and down the mountains behind Monaco *enthusiastically*).

To be fair, Button would insist that money didn't really make a difference to what he wanted, and pointed out logically enough that, if the motivating factor was money, what better than to be World Champion, with all the money that that would bring – not forgetting that you earned more and more money as you rose towards that? His motivation centred round the World Championship: he didn't care how long he took to get there and in that context it was not about money at all.

Nor was Button assured of success. Too many Formula 1 careers have reached a sort of plateau and, for whatever reason, the drivers have been unable to lift it from that towards the summit: Martin Brundle 158 races, no wins, Mark Blundell 61 races, no wins, Derek Warwick 147 races, no wins. They were very good drivers and in their time the backbone of Grand Prix racing. Across long seasons this seemed exactly what was befalling Button – despite his win in Hungary – and, worse, he was travelling downhill.

I want to set out, in precis form, Button's Formula 1 career because only when you consider that can you find the real context of 2009. These are his seasons, with finishing positions in each race (R = retired, * = classified but not running at the end, DNS = did not start, DQ = disqualified). Then I'll do the same for Barrichello.

2000, Williams:

R, 6, R, 5, 17*, 10*, R, 11, 8, 5, 4, 9, 5, R, R, 5, R
(12 points, 8th)

Button describes himself as a bad loser and doesn't accept that this is a weakness because, like all the others, he's in it to win and always has been. He'd talk of 'sulking' if things didn't go well but he'd find one aspect of Formula 1 frankly strange. You were a physical prisoner of the equipment you had – meaning the car – and you could only make it do what it would do. This is not so true of the lesser formulae, hence the strangeness.

2001, Benetton:

14*, 11, 10, 12, 15, R, 7, R, 13, 16*, 15, 5, R, R, R, 9, 7
(2 points, 17th)

Button would concede that 2001 was a bad time but insists he didn't feel he had lost his ability: to lose it from one season to the next would be an absurdity. What he did do was wonder why he couldn't solve the problems he confronted, but concluded that the Benetton was a difficult car and he was too inexperienced to do the solving. He felt, looking back, that learning across this lesson was no bad thing.

2002, Renault:
R, 4, 4, 5, 12*, 7, R, 15*, 5, 12*, 6, R, R, R, 5, 8, 6 (14 points, 7th)

Button would say that during these first three seasons he suffered some 'pretty bad experiences' because he'd reached Formula 1 so quickly so young, which, all else aside, prevented him from having the depth of knowledge to understand his car. In that sense, 2002 was a continuation of 2001.

2003, BAR:
10, 7, R, 8, 9, 4, DNS, R, 7, R, 8, 8, 10, R, R, 4 (17 points, joint 9th)

Team-mate Jacques Villeneuve was scathing about Button, likening him to a 'boy-band member'. Far from holding this against him, Button found they started having dinner together and, although the first few of these occasions were naturallty strained, it evolved into friendship.

2004, BAR:
6, 3, 3, 2p, 8, 2, 3, 3, R, 5, 4, 2, 5, R, 3, 2, 3, R (85 points, 3rd)

Only now did Button judge that he was 'ready', the apprenticeship served. He had his first podiums in a very strong, consistent season, prompting *Autocourse* to say he had 'truly emerged.' He was nowhere near winning the championship, however, because Michael Schumacher scored 148 points in the Ferrari and a certain Rubens Barrichello 114.

2005, BAR:
11*, R, R, DQ, 10, R, DNS, 4, 5, 3, 5, 5, 8, 3, 7, 5, 8 (37 points, 9th)

A nightmarish season with Button trying to get out of a Williams contract while the car had aerodynamic problems. He was disqualified at San Marino for a fuel system infringement on the car, which was suspended for Spain and Monaco. He crashed in Canada – a very unusual thing – after taking pole, and hadn't actually scored a point yet. He recovered.

2006, Honda:
4, 3, 10*, 7, R, 6, 11, R, 9, R, R, 4, 1, 4, 5, 4, 4, 3 (56 points, 6th)

The victory came in Hungary and was the moment Button felt he was now ready to go for a World Championship.

2007, Honda:
15, 12, R, 12, 11, R, 12, 8, 10, R, R, 13, 8, R, 11*, 5, R (6 points, 15th)

The second R was Canada, when Button's gearbox held him immobile on the grid while the others accelerated away into the race. It is always humiliating, for all the obvious reasons and not least because the driver has prepared his mind and body for exactly this moment – then nothing, an emptiness, almost a betrayal. What happened next was enacted in public and on television screens across the world, which can hardly have helped. In Canada the Honda was pushed away, Button shaking his head.

One of the ITV crew, Ted Kravitz, said a moment of two later: 'It's terminal for Jenson Button. They wheeled him back, they were trying to start him up … but they've given up. Jenson, from what I can see now, is absolutely furious.'

Four laps into the race Button was pictured striding down the pit lane unzipping his overalls, his whole face clenched so that it didn't actually betray anything.

Seven laps into the race Louise Goodman found Button. 'I think angry sums up the mood on Jenson's face at the moment,' she said. Then she said to him: 'You weren't best pleased with that, obviously.'

'It hasn't been a fantastic weekend,' he said, almost softly, 'but there is pace in the car on long runs so it's frustrating not to get off the line.' He looked away from the camera.'

'What happened?'

'I took first gear and it said it was in first gear and it wasn't, so I went back to neutral, went back to first gear again and there was no drive. It kept saying it was in first gear and that was *it*, I couldn't do anything.'

'Go and get yourself a cup of tea. Thanks, Jence.'

2008, Honda:
R, 10, R, 6, 11, 11, 11, R, R, 17, 12, 13, 15, 15, 9, 14, 16, 13 (3 points, 18th)

He'd known the truth about the car after his first few laps in it, because good drivers always do. He rang his father who could tell the truth by the tone of Button's voice alone. Button quickly confirmed it and they both gazed ahead to a barren season. Sometimes a car can be brought back to competitiveness, sometimes there's nothing you can do.

The final 13th place, at São Paulo, carried a heavy irony. Lewis Hamilton had just won the World Championship and, nearby, Button's Honda caught fire so that as Formula 1 surrendered to Hamilton Button was trying to put the fire out.

The years 2007 and 2008, seen here in starkest relief and culminating with the fire, were a disaster. *Autocourse* rated him the tenth best driver in 2007, itself a testament because he'd been 15th in the championship. *Autocourse* wrote: 'Talk closely to Button and he radiates a slightly detached, curiously enigmatic approach to his dilemma. He gives the impression of wanting to skirt around the subject, almost as if in reflecting in any more detail on a season that delivered him only six points would somehow drain the resevoir of his personal motivation for good. ... It must be heartbreaking to see your career evaporating in front of your eyes.'

Now consider that 2008 was worse.

'To drive that car,' Button says, 'was a handful. Every corner we got to we didn't know what was going to really happen, so it was a beast – but that's what we had to deal with. We knew that there were some very talented people in the team. We just hadn't produced the car that I think we expected to.'

Ross Brawn says he always rated Button highly but explains that until 2008 he had never worked with him and in 2008 the equipment wasn't good enough to let him make a finite, personal judgement. Brawn coins a telling phrase to encapsulate that: 'I still wasn't really able to judge that final strength that a very successful racing driver has.' The Honda team, who had of course worked with Button, assured Brawn that he had *it* – what it takes – and to wait. As a consequence the team decided to retain Button for 2009, primarily 'based on the expectations that he would do well with the right equipment.'

The decision, of course, would be amply rewarded. Just before half-season Brawn said this in response to the question 'Has Button changed?': 'Yes, he has a superior work ethic. Talent he had already. Now he knows how to be strong and it's different – it's solid – but he is still Jenson with a nice character.'

Louise Goodman, as we have just seen, worked for ITV as their 'finder' during the races. If someone crashed or broke down as they tramped back towards the pits they were sure to see Goodman waiting, microphone in hand, to find out what had happened. By definition she was intercepting young men who might variously be angry, deflated, close to tears, exhausted or breathless and with plenty of adrenaline still pumping. They might also sense they were vulnerable to saying anything in these circumstances and just walk on by. If you look at 2007 and 2008, Button was tramping back a lot – 11 times – and by definition had 11 chances to walk on by. He never did.

Goodman describes that touchingly, and broadens it to embrace all of Button.

'It's been interesting watching how he's changed over the years. What's so lovely about his success now in 2009 is that he's old enough and he's mature enough that he can put it totally into perspective to appreciate it. That's great.

'Jenson went through the same thing as Lewis Hamilton, didn't he? He was the blue-eyed boy and, OK, he didn't get the championship like Hamilton and he didn't get the success but he was very much the coming man and then he had the rug pulled out from underneath him. He made a few mistakes in the early years with his team selection and the way he handled the team selection, the way it was put out to the media. I think of a classic press conference one year in Hungary when there was talk of him changing teams – I can't remember the details. He sat there looking like a rabbit caught in the headlights. He said "No comment", "No comment", "No comment", really not knowing how to handle the situation. If he found himself in that situation now he would handle it in a very different way.

'I saw him at all the low points when he had to face me. I think actually by the time he got to the *really* low points he understood a lot more about how the business worked, how to make it better and how to move forward. He was a much more rounded person as a racing driver but also he was a lot more rounded individual, because he was so much older and he'd been through so much more. From a media perspective he was now handling it all very well.

'One of his strong points is that he never appeared to let his head go down. I can remember doing interviews with him when he'd come home 15th, he was telling me what a fantastic battle he'd had and he was dicing with so-and-so throughout the race – so even though the results weren't there he was still trying to maximise every opportunity. And there *must* be a difference between dicing for 15th or 16th and doing it for first and second.

'He never ducked away from the microphone – I think [paradoxically] a result of the lessons he learned early in his career when things were going well. We could edit what he said because it was on tape but ultimately we were going to transmit his words. It wasn't scary for me, not with somebody like Jenson – he wasn't going to let rip into the microphone. There was no fear of that [the 9.0'clock watershed!] with Jenson, no, no, never. He knew there was no point in directing his energy towards slagging off the team because that wasn't going to make anything get better.

'What he needed to do was direct his energies towards

building the team up and working behind the scenes to put himself into a better position. This is just my guesswork, but you wonder what he had learnt over the years from trying to jump from team to team and how it didn't necessarily work out. You look, maybe, at what somebody like Schumacher had done: his model was to have the right team around him and build it, then it takes three or four years before you start to get the success.

'I think also what had made a difference is that the last few years he's been working with a guy he trusts from a business perspective and so he doesn't have to worry about that kind of thing. He knows he's in good hands. You get the impression that they have a very strong relationship and he can just focus on the racing. Maybe that was him starting to build his own team around himself and work out how he had to get to where he wanted to.

'He's still very humble. It's almost as if he doesn't want to play the superstar at all and he's quite happy to take the mickey out of himself a bit. I don't think he's embarrassed [about himself], embarrassed is the wrong word. I think he's slightly self-conscious. He's not the type to shout from the tree-tops "Look at me!" He's still got the same friends as he had when he was a teenager.'

Button gave his own revealing view of who he was in an interview with *The Guardian* (29 March 2004). The context needs setting down. Damon Hill had said some time before that he didn't think Button would become World Champion, as he and Nigel Mansell had done, because to do that you needed to be a bit 'bonkers' – and Button was 'frighteningly normal'.

During *The Guardian* interview, which lasted half an hour before this topic came up, Button had been entirely himself, polite, engaging, good-humoured. Now he bristled and – *The Guardian*'s word – protested: 'I don't think I'm normal. How many ordinary guys can get up on the podium alongside Schumacher and [Juan Pablo] Montoya and talk about beating them? But I wouldn't want to be bonkers. I'm out to prove that you can be level-headed and win a World Championship.'

This is not at all as contradictory as it seems and it *is* revealing. Ordinary people – like me and like you – don't dedicate their teenage years to getting themselves into a place which could kill them, risking humiliation and defeat along the way, and, likely, financial devastation.

He was once asked whether a 14-year-old who was taken to a race track and fell for it should immediately approach his school's careers officer and ask how you became a racing driver? He replied that 14 was probably too late. He'd been karting for six years by then...

Ordinary people *don't* want to work day and night to get themselves on to a junior formula grid full of other young men in powerful cars, some of them Italian and fully charged for the lights going off. In this sense no driver reaching Formula 1, however fleetingly, is ordinary.

The driver who reaches it must by definition be dedicated, ambitious, brave and physically in excellent condition, none of which add up to bonkers. What Hill surely meant was that on top of all these qualities you need something else, perhaps a quality or two even the 'ordinary' Grand Prix drivers don't have. In Hill's case that would be overcoming the enormous, and debilitating, shadow of his father, financial circumstances so straitened that he worked as a despatch rider, and a very late entry to Formula 1, in 1992. He was 32, driving a shockingly uncompetitive Brabham, and was only able to qualify twice (in Britain, where he finished 16th four laps down, and Hungary, tenth, again four laps down). What saved him was test-driving for Williams and seizing a vacancy when it came: cumulatively a most unusual route in.

Mansell's struggles, and his unyielding determination to be entirely himself – his linguistics, his nationalism, his extraordinary self-belief, his ability to see himself in an heroic role against all-pervading adversity – is too well known to warrant another retelling here but, again, separated him from the man in the bus queue.

There is no doubt Jenson Button could have been in that bus queue, chattingly amiably to whoever stood next to him although he openly admired Mansell – because Mansell 'loved everything about Formula 1, the speed, the danger, the fans. He was very emotional about racing and I'm the same.'

There has never been any doubt that Button saw himself as a World Champion and 'I wouldn't be here if I didn't think that. That's always been my aim, and if I don't become World Champion one day I'll be very disappointed, but you have to be with the right team.'

Button's definition of normality – normal *but* saying publicly you can beat Michael Schumacher – seems a much more interesting balance than either Hill or Mansell found, especially speaking in 2004 two years before his first Grand Prix victory. You can emphasise this. During 2004 Schumacher would win 13 of the 18 rounds...

He reacted to adversity in the most normal way. Never mind Hill, he'd come under strong criticism from, among others, Bernie Ecclestone over one of his early team moves. His reaction in 2009?

'I don't need to poke anyone in the eye about what they've said about me in the past. There have been a lot of positive comments and those are the ones that you obviously enjoy. If there are going to be negative comments I have no reason to poke anyone in the eye for any reason. Things got very stressful and you read things in the papers that are very difficult to take. You want to say your piece but it is not really going to help because, if people don't believe in you initially, they are not going to believe what you have to say if you are not quick.'

He did not suffer a crisis in adversity, something he explains by pointing out that if you have been successful through karting and the lesser formulae 'you don't doubt yourself'. In fact, the last time he did doubt himself was when he was in karts at 14 and he asked his father if he *still* had it.

Interestingly that year he first went to Silverstone and would carry away (like so many other first-timers) a memory of how noisy the cars were. He managed to get into the pits, saw Ayrton Senna and thought '"Wow, bloody hell, a real live Formula 1 driver" – because I thought at the time they must be a different species.'

Since 14 he has not indulged in self-doubt at all, and not

sought reassurance from anyone else either. Instead, he looks 'within'.

That said, he was in no sense alone in the bleak and desperate December Christmas of 2008.

He'd pay tribute to the whole Honda/Brawn team for their support and his family 'for being so strong', although he felt his father was taking it harder than he was. He'd add that 'in those dark moments it's not good to be on your own. You think about things too much. That's why [lingerie model] Jessica [Michibata] has helped me so much. She's taken my mind off things when it's been needed and, to be honest, when it's not been.' That involved a holiday in Hawaii [there are consolations to being an unemployed Formula 1 driver, a model and Hawaii two of them]. That gave him something else to think about.

He was surprised by the breadth of people who rang to see how he was and to commisserate – people you might have thought would be probing him to drive for them. It wasn't. It was social, and more touching for that.

He even went back to his native Somerset because he was curious to experience *not* being a racing driver, and discovered that when he went out socially it involved a succession of people talking about the dole queue (which wasn't funny and wasn't a consolation).

Rubens Barrichello started, like Button and almost all the others, in karting. He came to Europe in 1990 and won the Formula Vauxhall Lotus. He moved to Formula 3 with the West Surrey Racing team, run by Dick Bennetts. Senna had driven for them and now Barrichello did what Senna had done and won the championship. He had 74 points, David Coulthard 66, Gil de Ferran 54. He moved to Formula 3000 and finished third (Luca Badoer 46, Andrea Montermini 34, Barrichello 27).

1993, Jordan:

R, R, 10, R, 12, 9, R, 7, 10, R, R, R, R, 13, 5, 11 (2 points, joint 17th).

Eddie Jordan signed him: 'He came to me with his father. I remember sitting in the front room of our house in Oxford and

I thought, *My God, this boy is the same age as our kids.* I'd seen him in Formula 3 and in 3000. He had a hugely mindful commercial head on him. He knew exactly what was going on and what a private team in Formula 1 entailed. He knew what he had to do technically and he had a great belief in his abilities.

'So I sat down initially and went through all the different video clips that I had of him driving. I put it all together and I thought, *You know, I can't really fault this, it looks really good,* for a young guy that we would mould into something that would be a championship hopeful – which is what we had to go on at that stage.'

On his debut in South Africa he qualified on the seventh row – in front of Gergard Berger in the Ferrari – and went to lap 31, when the gearbox failed. He qualified on the same row at São Paulo – alongside Berger now – but the gearbox failed after 13 laps. At the European Grand Prix at Donington, the fabled wet-dry-wet-dry race when Senna walked on the water, Barrichello ran second from laps 49 to 55, when he pitted, resuming fourth but after 70 of the 76 laps retiring with a fuel pressure problem. It seemed he had unlimited promise and might realise it quickly but the car wasn't reliable.

In the years to come, Paul Stewart would sign him for the Stewart team. He remembers Barrichello at Donington. 'Everyone goes on about Ayrton – well, Rubens came up from further back on the grid [12th] and as far as I was concerned he was the man of that race. That was classically how Rubens would perform. He wasn't put off by those conditions.' This race would prove a very accurate barometer of what Barrichello would do in similar conditions when he reached Stewart.

1994, Jordan:
4, 3, DNS, R, R, 7, R, 4, R, R, R, 4, 4, 12, R, 4 (19 points, 5th)

Imola in 1994, the fourth race of the season, remains a weekend cloaked in mourning. Barrichello crashed on the Friday, the Jordan pitched high. 'I don't know to this day how Rubens walked away from his crash,' Eddie Jordan says. 'That was massive, massive, massive, and everyone was frightened to death because the car took off and hit the top of the guard fence. Ayrton of course went to see him at the Medical Centre. I wasn't there next day when Roland [Ratzenberger] was killed because I was in the hospital with Rubens and then the day after, of course, was the fatal accident to Ayrton. That wasn't just an immense shock to Rubens, it was an immense shock to everybody – not just because Ayrton was a legend but also because he was such a great, great personality.'

They were both from São Paulo and, people said, Barrichello was Senna's protégé.

'At the end, I'm not sure. You know it's a bit like Michael Schumacher. When you're at that level you have to be inherently aggressive because you can't get there unless you are, but in Ayrton's case it didn't come across as obviously as it did with some other drivers. At the same time, Rubens was a competitor as far as Ayrton was concerned so he wouldn't call him by, he'd chop him up just as quick as he'd chop anybody else up.'

The Jordan designer Gary Anderson says 'Ayrton's crash was a big, big deal. It's a tricky one, I have to say, whether it makes you, breaks you or whatever. When Rubens came back he was a different person from before. His focus was harder – I don't know how you'd say it, but it was *something*. He lost a little bit of the fun part of it, but you can understand that.'

At Aida for the Pacific Grand Prix, Barrichello got the Jordan team its first podium, as Eddie Jordan says with undisguised delight all these years later. Eight races after Imola – Belgium – as Eddie Jordan says with equally undisguised delight, 'he got our first-ever pole position.'

'Rubens in my book is a good bloke,' Gary Anderson says. 'In his earlier days, 1993–1994, when he came to the races he had half of Brazil with him – that was all his family, his mother, his father, his sister, his aunt, his uncle, his brother, the ones by marriage or *something*: the whole family.

'I had this out with Rubens one day because he never had to make a decision in his life. He never made a decision about what bedroom he wanted at the hotel, what rental car he wanted, what flight he wanted to be on. He had everybody making all his decisions. I said to him at Monza "Rubens, if you arrive at that first chicane down there and you're side-by-side with somebody, you're going to have to make a decision. Are you going to try and pass the bloke or not? You've never made a decision in your life so how are you going to then? – because that's what life's about: making decisions. If you don't get the decision right, you think about it again, so start making some decisions. Get rid of that entourage. They're telling you everything. They know everything that's wrong and they know nothing that's right."

'That was the problem with Rubens at that point in time. *They* were in the garage looking around. I'd put my arm round Eddie Irvine or something – or Eddie Jordan would go and speak to Irvine – and they got the feeling there was an Irish mafia. They reported this to Rubens and that's when Rubens got into his sulks.

'As a person, Rubens was focussed and dedicated, and some of the spitting-the-dummy-out was because of that, and some was because of the advice from the outside world which was making him insulated form the real world. I like the sort of people who react as he did. Unless you do, you're nobody in life, are you? You're a passenger. You have to fight your corner.'

'Temperamental?' Eddie Jordan muses. 'I never really saw that side of it. He's very Latin. I would go and stay with him in Brazil, São Paulo – maybe twice every year. One day we'd do a launch and a Press day, and he would gather the most amazing bunch of people that you can ever imagine. At that stage Brazil was buzzing and then of course he became the leading light after the death of Ayrton, so there was a big responsibility. He took it on and there were times he never really quite delivered what he'd hoped to deliver at his home race at Interlagos. Maybe in recent years he's said things from his heart before he's actually thought them through but he is man enough to come back and apologise if he thinks they were wrong.'

1995, Jordan:
R, R, R, 7, R, 2, 6, 11, R, 7, 6, R, 11, 4, R, R, R (11 points, 11th)

1996, Jordan:
R, R, 4, 5, 5, R, R, R, 9, 4, 6, 6, R, 5, R, 9
(14 points, 8th)

'He was a team-mate of Martin Brundle's and quite clearly Brundle had a lot of experience, Brundle had been with me in the Formula 3 days in the early 1980s, and came back to drive alongside him,' Eddie Jordan says. 'I'm not sure how the championship finished [Brundle 11th] but I think you'll find that Barrichello was always ahead of him. We agreed after four years that he should go and spread his wings. He was still very young and he went to Stewart.'

1997, Stewart:
R, R, R, R, 2, R, R, R, R, R, R, R, 13, 14, R, R, R
(6 points, 13th)

Paul Stewart, running the team, remembers 'we had various choices, although the reality was we didn't have that many because we were a new team. You want to get somebody with experience and the really good drivers are not going to want to come to a new team – basically from Formula 3000 moving up into Formula 1. We talked to various drivers and I wanted to have somebody that had a combination of experience and that I knew was quick. I'd known Rubens since the European Vauxhall championship because we had Gil de Ferran and David Coulthard racing against him.

'We also raced against him in Formula 3 when he was with Dick Bennetts and I could see the guy had certain limitations. He wasn't the best at doing starts, for example, but he won the championship. He was just bloody quick.

'He came to me at, I think, the Portuguese Grand Prix. We were down there trying to hire Damon [Hill], knowing that he was out of a drive at Williams. Rubens and Gary Anderson came and saw me in the Ford motorhome. Rubens was really unhappy with the way things were at that time. I chatted to him although I wasn't seriously considering him because of Damon, who was a very big name and reigning World

Champion. If we were serious about what we were doing we had to make a bid for *him*. When that fell through I said "Well, what are we going to do?"

'I wanted to have a driver I could work with, that I could see eye-to-eye to, that I felt could be quick if we worked with him and build up his confidence. That was the key to it. I am still convinced it was the right choice for us at that stage in our development. He did a great job for us, it was fun to have him in the team and, whatever it was about our relationship, it enabled me to try and fix it when he was unhappy about something. Brazilians are sometimes a little more emotional than some other nationalities and it gave me pleasure being able to do things that made a difference to him and how he performed.

'And he was good technically. The debriefs with him were always very, good, very thorough. He was always very clear about what he needed. The Latin temperament? That's what I liked about him. He was emotional, but it wasn't as if he was just emotional or anything like that, he responded to "Right, here we go, what can we do for you, Rubens?" Generally, if you felt that you were doing the right thing for him he would respond extremely positively. That was very satisfying.'

The 2 in the 1997 season represents second place at Monaco, a wet race which Michael Schumacher won with Barrichello 53.3 seconds behind and Irvine, partnering Schumacher, third. The Stewart team were highly emotional and Jackie Stewart said he was more pleased with the second finish than if he'd won the race himself. Barrichello made only one small error, and separating the Ferraris was clearly something Ferrari noticed.

'That was entirely his performance, really,' Paul Stewart says. 'Rubens is particularly good in conditions of that kind. Obviously the car worked for him but Monaco was down to him, very much so. We made the right choice tyre-wise, and he would have been a key part of that decision. I loved having him in the team and he made a big difference to a lot of people in the team.'

1998, Stewart:

R, R, 10, R, 5, R, 5, 10, R, R, R, R, DNS, 10, 11, R
(4 points, 12th)

'There was a couple of times he was unhappy,' Stewart says. 'When Jan [Magnussen] would go quicker than him, for example. That would unsettle him. At that time we could change engines and we'd change his engine to make sure everything was right on his car. He never complained about new parts on Jan's car.'

Drivers frequently (and sometimes obsessively) imagine their team-mate is getting all the latest bits, giving them more speed. I mention to Paul Stewart how, in all my years of writing about it, only one driver has actually admitted his team-mate was just quicker.[1] Chuckling, Stewart said: 'Men, especially racing drivers, have this innate ability to deny, deny, deny – whether it's being caught with their pants down or finding a racing driver quicker than them.'

Nothing particularly to do with Barrichello. I just thought you'd like to know.

1999, Stewart:

5, R, 3, 9, DQ, R, 3, 8, R, R, 5, 10, 4, 3, 5, 8
(21 points, 7th)

In France, Barrichello put the Stewart on pole. It was the second of his career and Stewart's first (and only). Ferrari clearly noticed.

'He told me, of course, that he was thinking about going to Ferrari,' Eddie Jordan says. 'At that stage I was not his manager and I was not privy to those items in the contract but when I did look after Irvine in a similar situation it was not that clear about the role that Michael Schumacher played (contractually). I don't think it said that he was the Number One driver, but that doesn't mean he hadn't preferences. I don't want to be critical, but I'd like to have seen – if Barrichello's management had stood up to Ferrari – whether they would have to have given in. But I think Rubens was very happy to be driving at Ferrari and he drove there for a number of years.'

'I did know about it,' Paul Stewart says, 'I knew he was being romanced by Ferrari. When we went for Eddie [Irvine] after Rubens left, there were a lot of rumours about what we were paying him and there were all sorts of things going on. Whatever we paid him was approved and supported and budgeted for by the Ford Motor Company.[2] There were a few wild rumours that came out, and when Rubens heard them I think he was a little bit surprised and thought maybe he should have hung around for the negotiations! But, even then, Rubens had to drive for Ferrari, he had to tick that box for himself.

'I was happy for him and I was very realistic about the car that we could provide him with. Also, have you got the right to deny a man that sort of chance? I wasn't going to do that and I knew it meant a lot to him. If we were not delivering, and he knew he had had this Ferrari offer that he'd turned down, it would have been a major problem for us to manage. I felt that he would be able to challenge Michael on occasions but the team was programmed around Michael.'

2000, Ferrari:
2, R, 4, R, 3, 4, 2, 2, 3, 3, 1, 4, R, R, 2, 4, 3
(62 points, 4th)

That first win was in Germany when, significantly, Schumacher collided with Giancarlo Fisichella (Benetton) at the start, and in that instant team orders were destroyed. Barrichello had qualified 18th which, itself, made the win memorable. On the podium Barrichello's emotions overcame him and he wept openly. It was his 124th Grand Prix, a melancholy record (next Jarno Trulli 117, then Fisichella 110).

2001, Ferrari:
3, 2, R, 3, R, 3, 2, R, 5, 3, 3, 2, 2, 5, 2, 15, 5
(56 points, 3rd)

2002, Ferrari:

R, R, R, 2, DNS, 2, 7, 3, 1, 2, DNS, 4, 1, 2, 1, 1, 2
(77 points, 2nd)

The Austrian Grand Prix, sixth round, remains notorious because Barrichello commanded the race but was ordered to pull over and cede it to Schumacher at the very end. In the furore, it was easy to forget that Barrichello had just re-signed for Ferrari until the end of 2004. The grotesque finale at the A-1 Ring demonstrated that he would spend another two seasons in the equivalent of captivity.

2003, Ferrari:

R, 2, R, 3, 3, 3, 8, 5, 3, 7, 1, R, R, 3, R, 1
(65 points, 4th)

2004, Ferrari:

2, 4, 2, 6, 2, 3, 2, 2, 2, 3, 3, 12, 2, 3, 1, 1, R, 3
(114 points, 2nd)

2005, Ferrari:

2, R, 9, R, 9, 8, 3, 3, 2, 9, 7, 10, 10, 10, 12, 5, 6, 11, 12
(38 points, 8th)

Only Ferrari, Jordan and Minardi were using Bridgestone tyres so, all else aside, Ferrari lacked any real measurement for how good – or bad – the tyres were. It proved to be a crippling disadvantage this one season, Schumacher no higher than third in the championship (with only one win) and Ferrari third in the constructor's (Renault 191, McLaren 182, Ferrari 100).

It was time to move on again – to Honda.

Barrichello would say 'I was convinced to get away from my contract at Ferrari, and it is not anybody's fault I left, because I wanted to. When I got to the team I didn't find it how I was promised,' which makes you wonder why he stayed for six seasons.

'To this day,' Eddie Jordan says, 'I think that Michael would say to Rubens, "You know, you were a great, great team-mate."'

'The guy was quick,' Gary Anderson says. 'It's just so sad that he never won a World Championship and he didn't win more races, but when he had the opportunity, unfortunately, he was head-to-head with a bloke called Michael Schumacher. It wasn't head-to-head, it was actually head to about a hundred heads. I think he kept his head down very well at Ferrari. At the end of the day he left Ferrari to go to Honda because he thought he would be able to have free rein. Unfortunately he got caught up in Honda going downhill and he and his manager separated because of it. His manager said "Just take the money and shut up," but Rubens said "I want more than that, I want to win a World Championship. I had no opportunity to win a World Championship at Ferrari."'

2006, Honda:
15, 10, 7, 10, 5, 7, 4, 10, R, 6, R, R, 4, 8, 6, 6, 12, 7
(30 points, 7th)

2007, Honda:
11, 11, 13, 10, 10, 12, R, 11, 9, 11, 18, 17, 10, 13, 10, 15, R
(0 points)

2008, Honda:
DQ, 13, 11, R, 14, 6, 7, 14, 3, R, 16, 16, R, 17, R, 13, 11, 15
(11 points, 14th)

Reflecting on the season, Barrichello was asked if, knowing that all the development was going into the 2009 car, it wouldn't have been a natural course to take it easy across 2008. He replied that 'My mind was always aware that things would improve,' adding that there were reasons to be optimistic before the first race in Australia and further reasons with promised updates, but they proved a cruel disappointment. Nevertheless, 'When you are focused on your job, if you know you have given your very best, no matter where you finished, then that is great. And you have to fight to make sure the things that went wrong go right next time.'

He highlighted how, even in its moment of semi-triumph –

the third place at Silverstone in the British Grand Prix – the team wasn't functioning properly. 'On the Monday after the race we got everyone together because we should have finished second. We lost 20 seconds in the pit stop because there were too many people talking over the radio. For a team like us, we should never accept something like that.'[3]

These are not the words of a man taking things easy, or the words of a man who would even comprehend taking things easy.

'I think he is an outstanding man,' Eddie Jordan says. 'I think he's very, very fair on the racetrack. He would be everybody's delight as a team-mate because, apart from the fairness, he's easy, he's not political. He doesn't like and doesn't understand political things. That's probably why he says some of the outspoken things he's inclined to – because of things that go into his head, or things that he has seen, or things that he has believed. Of course some of them may not actually be there at all, but for racing drivers it's a very lonely world sitting in the car. You're racing your heart out for the two hours and you think things are different to the way they really are. That's what happened the other day.'

The 'other day' was the German Grand Prix at the Nürburgring, July 2009, and we'll be coming to that (see Chapter 8). Suffice to say here that Barrichello gave the team a broadside.

If he'd had his brain in gear, he'd have said 'I'll wait until I've had a good look at what happened.'

'He's not that kind of guy, is he?' Eddie Jordan says. 'He's inclined to say what's in his mind, he wears his heart on his sleeve. I enjoy him, I have to say. He's great company. I'm biased because he was so good to my kids and I think we were so good to him. He was part of our family.'

Gary Anderson is interesting about Barrichello's temperament. 'Rubens now is a much more mature person but he will "have it out" with anybody at any point in time and he showed that in the Nürburgring, when he did the big spit-the-dummy-out job with Brawn because he thought they'd lost him the race. That was him "having it out".

'At least you know what you're going to get. Yes, he has got

– I don't know what you'd call it – a Latin temperament, and you have to allow for that because they're different people. Different nationalities do have different characteristics, and he has a bit of that. I didn't find that detrimental. To be honest, if you sat down and talked to him he would ask the right questions, and he'd accept the right answers.'

Eddie Jordan offers a final evaluation before we set off on the long journey to Australia via Barcelona, and the astonishing 2009 season. 'He's driven more consecutive Grands Prix than anyone else, he's driven for Jordan, Stewart, Ferrari and Honda/BAR/Brawn. They're not bad teams. He's been pretty consistent for 16, 18 years and that is a long time. I think the only place that he was in a position to win a championship was at Ferrari and clearly he knew going there that that was never going to be allowed to happen.'

Could he do it at last? There were many, many questions begging for answers as the teams went to Barcelona and the testing which formed the season's prelude. The Barrichello question, as it turned out, would certainly be one of them.

When all had been fluid before the Brawn takeover Barrichello had attempted to answer the question himself. 'When I say I can still be champion it is because I really believe that. I am not worse than I was in 1993 in terms of speed. In terms of my physical condition I am better than ever so it is just down to the car and to the whole situation.'[4]

This seems an appropriate juncture to ask Nick Fry: *Do you think the drivers ever doubted themselves before 2009, or did you and the team ever doubt them?*

'The answer is an emphatic no to both questions. The secret here to keep people motivated is for there always to be hope. People have always to believe there really is light at the end of the tunnel, and I was always able to present that to them to some extent – although it might not have been completely convincing to some of them some of the time. We were building the wind tunnel, which was going to help the situation, and we were going to improve the machine shop, which was going to help our manufacturing facilities. They saw we were heading in the right direction. During 2007, which was awful, they all knew that we were hiring people and at the end of the year Ross joined us, so there *was* always something which was going to make the situation better.

'To the enormous credit of the drivers, neither of them ever gave up or stopped working hard. Through the whole period of 2007–2008 Jenson and Rubens just reset their targets. They knew that the best the car was capable of, for example, tenth or eleventh position, so if they came in eighth or ninth then they understood they had over-achieved. All they did mentally was measure themselves against the art of the possible, and if they managed to do better than that then they took credit.'

Notes

1. It was Jonathan Palmer who, at Tyrrell in 1989, found himself partnering young, ambituous Jean Alesi. Palmer realised that whatever he did Alesi was simply quicker. I insist (and I mentioned this to Paul Stewart, in passing) 'they were all going to beat Ayrton Senna if only they could get into the right car'. Drivers seem to need to believe this regardless of all evidence to the contrary.

2. One of the rumours was that at a board meeting in Detroit, Henry Ford demanded to know who 'Edmund Irvine' was – he was Christened Edmund, not Edward – and when someone asked why, Ford said 'because he's our highest-paid employee.'

3. Interview with Jonathan Noble (www.autosport.com/news/report.php/id/72531).

4. Ibid.

CHAPTER 5

STRANGE NEWS FROM SPAIN

There's a hallowed saying in motor sport which is usually expressed in fruity language but doesn't have to be. It is 'When the flag drops all the pre-season dreaming, scheming and claiming stops too.' What you get, instead, is that most disconcerting thing, reality. Until this moment all the teams are going to beat all the other teams, all the cars are going to beat all the other cars and, especially, all the drivers are going to beat all the other drivers (see Note 1, previous chapter). After this moment, mostly they aren't.

These days the flag is five red lights that come on to hold the cars on the grid and go off to release them. The methodology changes nothing.

In one way, the saying perfectly encapsulates what happened between 9 and 29 March, but in another way it didn't, because pre-season 2009 turned out to be very strange, as if Ross Brawn and his team had found a way of suspending reality, or circumventing it, or bending it to their will. Nobody was sure which and at moments you felt *they* weren't sure, either.

The team went to the communal pre-season testing at Barcelona, which was three days after the car's shakedown at Silverstone – that is to say, the first time it actually turned a wheel.

All ten teams would be at Barcelona, permitting direct but potentially misleading comparisons because, in testing, teams are free to do whatever they want. As anyone will tell you, testing may be a guide but you really do have to wait until the lights go out before you see, forgive me, the cold light of day.

This testing, and three subsequent days at Jerez, demand to

111

be examined in some detail because they were so remarkable and so accurate a pointer to what *would* happen next. The statistics are eloquent, as they always are in motor racing, and they are given, I hope, without overloading the narrative. Something powerful was happening, and happening very quickly despite all possible misleading comparisons. In a word, it was impetus.

In 2007 and particularly 2008 that had belonged to Lewis Hamilton in the McLaren who, in such an astonishingly short time, had become what Button ought to have become a decade earlier: a handsome, softly-spoken and articulate World Champion. Since his debut in 2007, Hamilton seemed to be ushering in his own era and approaching the Barcelona test he could contemplate a career of 35 races which had yielded nine victories and 207 points. In wins alone, he *already* had more than John Surtees, Gilles Villeneuve, Keke Rosberg, Eddie Irvine, Juan Pablo Montoya and Mike Hawthorn, to select random names.

In points alone, he *already* had more than Alan Jones, Ronnie Peterson, Bruce McLaren, Stirling Moss, René Arnoux, Jacky Ickx and James Hunt. This comparison is unfair because the points were increased in 1991 to 10 for a win, then 6 and 4, increasing again in 2003: still 10 for a win but then 8 and 6, descending to a single point for eighth. This did not disturb the feeling that, after the Clark Era and the Senna Era and the Schumacher Era, here might well be the next.

Round the busy, bustling Circuit de Catalunya some 12 miles north of Barcelona there would be a great deal to watch and try to understand, but the main focus would have to be on Hamilton and McLaren. In theory all the others were trying to catch him.

Fernando Alonso, twice World Champion, was hungry for a third at Renault and, as he proved in 2008, could conjure victories from the most unpromising positions. His CV: 122 races, 21 wins, 551 points.

Felipe Massa and Kimi Räikkönen were both fast and they had the wealth of Ferrari behind them. Massa had come within a breath of the championship in 2008 and was visibly maturing into a front-runner. Massa's CV: 105 races, 11 wins, 298 points. Räikkönen remained a compound of awesome speed or vanishing into the pack and you could never quite tell which it was going to be. Räikkönen's CV: 139 races, 17 wins, 531 points.

BMW Sauber had been constantly advancing since BMW took over Sauber at the end of 2005 and their drivers, personable Nick Heidfeld, who was easy to underestimate, and Robert Kubica – already a race-winner – promised much. Heidfeld's CV: 150 races, 0 wins, 200 points. Kubica's CV: 40 races, 1 win, 120 points.

Toyota had been toiling these many years but Jarno Trulli could himself win races, and logic, if nothing else, suggested that one of these days the enormous Toyota investment would *have* to bring reward. Trulli's CV: 199 races, 1 win, 214 points. His team-mate Timo Glock, eight years younger, was coming along at a gallop. Glock's CV: 22 races, 0 wins, 27 points.

Almost from nowhere the young, fresh-faced German Sebastian Vettel might beat the lot of them in the Red Bull. He, too, was already a race-winner and his team-mate, Mark Webber, ought to have been. Webber was unlucky. What would happen if and when his luck turned? Vettel's CV: 26 races, 1 win, 41 points. Webber's CV: 121 races, 0 wins, 100 points.

You had to factor in Nico Rosberg at Williams, another man visibly maturing and with the great virtue of being straightforward. Rosberg's CV: 53 races, 0 wins, 41 points.

Cumulatively, this was a strong, broad and deep cast of opponents which Brawn would have to confront, and confront them as a team which had been all but killed, moved to intensive care, put on life support and were only here courtesy of a kiss of life.

The timeline had become:

Friday 5 December: Honda announce withdrawal.

Thursday, 5 March: Fry announces a deal is imminent.

Friday, 6 March: Brawn announces he owns the team, and Button shakes the car down at Silverstone.

Monday, 9 March: the four-day Barcelona testing begins.

The Brawn team, of course, had been in no position to test

the car. The context with that can be expressed in a direct comparison. Ferrari tested at Jerez from 9 to 11 December. On the first day Räikkönen did 48 laps; on the second day 89 laps and Massa 27; on the third day Räikkönen did 82, Massa 72. Ferrari then decamped to the new circuit in the Algarve, Portimão, between 15 and 17 December. On the first day Massa did 36 laps; next day test drivers Luca Badoer (71) and Marc Gené (51) took over; Badoer did 75 laps on the final day.

Ferrari gave their new car, the F60, a debut run at Mugello early in the New Year then, at the same circuit from 19 to 22 January, began serious testing. Räikkönen did 54 laps on the first day; 42 on the second; Massa did 104 on the third and 103 on the fourth.

They went to Sakhir between 10 and 19 February. Massa covered a total of 328 laps and Räikkönen did exactly the same. They went back to Jerez from 1 to 5 March where, successively, Massa did 63 laps and 135, Räikkönen 105 and 112.

That's 1,925 laps with the new car.

The comparison becomes totally stark in statistics. Brawn: 0 laps.

Barrichello and Button had enormous experience between them, as we saw in the last chapter. Barrichello made his debut in South Africa in 1993 (but would say, delightfully, 'Well, I feel younger than most of them'), Button in Australia in 2000. It seemed their fate was as eternal bit-part players, and at 37 Barrichello wouldn't be doing even that for much longer. Barrichello's CV: 268 races, 9 wins, 530 points. Button's CV: 153 races, 1 win, 232 points.

That first morning at Barcelona drizzle fell but it soon cleared and the track was in good, serviceable condition. Ten cars would exploit that, although whether anybody expected much from the Brawn so soon after it came off life support wasn't clear. Ross Brawn believed, and said, the car was a good one. *He* had the enormous experience we have seen, of course, and wouldn't say such things unless he was sure of his grounds, but, I repeat, all cars were going to beat all the other cars and all teams were going to beat all other teams until the lights went out in Melbourne only 19 days after the Barcelona test finished.

Button sat in the car in the pits with Brawn, earphones clamped to his head, watching benevolently. The car was virgin white and soon to become Virgin white but at this stage looked naked of sponsor's decals. Half a dozen other team members watched intently. Brawn never betrays anxiety and neither did they, although they must have felt it. The jackmen at the front lowered the nose of the car and scampered clear. The engine growled like – as a poet once wrote – a God yearning in pain, and the sound echoed back off the pit's walls.

Button brought the car gently, smoothly forward and twisted it right into the pit lane. He stopped because another car was coming past, the engine yearning so loudly now that a man nearby had to clamp his hands to his ears.

Then Button went down the pit lane and out into the 2.8 miles.

The great adventure had really begun.

When Button had gone Brawn stood astride the pit entrance. A photographer came up and they shook hands warmly. If Brawn never betrays anxiety he invariably reacts normally even though for him, out there through the 16 turns, something momentous and inescapable was beginning.

Button knew the circuit because every experienced Formula 1 driver does after all the testing there over the years. Button would say the race there was almost like your home Grand Prix. He knew you needed confidence in the car to negotiate the high-speed corners and establish a proper rhythm to master the slower ones. In its differing demands, Barcelona may well have been the perfect test of a new Grand Prix car.

He sensed after just four laps that the Brawn was competitive. James Hunt once said that you know almost immediately if a car is good or not and, if it's not, it's already too late. You'll have to live with it, whatever it is. The opposite is also true and the good car tells you it is good just as quickly, especially if you've been driving Grand Prix cars for almost a decade and a depressing number of them were not very good at all. It gives you a very accurate yardstick.

I put it to Brawn: *Jenson said after the four laps.*

'Yes, I am sure the drivers do know. I knew, yes. You look at the lap times and you look at the data when the car was settled

115

and balanced. There was nothing strange happening and the lap times were good. We knew what fuel we had on board even if people were insinuating we were messing about because we didn't have sponsors. We knew very quickly and there were reasons. There are very few fortunate accidents [of pure good fortune] in Formula 1. You get what you put in. It's a very good engineering team here and they just needed that opportunity to be able to display what they could do.'

They'd just done that at Barcelona all right.

Others sensed that the car suited Button's style, neat, fluid, unhurried, and so smooth it put people in mind of Alain Prost and, before him, Jackie Stewart. Like Prost and Stewart, Button's style did not radiate speed and was the more deceptive for that, just as they had been. His style meant he was light on cars, light on tyres, and rarely made mistakes. Like Prost and Stewart...

He brought the car back to the pits and six mechanics pushed it rearwards into the pit, Brawn padding along behind it; then a white screen was drawn across to protect it from prying eyes. Button clambered out, examined the times and had all the confirmation he needed. He understood in those few moments that the decision to remain with the team had been a wise one. Nobody – *nobody,* not Button or Barrichello, Brawn or Nick Fry – knew how wise.

Button spoke about how well the tyres suited the car, judging that the season before they'd been 'reasonably' good. This is not as trivial as it sounds, and another hallowed saying in motor sport sums that up: 'There's time in the tyres.' This would become one of the dominant themes of the whole season for every car and every driver, as we shall see.

At lunchtime Button was fastest. The top three:

Button	1m 21.1s
Jarno Trulli (Toyota)	1m 21.8s
Nelson Piquet Jr (Renault)	1m 22.0s

While resisting the temptation of comparisons (and, with the benefit of hindsight, cheating), it's legitimate to point out that

Räikkönen in the Ferrari did 1m 22.8s and Heikki Kovalainen in the McLaren 1m 24.2s.

The afternoon was a little windier and Button carried through solid work to finish the day with 82 laps covered. By then the gearbox was being a little naughty but, because the team had done no testing, this neither surprised nor disconcerted him. He was perfectly well aware something like that might happen. 'Fortunately, it's a minor problem that is easily addressed.' He spoke almost guardedly about how the day had been 'positive' and they were on their way, although he didn't add to that. He was mature enough to know that *nothing* was conclusive yet, although, privately, he was anxious to tell his father just how good he found that the car was.

The day finished:

Heidfeld (BMW Sauber)	1m 20.3s
Räikkönen	1m 20.9s
Trulli (Toyota)	1m 20.9s
Button	1m 21.1s
Piquet	1m 21.6s
Sébastien Bourdais (Toro Rosso)	1m 22.1s
Mark Webber (Red Bull)	1m 22.2s
Adrian Sutil (Force India)	1m 22.4s
Kazuki Nakajima (Williams)	1m 22.8s
Kovalainen	1m 22.9s

Brawn explained that 'on the basis of our simulations we knew what lap times this car would do theoretically at Jerez, Bahrain and Barcelona. When we saw the times of the competition, we were surprised they were not quicker.' He didn't add to that. He, too, was mature enough to know that *nothing* really was conclusive.

Virgin white and naked? The team lacked sponsorship, although the car did have a green and yellow strip down the middle, unlike the other cars which looked like the usual mobile advertising hoardings. Seen flank on, the Brawn bore two names and two only: Brawn and Bridgestone.

Now the insinuations began that the car was running light

precisely to set fast times and attract sponsorship. Ross Brawn emphatically denied this, and subsequent events vindicated him in an overwhelming way. This is what, smiling in that benevolent way, he said: 'If everyone knew how much fuel we had on board they would be surprised. Even Mercedes didn't believe it when we told them.'

Norbert Haug, running the Mercedes racing operation, was impressed. 'I believe the people around Ross Brawn and Nick Fry have done good work. All the conditions to build a competitive car remained [when Honda left]. Ross knows how to develop a team to a competitive state, which he has proved often enough.' It is what people say, especially in Formula 1, but this time it was true.

Barrichello took over on the second day and, like Button, knew he had a competitive car after 'just four laps' and knew it would 'take us to a different level'. That morning Räikkönen went fastest, Barrichello next and only 0.6 of a second slower. The top three:

Räikkönen	1m 20.3s
Barrichello	1m 20.9s
Trulli	1m 21.3s

After lunch Button gave an interview to camera behind the pits, looking perfectly at ease with himself and perfectly comfortable with the microphone craning towards him. As he spoke, the unseen passing cars on the start-finish straight howled by. The testing, he said, 'has been going really well. The car's good to drive, it definitely suits my style – which is great – and I think we've done a good job aero-wise, mechanically, and we've got a good lump [engine] in the back of it so the pace is good. What we don't know is how we are compared to our competitors. You never know what fuel loads people are running on. All I know is we started off very well and the car is reasonably reliable [note the English understatement], which is what we have been working on so far this week.'

Brawn faced the same camera and microphone. 'We are obviously glad to be going to the first race, because that wasn't a certainty up until a few weeks ago. We have a good car and the issue will be building in reliability and building in team performance, because we've only got this test prior to the race. We'll start race simulations, pit stop practice and things like that tomorrow' – the Wednesday. 'They've been practising back at the factory but working with the car is crucial and so it will be a big challenge. I think the fact that we are there is a major achievement, but I guess that will be gone very quickly and our results will have to be the things that speak for us.'[1]

Nakajima took the Williams up to second-fastest in the afternoon while Barrichello concentrated on sustained running. By day's end he'd have covered 111 laps.

Räikkönen	1m 20.3s
Nakajima	1m 20.9s
Barrichello	1m 20.9s
Trulli	1m 21.1s
Webber	1m 21.3s
Heidfeld	1m 21.6s
Sutil	1m 21.8s
Alonso (Renault)	1m 21.9s
Kovalainen	1m 21.9s
Bourdais	1m 23.0s

Button returned on the third day, overcast and the sun hiding until later. He covered 130 laps and confirmed everything with a lap of 1m 19.1s, Felipe Massa in the Ferrari next with 1m 20.1s. That's a full second that, in the kingdom of fractions, makes you ruler of all you survey. Significantly, because a pattern was emerging, Hamilton in the McLaren could summon no more than 1m 21.6s, slowest of the ten runners.

Button did a race simulation of 66 laps (including two pit stops) and lapped consistently in the 1m 20s and 1m 21s. Räikkönen's fastest qualifying time at the Catalunya circuit in 2008 had been 1m 20.701s, so the Brawn was on the pace however anybody defined it.

On the morning of the fourth day Nico Rosberg in the Williams became the second driver after Button to dip into the

1m 19s, Barrichello the third – and in the afternoon Barrichello blew that away with 1m 18.9s as well as covering 103 laps, including a race simulation. He, like Button, was consistently fast and the magazine *Autosport* calculated that, 'using the first 18 flying laps of a stint, Barrichello's run was almost six seconds faster than the best runs of Felipe Massa and Timo Glock, who were very similar in their net pace over their runs.' The final times need to be set out in full:

Barrichello	1m 18.9s
Button	1m 19.1s
Rosberg	1m 19.7s
Glock	1m 20.0s
Massa	1m 20.1s
Robert Kubica (BMW)	1m 20.2s
Räikkönen	1m 20.3s
Heidfeld	1m 20.3s
Vettel	1m 20.5s
Alonso	1m 20.6s
Hamilton	1m 20.8s
Nakajima	1m 20.9s
Trulli	1m 20.9s
Sébastien Buemi (Toro Rosso)	1m 21.0s
Giancarlo Fisichella (Force India)	1m 21.0s
Webber	1m 21.3s
Bourdais	1m 21.6s
Piquet	1m 21.6s
Sutil	1m 21.8s
Kovalainen	1m 21.9s

Barrichello expressed delight, particularly at the distance he had been able to cover, and insisted it was useful for Melbourne, although before that they'd go to the three-day test at Jerez. 'The car has proved fast and reliable throughout the week so we go to Jerez feeling positive and pleased with the results.' Like Haug's words, it is what people say but, like Haug's, it was true.

At Jerez he went quicker (1m 19.2s) than Alonso in the Renault (1m 19.8s). Alonso responded the next day by going faster (1m 18.3s) than Barrichello (1m 18.3s), who covered 62 laps, The Brawn drivers swopped the car at midday. Button covered 12 laps in a Grand Prix distance simulation before another gearbox problem struck and stopped him out on the track. He had a best time of 1m 18.8s, making him third.

On the third day (and Brawn's last) – 18 March, the Australian Grand Prix meeting beginning the week after – Button delivered a thunderous message to each member of that strong, broad and deep cast of opponents.

1m 17.8s.

In the kingdom of fractions, where the going rate is invariably calculated by tenths and hundredths, this was a full half a second quicker than Alonso's 1m 18.3 the day before. Hamilton, fourth, did a 1m 19.1s, and you don't need to be a candidate for Mensa to grasp the full implications of how slow that was.

Brawn was typically candid when he explained that the team had vaulted the first 'hurdle' – just physically getting to Australia – but while its structure would take them into the medium term, the longer term still had to be resolved. The team were behaving quite normally because, as Brawn confided, they were already working on upgrading the car for first European race, the Spanish at Barcelona, on 10 May.

Barrichello used all his experience to evaluate the testing. He estimated that when he was at Ferrari, and they were dominant, the cars covered perhaps 20,000km before the first race. 'This is very, very different. I had three tests. I have been in the gym every day but, even saying that, I don't think we are physically prepared to go flat out from the beginning of the race because driving the car gives you what you need, neck muscles and so on.' The testing 'prepared us very well, but I'm just saying that compared to those times, it's very, very different.'

And to anyone who still believed the car had been run light, when the lights did go out at Albert Park, Melbourne, the dreamers, schemers and claimants would all find out what reality was telling them. In that, the whole Brawn team had to be included.

Some perspective from Nick Fry, and first his own reaction: 'I think it was clearly excited and pleased after the shakedown and test, but partly not surprised. When I say that, I mean that we had invested from Silverstone 2008 onwards. We really stopped development of the 2008 car about halfway through the year and we had invested a lot of our resources very heavily in the specific design and development of this car.

'We had actually started the aerodynamic developments well before that. It was a long run-in, but also it was a long run-in against a background of fantastic facilities, which had been developed over the previous three-plus years. There had been a substantial amount of hiring, which to Honda's credit they allowed me to do. The dilemma that I had in 2007 was that I couldn't guarantee that I was going to get Ross. I had to go ahead during 2007, with Honda's back-up, hiring some very significant people like Loïc Bigois who runs the aerodynamics, John Owen who is one of his assistants – they were all hired in 2007 because we had to work on the basis that we couldn't wait for a new Technical Director and maybe someone like Ross wouldn't come along anyway.

'So when we were successful at Silverstone and Barcelona – and it *was* a good result – the reason I say I wasn't entirely surprised is because we'd put in so much effort over the previous couple of years to reach that point. It was a relief that it had all come together, but it wasn't altogether surprising.'

It would have been very easy to over-react to the Barcelona test because of all the traumas before but did you honestly see what was going to happen next?

'In sport everyone is, deep down, quite superstitious, and after so many disappointments you don't want to raise your hopes too high. However, did I believe we would win races in 2009? Yes. Did I believe that we would win so many races? Absolutely not. I don't believe anyone in their wildest dreams could have anticipated that.'

There was also the matter of the legality of the rear diffuser on the Brawn (and Toyota and Williams), which was already subject of a complaint from Red Bull. Of this, more later.

Bridgestone were the sole tyre supplier in 2009, and although the Formula 1 enthusiast is naturally drawn towards supporting individual drivers and, more rarely, individual teams, tyres were no longer a boring (and slightly incomprehensible) technical matter that could be safely ignored while you settled down to watch the race. In a disconcerting number of situations the tyres *were* the race.

Bridgestone took two batches to every race:

The first batch were intermediate and full wets in case the Heavens opened. These were understandably the same throughout the season and were only to be used when the weather made them necessary.

The second batch were dry-weather tyres for normal usage, made in four compounds: super soft, soft, medium, and hard.

Bridgestone would take two of these compounds to each race, and decide themselves which two. The subtlety began there, because each team had to use *both* compounds in qualifying and the race. *When* they ran them during the race was at their own discretion – and they would find some compounds suited their cars better than others. That depended on several factors but mainly the car's characteristics. It would bring Brawn delight and despair in equal measure. The tyres became a tactical choice: if a team was running a two-stop strategy, for example – that's three sets of tyres – and Bridgestone had allocated super soft and medium, which did you pick for which stint? (In a wet race the teams did not have to use anything but wets or intermediates.)

The tyres had more than ordinary relevance to Brawn because the car didn't always like the tyres, causing particular problems and making both drivers vulnerable, but early on when it did – especially in warm weather – the car floated forward and was very hard to beat. Button's driving style guaranteed he really was light on tyres but even he would find them graining and chewing at crucial moments.

The harder tyres were known as 'primes' and the softer as 'options'. It's important to know that because it's the shorthand the drivers and teams would use.

This was the Bridgestone choice up to Monza:

Australia	Super soft, medium
Malaysia	Soft, hard
China	Super soft, medium
Bahrain	Super soft, medium
Spain	Soft, hard
Monaco	Super soft, soft
Turkey	Soft, hard
Britain	Soft, hard
Germany	Super soft, medium
Hungary	Super soft, soft
Europe	Super soft, soft
Belgium	Soft, medium
Italy	Soft, medium

Gary Anderson explains what this meant, and would mean during the season.

'What the FIA wanted to do, in saying teams have to use both compounds, is spice up the action.'

This is how.

'Monaco was to be super soft and soft, which means the compounds are next door to each other, and Hungary the same. The other races would be two doors apart, say super soft and medium. There is probably a quarter of a second difference between two "next door" compounds at any given track – no big thing – but when the compounds are two doors apart that becomes half a second, a much bigger thing.

'For example, you take Monza, which has big, long straights. The tyre generates a lot of heat in its carcass and shoulder but the corners themselves are relatively low-speed so the lateral forces are not that high. The surface of the track makes a difference to the tyre, too, so only Bridgestone know what their tyre is really like for a given scenario.

'Bridgestone know best which of their tyre constructions and their tyre compounds will suit a given track – as far as the heat durability is so it doesn't blister, as far as the surface roughness or the surface texture of the track is relative to the tyre compound. All that is taken into account.

'What we saw last year was two compounds and you

couldn't really tell the difference because the grooved tyre was the dominating factor and once you'd done three or four laps the tyre was knackered anyway. This year, I think it does spice it up. It's more critical when you use them and the tracks are changing all the time so you have to think on your feet. I enjoy the pit stops and I enjoy the tyre decisions.'

Repeating, all this would have more than ordinary relevance to Brawn.

The Formula 1 season has evolved into a global activity, although Europe remains the backbone and, in a real sense, home. The first four races involved immense distances and absolute culture changes. Australia was well established (Adelaide from 1985 to 1995, Melbourne from 1996), China first staged a Grand Prix in 2004, Malaysia in 1999 and Bahrain in 2004. Whatever the distances and cultures, they were just circuits which, in turn, became stepping-stones into the season. By the time the teams boarded their planes after Bahrain on 26 April to come home the season would have a definite shape. The dreaming, scheming and claiming would be a long, long time ago.

Button expressed excitement at arriving in Australia because the car was competitive. He described the team as a tight unit and the circuit as 'fun'. He'd always qualified well, despite the quick changes of direction, the bumps and the problem 90° corners always posed. More generally, he explained, 'You can say it is a very good car but you still need to get the laps in and make it your own.' He hadn't been able to do that yet. To accommodate European television schedules, one practice, qualifying and the race would be run late in the afternoons. The schedule, local time:

Friday	First practice 12:30–2:00	Second practice 4:30–6:00
Saturday	Third practice 2:00–3:00	Qualifying 5:00–6:00
Sunday	Race 5:00[2]	

Brawn explained that Albert Park was 'very different' from Barcelona and Jerez and so the team concentrated during the

Friday on setting the car up for the conditions and the way the drivers liked it.

During the first free practice on Friday, Rosberg went quickest (1m 26.6s), Barrichello fourth (1m 27.2s), Button sixth (1m 27.4s). Free practice resembles testing in that you don't know what the others are doing, or trying to do, so all times must be approached with caution. Everybody knows, as Ron Dennis of McLaren once pointed out volubly, that you don't win races on Fridays: you take your own steps towards winning them on Sundays.

In the second session Rosberg went fastest again (1m 26.0s) from Barrichello (1m 26.1s), Button fifth (1m 26.3s). 'Track conditions improved considerably in the second session,' Brawn said. 'However, we are clearly not alone in finding the experience of running slightly later in the day less favourable than anticipated. It is a useful indication of what we may find when the race runs at a similar time on Sunday.'

Button found 'a few little niggly problems' with the set-up but said the pace was fine and, intriguingly, added 'we didn't want to show our hand too much. The long run performance looks competitive, particularly on the harder tyre. We still have some work to do on the softer tyre so that will be a priority for third practice. I had traffic on both of my new tyre runs at the end of the day, which was a shame – we don't know how quick we are over one lap yet but there is plenty of time to find that out.'

Barrichello, like Button, was delighted to be in Australia at all and, like Button, found the delight compounded by what the car had already shown despite the limited time it had had to do that. 'We evaluated both tyres and are happy with the overall performance so I think we have a good chance of a strong qualifying performance.'

Ross Brawn's insight: 'The car performed well and we are pleased with the day's work, experiencing only minor issues which are to be expected with our limited testing mileage. A good start to the weekend.'

It was about to get a lot better. Sir Richard Branson, at the circuit, announced that Virgin would be sponsoring the team and the car known as the Virgin BGP 001. Branson pointed out that Bernie Ecclestone was in the midst of a campaign to curb costs in Grand Prix racing – potentially a divisive and explosive move, however much it represented common sense to an outsider – and new teams would be able to come in without a king's ransom.

'That will encourage a lot of new companies to get involved with the sport and make it much more exciting,' Branson said. 'Those financial costs are less than they were a year or two ago but so they should be because the world is in a very different state compared to then. The sport will benefit from the costs coming down right across the board and with engineers using their skills rather than the teams using a chequebook in the future to produce great cars.

'As far as "clean" fuel is concerned, we have invested quite a considerable sum of money in a company called Gevo. One of the tasks they have had is to see if they can come up with a fuel for Formula 1 that is clean, doesn't emit any carbon, and can perform as well as the dirty fuels used in cars to date. I'm delighted to say they have come up with such a fuel. Over the next few months we will be trying to talk to Formula 1 and the various car companies to see if we can have it introduced as the one it uses so it can go from being a slightly polluting sport to a clean one. As far as I'm concerned I'm looking forward to working within the sport to try to change it.'

Branson reportedly had designs on introducing bio-fuels to the airline industry.

Jackie Oliver texted Ross in Australia as team owner and said: 'You are about to find out whether the ability to raise money is part of your capabilities as well' – the 'as well' being on top of technical skill, organisation and man-management. Oliver, who has enough personal experience after running Arrows, points out that raising money is another kind of skill and wondered [he was speaking in mid-season 2009] if Brawn possessed it. 'Colin Chapman did. He was all things to all people and the business models weren't the same then. Ron Dennis is a good example of someone who was extremely successful at generating money within Formula 1 but he did it in a completely different way than I used to. He did it corporately. Winning races is not just Ross Brawn's technical capability and the driver's skill, it starts with the guy who is able to give money to those guys so they can do the job. Success in that area requires a different management style. You're talking serious money these days and Ross is going to find out whether he and Nick Fry, as a combination, are going to be able to do it.'

This was not an immediate question, although the financial amount of Branson's sponsorship was not announced (they never are). At some point in 2009 Brawn was clearly going to need the serious money. That could certainly wait until after Australia but it wouldn't be going away.

In the third practice, on Saturday, Rosberg went fastest again (1m 25.8s), Button third (1m 25.9s), Barrichello sixth (1m 26.3s), and it's worth stressing again that these sessions are indicative but not definitive. Button described it as 'pretty good on both tyres' – medium and super soft, remember – and said 'I was reasonably happy. We didn't know what other people's pace was and you don't until you get to qualifying.'

Exactly. Qualifying is a preliminary reality check before the lights go out.

The qualifying hour, divided into three sections of sudden death, and abbreviated to Q1, Q2 and Q3, was not just a nervous, taut place but one of subtleties because of the tyre regulations. Here, a team *had* to use one set of medium tyres at some point during qualifying. Since the difference between the two compounds was estimated at half a second – by Gary Anderson and everybody else – *and* the medium tyre needed some laps to find its optimum performance, dare a team risk them only to find that slower cars on the super softs were going *much* faster? It might mean sudden death in Q1, which is in the nature of a great humiliation for a big team.

In Q1 the Brawns were the only cars which could run happily on the mediums, saving the super softs for Q2 and Q3. It was already a significant advantage because even the fast men in the other teams didn't dare to risk being half a second off the pace by using the mediums. If they did, slower cars on super softs might hustle them towards Madame Guillotine and her sharp, sharp blade at the end of Q1. The top four:

Barrichello	1m 25.0s
Button	1m 25.2s
Webber	1m 25.4s
Glock	1m 25.4s

Since each car had four sets of super softs for the whole qualifying hour, they'd used (apart from the Brawns) one set: three left. In Q2 they felt that they had to make two runs to be sure of surviving, and that meant two more sets of super softs, leaving only one *and* the medium for the Q3 shoot-out.

Button said that the other cars were 'a little bit closer' than he'd anticipated in Q1 and Q2 – one- or two-tenths behind. They proved 'more competitive than I thought they were, so it has been a little bit harder than I expected. There were four or five cars sitting on the same lap time and that was only two-tenths behind me. I was struggling on low fuel for some reason. I just could not get the car working right but when we put fuel in it, it felt a bit more normal.' The Q2 times:

Barrichello	1m 24.7s
Button	1m 24.8s
Vettel	1m 25.1s
Rosberg	1m 25.1s

Clearly, with their two sets of super softs available, pole lay between the Brawns, but which? Barrichello's first run proved half a second slower than Button. 'My car was fantastic on low fuel, it was really, really good, but then in Q3 for some reason I developed some understeer. We tried to move the wings a little bit more, add a little bit more front wing but the car kept going to understeer so I was very limited and it was difficult,' Barrichello said.

His car was fine-tuned and he went out for his second run confident of pole. He managed to go a tenth faster than Button but Button went even faster. As the two cars crossed the line Branson, on the pit wall, had a smile as wide as Albert Park itself. He clapped like a schoolboy while Brawn's face impassively scanned the TV monitor a few feet away. When Button was out of the car Barrichello embraced him.

Button	1m 26.2s
Barrichello	1m 26.5s
Vettel	1m 26.8s
Kubica	1m 26.9s

Hamilton suffered a gearbox failure before Q2, relegating him to the back of the grid. In Q1 he had done 1m 26.4s – 15th. Kovalainen only just escaped the guillotine but didn't survive into Q3. The McLaren team were in trouble, the Hamilton Era was temporarily suspended and Button was suddenly the boy.

Barrichello insisted 'the first row for both of us is a credit and we must be happy. This car is a wonderful car to drive, well balanced and looking after its tyres, so we have everything that we need to carry on.' He beamed, looked in good form and parried a question about team orders governing turn 1. 'Right now my ears don't hear words like that. I've been long enough in this not to hear anything at all!'

Button, delighted, faced the journalists wearing a Brawn white peaked cap and designer stubble. 'It has been a long time since we had a car that has been competitive. It is 2006 since I put it on pole here. It has been very tough and there are a lot of people who stand by you but there are obviously a few people that don't and they forget and they don't believe. The important thing is that the people within the team believe and that is all we care about.

'Testing was good but you don't want to get too excited, people always tell you. Maybe you shouldn't be thinking about going out for the pole or for the win, but why shouldn't you? It doesn't change anything thinking about it. It is good to go into the weekend positive. You don't need to let anyone else know what you are thinking. I came into this weekend positive and I am sure Rubens was the same. Going past the garage just after we weighed, and seeing all the guys' faces and the smiles on their faces – I didn't think it still existed because it has been two years since we thought "Wow, that was fantastic."'

He seemed, as he so often did, a man at ease with himself in almost all situations and by now at ease with the snake-like battery of microphones thrust towards his face.

Since the starting time of the race had been put back to 5pm, and since Albert Park is in fact a park (complete with trees) there was the question of shadows and light. 'It is difficult here with the shade and the low sun because it is not a normal circuit,' Button said. 'The sun shining through the trees makes it very difficult, as Sebastian [Vettel] will tell you from yesterday. Turn three' – the 90° right-hander which Button estimated at 57mph and 1.7G – 'was very difficult.'

Vettel commented: 'It was my mistake. You go down the main straight and the sun is very low and you cannot see the white line when you exit the pits, so you just keep right and hope you are far enough right. It is the same when you go through turn 3 with the trees. It is quite tricky: you have a lot of shadows there. Obviously I was a little bit too optimistic and went on the grass.'

The late start time also posed a tyre problem. The track temperature, Barrichello said, 'is dropping so everyone is sliding around that much. We needed some hotter temperatures. The tyres seemed to perform better in the two o'clock practice this afternoon than in the evening session.'

One other question needed to be addressed: KERS, which Brawn hadn't got. The system gathered energy under braking and made it available for a short burst afterwards, allowing a car with it to surge past a car without it.

'You can say that we can't afford to develop it at the moment,' Button commented, 'but from what I've heard people who are running KERS think that there is an advantage of two- to three-tenths on the circuits that have long straights. This circuit doesn't have long straights and maybe when we get to a circuit like Malaysia we will see that they have a little bit more of an advantage than the cars not running KERS.'

Ross Brawn's insight: 'The track conditions were more favourable than we experienced yesterday and we found that the tyres worked in a more conventional way. In addition, the changes we had made following yesterday's practice sessions proved positive and both drivers had a well-balanced car which allowed them to concentrate on maximising the lap times.'

Before the race, Button's fourth gear had been replaced because there were worries over the transmission. Brawn explained that 'the dynamics of the Mercedes engine are very different to those of the Honda so the software needs to be more fully developed to reflect that and there simply hasn't been enough time to effect it yet.'

As the red lights went out Button made a perfect start but Barrichello's car lurched forward so slowly that the column of cars behind jinked out to miss him. 'Basically when the car first moved it hit anti-stall and then it was into neutral. I don't know why. Anti-stall is a protection from the engine that you have. You jump into neutral if you don't have the right revs. I had to recover and get the clutch back on and go. When you do that, you use a lot of throttle and there was a lot of wheelspin, so I lost a lot.'

By now the cars were streaming towards turn 1, Button carving a path to the left and swooping right through the corner with all the grace of a bird of prey. The dreamers, schemers and claimants were faced with reality. All the others had journeyed to Melbourne believing they could win. Now they knew they couldn't unless the Brawn team lost the race.

Barrichello, in the pack and over to the right, found a Red Bull (Webber) angled across him and a McLaren (Kovalainen) pounding up behind. Barrichello insisted he was able to brake for the corner but 'the McLaren came up too fast and threw me into the side of a Red Bull. I thought that that was it for the race. Fortunately the car is very strong and kept me going.'

Button was gone into the shadows which fell across the circuit already, gone alone into the distance, the others a mewling, scrapping horde already far, far away. It was as extraordinary as the pole position. *This was by turn 3.*

Barrichello ran seventh.

Button found himself four full seconds clear of Vettel and on lap three that had become 4.4, but Vettel clung on so well that they were trading fastest laps.

The team were telling Barrichello on the radio, 'You have some damage left-hand side and the front flap. We think it's best to stay out.'

Vettel cut three-tenths of a second from Button's lead. Button responded by setting a new fastest time in the first sector then Vettel matched it. Button responded to that with a new fastest lap, 1m 28.7s. After five laps Vettel was 4.2 seconds behind, Massa at 6.7, Kubica at 8.5.

'The first few laps of the race,' Button would say, 'were great for me and I could settle into a pace. I was keeping Vettel's times in check, just knowing what he was doing. I said on the radio to my engineer "Can you please pinch me next time round" [to prove all this is really happening]. It was after five laps when I had a five second lead or something.'

On lap 9 Rosberg muscled and elbowed past Räikkönen for fifth, Barrichello poised to attack Räikkönen. In turn 3 he tried to go inside, the Brawn visibly wobbling. Räikkönen resisted and there was contact. Räikkönen drifted wide and Barrichello drove round the outside of him. 'On my first stint my nose was falling apart and I lost the braking stability when I hit Kimi as well. He closed the door and I couldn't avoid him.' Barrichello eased away.

Vettel closed the gap to Button to 3.7 seconds and made his first pit stop on lap 16 and Button, sensing he could settle the whole race, rapped out another fastest lap. Then Nakajima in the Williams crashed, leaving debris strewn across the track.

Barrichello pitted on lap 18, Button a lap later, and the Safety Car emerged...

'I struggled massively to get heat into the tyres,' Button said. 'The car was hitting the ground and just before the Safety Car pulled in I flat-spotted the tyre pretty severely.' You could see smoke coming from the front left as the Safety Car released them to race again. Vettel, of course, was directly behind – more like a predator than a bird of prey. The gap was slightly more than a second. Button applied the pressure, eased away and took the gap to four seconds again despite the fact that 'we were struggling for heat. I just couldn't get any heat in the tyres in the second stint.'

The shadows were lying heavier across the track, the cars making their own shadows.

A gap came up on the screens, 4.8s.

Button	Vettel	
Lap 39	1m 28.4s	- 0.1s
Lap 40	1m 28.7s	- 0.2s
Lap 41	1m 28.7s	+ 0.1s

With 17 laps left Button still led by 4.8 seconds. Almost unnoticed, Barrichello had worked a passage to third, albeit 25 seconds away. Vettel made his second pit stop on lap 45, the super soft tyres on for the final assault. He emerged just as Barrichello arrived and they waltzed through turn 1, waltzed towards and through turn 3, Vettel holding the middle of the track, Barrichello probing left and right.

Massa limped back towards the pits with a broken upright and travelled slowly into the pit lane just as Button arrived to make his second stop. The stop went wrong, a wheel sticking, the fuel hose late, so that Button was stationary for 13.2 seconds.

'You know, I really made a mistake and it was frustrating,' Button would say. 'I overshot the pit a little bit. I was in second gear when I came in and the neutral didn't work. It only works in first gear but I was just confused with Massa in front and that lost us a hell of a lot of time. They just about got the nozzle on after they had done the tyres. That cost me five or six seconds.'

Button emerged with Vettel – and Barrichello – roaring down the start-finish straight towards him. The gaps after lap 50 of the 58:

Vettel	@ 1.6s
Barrichello	@ 3.4s
Kubica	@ 4.4s

Barrichello made his second stop on lap 51, super soft tyres on. He emerged fifth, behind Rosberg. Button covered that lap in 1m 29.2s, Vettel nibbling 0.071 of a second – the sort of statistic which does have currency in the kingdom of fractions. A gap flicked up, 1.8 seconds, and now Vettel could see Button wheeling and turning just ahead. Kubica was coming – fast.

Six laps remained and a television camera caught the mounting drama by showing Button, Vettel and Kubica all on the start-finish straight. The sun was glinting through the trees, lower and lower.

'It was really difficult,' Button would say. 'It is strange for such an open circuit. You could not see the exit of the corners at all. I used a visor that was slightly tinted and that was the correct thing to do, but with the glare from the sun and the change in light from the trees it was difficult. You could so easily put a wheel wrong.' He added that 'the bad light was always on the most difficult corners.'

Barrichello fled past Rosberg – simply outpowered him – and set off with visible urgency after Kubica.

With four laps to go Button had squeezed a lead of 2.5 seconds, Kubica at 3.8s. The smoothness of Button's style was clearly protecting his super soft tyres, and so was the smoothness of the Brawn. Others, like Rosberg, were not faring so well. Kubica was the only front-runner now on medium tyres, which made him a growing threat to Vettel and, by extension, to Button.

'I wasn't worried, actually,' Button would say. 'I knew when I came out in front of Vettel that I would be fine because we could look after the tyres. The thing with the last stint was not to push and try and see what was the best time I could do. I was purposely driving very slowly for what pace I thought we could do to look after the tyres. I wasn't turning in aggressively to any corners.'

At turn 3 Vettel braked early and Kubica was alongside. Vettel went into him, rotating Kubica who – helplessly – nosed him on to the grass, shards of bodywork showering everywhere. Vettel went a little further and skewered into the wall broadside, Kubica went a little further before thrashing round and round on a thin strip of grass.

Barrichello was trying to protect his super soft tyres when 'all of a sudden I heard on the radio "Crash, crash, crash – be

135

careful." Then I saw the two cars going off and it gave me second position, which was great.'

The Safety Car came out. 'I wasn't thinking *I'm going to cross the finish line with the Safety Car out,* it was *Oh dear, another Safety Car,*' Button said. It waited at the end of the straight for the cars to appear and come to it, then it circled at an even pace for the remaining three laps, Button following, then a lapped Red Bull, then Barrichello. The Safety Car pulled off, leaving Button to race the final two corners.

'When I crossed the line I'd won the race,' Button said. 'I crossed the line first and it doesn't matter how it's done. It's the same emotion, exactly the same emotion, because you've won.'

On the slowing-down lap Brawn murmured on the radio, 'Sensational job, sensational job, Jenson. Well done.'

The podium and the aftermath were purest delight, although Button – the designer stubble seemed to have grown into a moustache and neat little beard – did say that he'd like to thank all those families of team members 'for putting up with us lot over the winter, because I'm sure we've been very grumpy. Some people might say it is a pity it finished under the Safety Car but I don't care. I won the race and that is all I care about. You don't find Ross speechless very often but the last 15 minutes I would be surprised if he said a word. When we saw him when we went up to the podium he had nothing to say. The big bear was just there speechless. It was good to see, because it was a very emotional day for him as it is for us as well.'

Barrichello said 'we had 1,500 kilometres testing each and one day for the mechanics to get used to things. They didn't have a lot of sleep before they came here so it's all a dream really. It was funny to see Ross that way because not even at Ferrari did I see him like that. It looked like it was his first win so it was really amazing. I had a lot of mixed emotions during the race and honestly I am so delighted to have achieved second.'

If Brawn lost some of his composure in the aftermath, he'd recovered it when he gave his insight: 'We have worked incredibly hard for this victory and to see the dedication, commitment and sheer hard work come to fruition with Jenson and Rubens bringing home a one-two finish for Brawn GP at the first race of the season is immensely rewarding. After everything that our team has been through over the past four months, this is quite simply a sensational result. It is just the beginning for us and it wasn't a perfect race by any means so we will learn from it and continue to improve. We have to keep developing the car throughout the season if we want to challenge for further wins and the championship.

'I would like to express our sincere thanks to Norbert Haug and Mercedes-Benz High Performance Engines who have been so supportive over the past few months and have worked closely with the team to ensure we were in a position to go racing this year.' He thanked Virgin, Henri Lloyd (the team's official clothing and footwear supplier) and 'all our team partners for having the vision to see what the team could do and wanting to be a part of it. It's difficult to put into words what this win means to our team but I'm sure that I speak for every single one of them, here at the track and back at the factory in Brackley, when I say it has been a wonderful weekend.'

Button promised to celebrate, although in moderation. He had a few drinks – 'You've got to' – but insisted the morning after that 'my arms and legs are still working.' Just as they had been for one hour thirty-four minutes and fifteen seconds on the Sunday.

Constructor's: Brawn 18, McLaren 6, Toyota 5, Renault 4, Williams 3, Toro Rosso 3.

Driver's: Button 10, Barrichello 6, Hamilton 6, Glock 5, Alonso 4, Rosberg 3, Sébastien Buemi (Toro Rosso) 2, Sébastien Bourdais (Toro Rosso) 1.

Historians pointed out that the last time a team making its debut had finished first and second was at the 1954 French Grand Prix – although in any meaningful sense Brawn were not making their debut because they were not a new team, they were an established team with a new owner and a new name. No matter. In 1954 it had been Mercedes, the self-same Mercedes who made the engines which Button and Barrichello wielded to such devastating effect. Another hallowed saying, albeit French, suddenly seemed appropriate: *The more things change, the more they stay the same.*

Appropriate? Well, maybe and maybe not. The Brawn team were about to prove that things had changed and weren't the same thing at all. Brawn himself said something like that, referring to championships. 'We didn't start out with such thoughts. Normally you start the year, try to win as many races as you can and just see where it goes. If we react the right way we have a chance. We've done the painful restructuring, so who knows? I told the team recently that we are now as good as everyone else in the business, so why shouldn't it be us?'

Fry says that 'for very different reasons Australia was extremely emotional, because we were all so tired after a winter of fighting for survival and all the challenges that presented themselves. That was the tearful race, partly because we were all worn out, secondly because of what we had achieved and thirdly because we knew what was coming, which was having to go back and reduce the company in size. So that was a very emotional situation.'

It fell to you to prune the staff.

'Yes. The advantage of our situation is that I believe, and I am sure Ross believes as well, we have very complementary skills. Ross is expert technically and in the time he has been here – especially this year – has become increasingly good on the commercial side, which is something he'd never really had to get into too much before. I'm more commercial with an engineering project management background. We know a little bit about each other's business but on the other hand we don't try and compete with each other.

'I went with Ross to Melbourne. We knew we were going to get a lot of attention and having the two of us at the race was necessary. We had Mr Branson there and so on. I came back immediately and unfortunately had the job of wielding the axe. It was very difficult indeed, not only for me but for everyone here because you must remember that many of the people who sadly had to leave had been with this team in some cases since it started. That was not only very difficult for them but also very difficult for their colleagues.

'I haven't had to do this many times in my career – at Aston Martin with Walter Hayes, I had to do something similar. I think the secret, if there is one, is to be quick and fair. The longer you draw out the process the worse it gets. People want to know where they are, they want to know are they in or are they out? Then they can deal with either situation. It's when they *don't* know – quite naturally everyone is on tenterhooks. I sometimes liken it, even slightly trivialising it, to being a bit like going to the dentist. The fear before you go for your filling or extraction or whatever is a bit worse than the reality.

'When people know that we can't keep them at least they can get on and plan their lives around that. We had no choice and everyone understood we had no choice. The process, upsetting though it was, actually went very smoothly because everyone in the company realised that it was either reduce the workforce by a very significant number of people or everyone went. Those who remained were upset that their colleagues had gone but realised they wouldn't have a job unless we did that, and those that had to leave realised that the management was in no position to do anything else.

'It's one of the things you have to get on with. Having John Marsden, the Personnel Director, helped. He was also my Personnel Director at Aston Martin, so when I came to BAR as it was in those days he was one of the first people I called. In these difficult situations, having someone that you can rely upon – and somebody who's been through it before – is very important. John is very experienced and knows the law inside out. He's one of these people who, because he's had to do it before, is able to do it with confidence and quickly, in the full knowledge that he is doing the right thing.

'In our negotiations with Honda we had all agreed that a redundancy programme would be necessary and we, as the new owners, had also agreed with Honda that we would give the staff the same terms that they would have had if Honda had closed down the company. Honda proposed somewhat enhanced terms versus what is legally required and obviously, as the new management team, we were happy to do the same thing. It was the right thing to do.'

Brawn said the 'unfortunate restructuring' had been 'very focused on performance. It would be no good having a team with fantastic production facilities and no ideas, so the team has been structured very strongly around maintaining a good development programme. We've tried not to impact the technical areas too much and, yes, the development is on-going.'

It certainly was.

Notes

1. www.motorchili.com/video/3321/Brawn-GP-2009—Jenson-Button-and-Ross-Brawn-Interview.

2. I'm indebted to Laura McLachlan, Media Operations Manager, Australian Grand Prix Corporation, for providing these local times.

CHAPTER 6

COME FLY WITH ME

After the retirement of David Coulthard at the end of 2008 only two British drivers remained in Formula 1, Button and Hamilton. Their similarities – well spoken and articulate, well presented, well balanced and, if they'd made a mistake, liable to admit it – could not mask the difference in their trajectories.

Hamilton arrived in Formula 1 borne by formidable records from karting through the lesser formulae just as Button had, but then, as we saw in Chapter 4, Button's trajectory flat-lined while in 2007 Hamilton put together the most accomplished debut season in World Championship history. He began with a third place in Australia, worth of course six points. Button would drive all 17 rounds and finish with a total of ... six.

Hamilton's sequence continued 2, 2, 2, 2, 1, 1, which meant that after his first seven races he had won twice as many Grands Prix as Button, then completing his 125th. Astonishingly, Hamilton finished the season runner-up in the championship (Räikkönen 110, Hamilton 109) – Button 15th – and went on to win it outright in 2008 after a drama-haunted climax in the rain at São Paulo, the final race. Britain had found a new sporting hero who looked and behaved like a *genuine* hero and, in those heady days, it didn't seem to be stretching a point to say that the *world* might have found one, too. The fact that Hamilton was mixed race and uncannily like the iconic golfer Tiger Woods merely strengthened that view. Button finished 2008 18th with three points: even Hamilton's fifth place at São Paulo – four points – was worth more.

Brazil, which brought so many riches to Hamilton, had been on 2 November.

The Australian Grand Prix, which brought the kiss of life to

Button after the Brawn team had been given it themselves, was on 29 March.

In that comparatively short space of time Hamilton's career imploded exactly in tandem with Button's exploding. It was a perplexing and hypnotic spectacle both ways. Hamilton's plight centred on an incident in Australia with Jarno Trulli while the Safety Car was out. The exact circumstances need not detain us here – a disputed overtaking move – except to say that McLaren were a great deal less than candid to the stewards, one senior employee departed the team at the speed of a Formula 1 car, and Hamilton's reputation for probity came under the closest scrutiny. He did not emerge well. For long, surreal moments McLaren risked losing Mercedes and Hamilton.

Hamilton had worked his way up to fourth, which became third when Trulli was disqualified and then became nothing when Trulli was reinstated and Hamilton disqualified instead. In this chaos you could not mistake that the McLaren was a car far off the pace, possibly condemning Hamilton to a *Buttonesque* season, assuming he stayed, and you could not mistake Button controlling the Australian Grand Prix from pole to flag, everything under control, in the most *Hamiltonesque* way.

There are precedents for a successful team one season being far off the pace the next, and precedents for it happening the other way round, but never surely together and on this scale. To continue analagy and comparison, Button took from Australia more than three times the points he had taken from the whole of 2008.

There was, needless to say, the Great Diffuser Controversy moving along towards the FIA's Court of Appeal, and the verdict there gave the days after Australia a feeling of uncertainty and impermanence. Button and Barrichello said, inasmuch as they could say anything, that there was nothing they could do except wait. Here is Barrichello: 'One thing is clear: everyone here has a diffuser. It's not that we have one and nobody else has. We just found a different interpretation. We stayed calm, but yes, there was the fear that something might go wrong.'

Ross Brawn sounded circumspect. 'We have this appeal

hearing next week or the week after next and we need to see what comes out of that, because it may change direction. I'm reasonably confident but you can't be 100 per cent.'

Yes, the more things change the more *some* of them do stay the same.

(The diffuser is a device positioned on the floor of the car at the back, between the wheels. It channels air to create downforce – and it's not one of those esoteric things peculiar to racing. As Gary Anderson points out, 'If you look at some road cars – a Ford Focus RS, say, or a Ferrari – you might see a diffuser.')

The second race of 2009, Malaysia, was initially confusing and offered Brawn's opponents hope.

Friday practice 1

Rosberg	1m 36.2s
Nakajima	1m 36.3s
Button	1m 36.4s
Barrichello	1m 36.4s

Friday practice 2

Räikkönen	1m 35.7s
Massa	1m 35.8s
Vettel	1m 35.9s
Rosberg	1m 36.0s
Webber	1m 36.0s
Barrichello	1m 36.1s
Button	1m 36.2s

Brawn pointed out that this was 'our first experience of higher track and air temperatures so we made the most of the available running to learn how the car, tyres and engine work in these conditions. We struggled a little with the balance of the car and at the moment it is not performing quite as well as in Australia. However, I am confident that we are on the right path and with some hard work we should be in a good position.'

Barrichello spoke of a positive day on a circuit where the right balance is always elusive and he felt the work evaluating both types of tyre would bear fruit.

Button described the day as 'useful' in finding the balance. 'My biggest problem was that we are locking the tyres and brakes very easily so we need to have a good look at this. We're not quite there yet.'

Saturday's third practice hardly suggested progress or answers. Rosberg (1m 35.9s) went fastest again from Webber (1m 36.0s), Barrichello ninth (1m 36.519s), Button tenth (1m 36.541s).

Qualifying was something else. 'At the start,' Brawn said, 'there was a distinct possibility of rain so we went out early in Q1 to bank some dry running. From there it was a busy session with the track evolving incredibly quickly.'

Button did no more than 1m 35.0s – seventh – but was the only driver using the medium compound tyres. That carried enormous consequences and negated the fact that four drivers (including Barrichello) went into the 1m 34s.

The overnight changes to Button's car cured the balance problem, the rear-locking under braking was gone and the car felt really good immediately. 'It's a big turnaround. We had to put in a bit of mental work but that's the difference to last year. Now when we change something we notice it on the car. Last year you could do what you wanted and things always remained the same,' Button said.

Ferrari decided one fast run would be enough and it wasn't. Massa missed the cut. (Räikkönen did survive to Q3 but finished only ninth and Button said he'd anticipated that the Ferraris would be stronger).

In Q2, Button put on super softs and on his first run did 1m 33.7s, which would remain fastest from Trulli (1m 33.9s), Barrichello sixth (1m 34.3s). He was grappling with a touch of understeer and the team couldn't resolve it. Hamilton and Kovalinen both missed the cut.

In Q3 Button carried fuel worth two more laps than Trulli and still took pole:

Button	1m 35.1s
Trulli	1m 35.2s
Vettel	1m 35.5s
Barrichello	1m 35.6s

Barrichello had to have the gearbox changed, demoting him five places so that he'd start on the fifth row. 'Rubens was struggling for grip under braking,' Brawn said, 'which resulted in understeer and he was never completely happy with the balance of his car. With the replacement of his gearbox, this puts him further back on the grid than we would have hoped. However, his experience will stand him in good stead in the race.'

Barrichello explained that 'with more fuel on board the car started to understeer. This especially hindered me in the middle-fast corners. I had to wait ages before I could hit the accelerator.' That, of course, is ages to a Formula 1 driver, not to you and I.

'The whole of qualifying was exciting,' Button said into the microphones, grinning broadly, 'especially Q3.' He pointed out that in all these long years he'd never had two consecutive poles and he liked that feeling, not least because it proved the car worked well on radically different circuits. 'We are hoping that the rain stays away but you just never know at this circuit. We've never driven with the car in the rain. That could become a whole new experience and I'd rather not undergo it during the race.'

The subsequent irony in these words would be a thing of wonder. The race was due to start in early evening (the European television schedules, never forget) which, as the locals would tell you, is a risky time of day in a risky season – unless you like monsoons, of course. Formula 1 cars, attuned to every nuance of dry tarmac, regard *water* as hostile terrain, never mind monsoons.

When the red lights went out it was, however, nice and dry and normal. Button made a hesitant start ('pretty bad') while the shoal of darting cars – Barrichello in the midst of them – surged towards him. Button stayed over to the left for the first corner, a right-hand spoon.

'I was surprised at the lack of grip on my side of the grid. I had a lot of oversteer and I don't think I got heat into the rear tyres. The KERS cars came up so I lost time there. Turn 1 was messy, really. I went in deep and got a big snap of oversteer which dropped me to fourth.'

The first spoon was followed by a tighter second and in that Alonso had hustled past, giving an immediate order of Rosberg, Trulli, Alonso, Button, Räikkönen and Barrichello.

In turn 4 Barrichello went round Räikkönen, cleanly, on a simply power play. As the lap unfolded Button tightened onto Alonso's Renault. Into turn 13, a long, almost languid right curve, Alonso went wide and Button moved through the empty space.

It was deft, neat, and very quickly done. 'I was really, really struggling with the rear end when Alonso was in front of me. I have never seen a car so sideways before,' Button said wryly.

Along the pit lane straight Alonso tried to mount a counter-attack, but now he had Barrichello tightening on to him. The order from Rosberg, completing the lap:

Trulli	@ 1.2s
Button	@ 3.9s
Alonso	@ 4.4s
Barrichello	@ 4.6s
Räikkönen	@ 5.6s

Button moved way from Alonso, Barrichello still tightening. On lap 3 Barrichello stole up the inside but went wide and Alonso was in front of him again in the final corner. The order from Rosberg, completing the lap:

Trulli	@ 1.3s
Button	@ 2.5s
Alonso	@ 8.7s
Barrichello	@ 8.7s

Into turn 1 Barrichello outpowered and seemingly outbraked Alonso to take fourth. 'I was really happy with how the car was performing in the dry in the first stint,' Barrichello said. 'After a good start I felt I had the pace to catch up with the front-runners and score some good points.'

Button set fastest lap and drew fully up to Trulli. In the distance the clouds loomed heavier, tinged with an ominous purple-blue. On lap 4 Rosberg responded with a new fastest lap, Button exactly one second behind Trulli. Now, towards the grandstand, the bowl of sky was mutating into blue tinged with a more ominous black. Barrichello set the fastest lap, 1m 37.9s.

During lap 9 a voice on one of the team's radioes said 'We expect rain in about ten minutes.' The light was darkening now, thunder echoing.

Rosberg forced the fastest lap time to 1m 37.6s. Button forced it to 1m 37.5s. The order from Rosberg, completing lap 11:

Trulli	@ 3.0s
Button	@ 4.2s
Barrichello	@ 10.3s

Rosberg pitted on lap 15, Trulli inheriting the lead. Button pursued him and the sky darkened further. A gap flashed up, 0.8s. Button was increasing the pressure on lap 16: in the first timing sector he took 0.2 of a second, 0.02 in the second, 0.2 in the third. Trulli pitted on lap 17.

Barrichello reminded everyone that he could go a bit, too, with a new fastest lap.

Button had two laps before he pitted. This was hallowed Brawn-Schumacher territory at Ferrari, like taking a key to a race which had been padlocked to keep you out. It was also classically simple. The car or cars in front – the padlock – had been holding you up and, now they were gone, you held the key. To open the padlock you had to raise your pace to such a pitch that you gained whatever you needed to enable you to pit and come out in the lead.

As we saw in Chapter 3, Schumacher had been able to do this at circuits like the Hungaroring, and therein lies a tale. When Brawn was at Benetton and Schumacher left to join Ferrari, Gerhard Berger and Jean Alesi came from Ferrari in a direct swap. Brawn discovered the difference because when he asked Berger and Alesi for some rapid-fire laps they couldn't oblige, however much they wanted to. They were already at their maximum. Whenever he'd asked Schumacher the rapid-fire laps came on demand, Schumacher exploiting the spare capacity he had even when he was going fast – or, as Schumacher described it, moving into a long sequence of qualifying laps.

Button was being asked it now.

Rosberg had pitted on lap 15, Trulli on 17. Button set new best sector time after new best sector time. Trulli was stationary for 9.8 seconds – the sky satanic – and Button did 1m 36.6s. It was 0.8 of a second faster than Barrichello's fastest and, in the kingdom of fractions, this was big, the kind of big that wins races. He moved into his in-lap and that was fast too.

He'd say, with that very English modesty, that 'I could put in a couple of quick laps. It got me in front and it seemed like it was going to be fine until I looked up and saw the clouds come over and it started raining.'

The Ferrari mechanics wheeled out wet tyres for Räikkönen. Rain evidently had begun to fall somewhere and they put the wets on.

Button pitted, the satanic sky closer. He was stationary for 8.7 seconds while fuel went in and a new set of soft tyres was fitted. When he emerged, the rest were nowhere to be seen. Barrichello pitted on lap 20, the rain coming from the far side. He had soft tyres, was stationary for 9.4 seconds and emerged fourth. Button led by 11 seconds.

On lap 21 rain smeared Barrichello's visor. Alonso was off on the grass, his tyres glistening. Button pitted on lap 22 for wets. 'Unusually for Sepang it started spitting and we went for the full wets thinking it was going to chuck it down, but it didn't to start with. A few other people made the correct choice but we had a 16 to 18-second lead at that point so I carried on,' Button said.

Suddenly the pit lane was choked with the others doing that: 11 of them. A fork of lightning pierced the gloom, the wind rising, the light even darker. It had become a twilight race and out on the track the cars were leaving little, almost ephemeral, whisps of spray behind them.

Button led Rosberg by 15.8 seconds, Trulli third, Barrichello fourth. The rain fell harder. Button, of course, had moved from the kingdom of fractions to the land of the completely unknown: the Brawn hadn't been on wet tyres before. 'The balance was definitely not right on the full wets,' Button said. 'The circuit was reasonably dry so it was difficult to get a balance. I had massive oversteer on the first couple of laps and then the front started graining.'

Timo Glock in the Toyota was on intermediate tyres and travelling faster than the rest. Were they all vulnerable to him? He was sixth on lap 25, although 34 seconds behind Button. Forks of lightning streaked high above. Barrichello nipped past Trulli in turn 12 and held it through 13.

Rosberg pitted for intermediates, then Hamilton.

Barrichello drifted wide and still Glock came, second and 24 seconds behind Button. Barrichello pitted for intermediates. Button pitted for intermediates, stationary for 6.2 seconds, and now the cars were throwing up rolling balls of spray: not yet tidal waves, not yet waterfalls, but still visible from a distance. Glock led Button by 3.3 seconds, Button pulled alongside as the pit lane entrance loomed and Glock went into it for full wets.

He'd tell the tale graphically enough. 'In the middle of the race I saw the rain was coming, the rain was coming, but it took so long that I thought *OK, when it takes so long then I go for intermediates* because everybody else was already on heavy wets. I saw they struggled and destroyed them. I said "We go for inters and take the risk." I was driving around, driving around, overtaking cars, overtaking cars, and found that my tyres were going off as well but my engineer told me "You're still the quickest on the track, you're still the quickest." I think it was worse in turns 7 and 8 and that was the direction the rain was coming from. It reached the point where I had to pit because my tyres were going off completely. I said "OK, I *have* to come in." It was just at that moment that Jenson overtook me again.'

And the heavens opened.

Three bolts of lightning struck the top of the grandstand.

Fisichella in the Force India slid gracefully off sideways into gravel. Vettel waltzed slowly off, his Red Bull halting and the rain stabbing at it.

Button eased into the pits, was stationary for 6.3 seconds while fuel went in but more importantly wets went on. He'd recount the sequence of events leading to this: 'We'd gone for the full wet tyre, it just destroyed itself and we saw Timo flying up behind us on the inter, so we put the inter on. Then, just as he came by, I saw his tyres were bald and it was raining out the back. He was struggling quite a bit and had to pit. I got one lap in on the inter with reasonable pace and I was able to get in and put the wet tyre on and come out in front. You've got to say we made all the right decisions when it came to when to pit for which tyres.'

By now the cars down the pit lane straight were leaving spray for huge distances behind them. Through the gloom Button *seemed* to be leading from Glock and Heidfeld, Trulli fourth, Barrichello fifth.

Button ploughed through standing water and the cars were virtually travelling within a constant circuit of spray. A few moments later Button was ploughing through deep water. The Safety Car came out, its twin yellow arc lamps making it seem like a monster surging through the satanic weather. Then red flags were waved, stopping the whole thing before the racing cars had reached the Safety Car. Hamilton waltzed, caught that, continued. Heidfeld, going very slowly, executed a complete spin. Fisichella, having recovered, spun lazily off backwards.

'You could not actually see the circuit,' Button would say. 'It was that bad. We were behind the Safety Car and the team said "All you have got to do is drive around" – that was difficult enough. For a few moments I was almost off the circuit. We were going around at running pace, that slow, and the Safety Car was pulling away from us. When the Safety Car is pulling away at 20 seconds a lap, you know it's too wet for a Formula 1 car.

'All I had to do was stay on the circuit. How slow it looks – embarrassing! – but that was as quick as we needed to go and if I'd gone any quicker I think I would have ended up in the gravel. People might say that we're supposed to be the best in the world so we should be able to drive in whatever conditions but that's not the case' – and this said with the gentlest, self-depreciating smile, his eyes sparkling. 'These conditions you're doing 60 kilometres an hour maximum, and even then you've got a very good chance of putting it into the wall.'

Glock had a slightly different perspective. 'We tried to follow the Safety Car and that was difficult. I was swimming around. I couldn't believe it because Jenson was sometimes going quite quickly and I was just *swimming…*'

The cars parked on the grid – well, all over the grid, their red warning lights blinking on and off like little lighthouses in the storm. A darkness tinged with grey enveloped them and nobody seemed to know what to do. Webber went here and there consulting drivers hibernating under umbrellas – *Should we race again, will we race again, what's our position?* 'The guys made the best call to stop the race when they did,' Webber said. 'It would have been nice to have had some more laps to give us a crack at getting on the podium but that's how it is, so I've got mixed emotions. It's dark now [7:00pm] so it was the right call not to make a restart.'

Räikkönen sipped a Coke knowing the race was over.

Button sat in the cockpit. There was, he said, always a possibility of a restart and 'as far as I knew we were always planning for a restart. That's why all the cars were moved around [on the grid] but the problem was that so many cars spun off on the last lap that I think it was very difficult understanding who was in what position – so that was why we were all moving around a lot on the grid. I'm happy it didn't start again because we would have spent ten laps behind a Safety Car and every lap, every corner you got to, you would be scared that you were going to throw it off – it's out of your control, it's a matter of what position the river is in on the apex of a corner and you can't see it.'

No race can last more than two hours under the rules but now the organisers froze the time when the race had been stopped [55m 30.6s] so that if a restart did prove possible racing could resume – theoretically for another hour and five minutes. The darkness made that irrelevant.

Suddenly, after 40 minutes, team members were leaning over shaking Button's hand and he was beaming. The race had run 32 laps but would be counted from the end of lap 31, half points awarded. He'd won. He stood in the cockpit, bareheaded, and people slapped him affectionately. He waved both arms to the crowd.

Heidfeld was second, Glock third, Trulli fourth, Barrichello fifth, Webber sixth and Hamilton seventh.

Constructors': Brawn 25, Toyota 16.5, BMW 4, Renault 4, Williams 3.5, Toro Rosso 3.

Drivers': Button 15, Barrichello 10, Trulli 8.5, Glock 8, Heidfeld 4, Alonso 4.

Ross Brawn's insight: 'I am pleased with how quickly we were able to react to the changing conditions to maintain the lead that Jenson had achieved in the first stint of the race. However, it was not perfect because we could have had both cars in the top three if we had been a little bolder in bringing them in for their third stops for intermediate tyres.'

Button said, wonderfully, that so far in this season of astonishment 'I still haven't seen the chequered flag without a Safety Car in front…'

Brawn went to Paris to argue the diffuser case and the FIA Court of Appeal sustained its legality. This immediately safeguarded the points already won and allowed the team to continue using it.

The Paris hearing was not one of decorum and civility throughout. Ferrari's legal representative, Nigel Tozzi, accused Brawn of not acting 'within the regulations' and added that 'only a person of supreme arrogance would think he is right when so many of his esteemed colleagues would disagree.' Nobody at Ferrari had ever seemed to accuse Brawn of that when he was plotting and conjuring Schumacher's championships, but never mind.

Brawn was unmoved. 'I never took it personally but my wife did! If it had been Stefano Domenicali [running Ferrari's Formula 1 team] saying it I would have been upset, but I was quite strong in my own presentation. Tozzi is just a hired gun and knows how it works, though I feel his style of argument has probably had its day. The mood was moving in an acrimonious direction but if it was intended to put me off it had the opposite effect. As soon as he started with the personal remarks I assumed he was struggling with the rest of his case.'

Did Brawn feel vindicated? 'I don't think of it that way. It's unfortunate that this argument reached the extent that it did. We all need to learn how to handle these things. I can see it from both sides, but I really feel we have just got to accept the arbitrators' decision and get on with it. It's a bit like a football match and the referee's decision. Sometimes it goes with you, sometimes it doesn't. When we came up with the concept we didn't think it was radical. We thought it was clever, but it wasn't a "Eureka!" moment. It was no surprise to us that other teams had it at the beginning of the season. In fact, the surprise was that there were not more.

'We respect the right of our competitors to query any design or concept used on our cars through the channels available to them. The FIA technical department, the stewards at the Australian and Malaysian Grands Prix and now five judges at the ICA [International Court of Appeal] have confirmed our belief that our cars have always strictly complied with the 2009 technical regulations. The decision of the ICA brings this matter to its conclusion and we look forward to continuing on the track the challenge of what has been a very exciting start to the World Championship.'

The Italian Flavio Briatore, the man running the Renault team, became very Italian because he might now have to spend a lot of money getting a diffuser on to the Renault. He fell back on tried, tested and extremely tedious tactics. He played psychology and politics simultaneously, first by suggesting that when the Formula One Team's Association (FOTA) next met they should prevent the Brawn team getting some £25 million as its share of television revenue because as, technically, a new team they were not entitled to it. One report (*Autosport* magazine) suggested FOTA had agreed the month before to regard Brawn as a continuation of Honda, taking the rights with it. Brawn had certainly pointed out that in the team's present condition the £25 million might have consequences for the team's survival.

Briatore said that Brawn should relinquish his post as FOTA technical director and now Briatore was into his stride. He said that the season was in effect already over. 'I don't know how we can say we have credibility. It is impossible to recover the ground we have lost on those teams [with diffusers]. In three or four races the championship will be decided and I don't know what the interest of the TV viewers will be when Button has 60 points and Nakajima has 50. It will be better to listen only on radio and watch something else.'

In view of what was to happen to Briatore later in the season, his words at this point would become grotesquely ironic, almost tragic.

Briatore turned on the Brawn drivers, firing this barb: 'And then you have a Brawn driver who was almost retired [Barrichello] and another who is a *paracarro* fighting for the championship [Button].'

This sent the media scurrying for Italian dictionaries, or anybody who was – or could speak – Italian, to find out what a *paracarro* might be. Some thought it was a kilometre post at the roadside, others just a concrete roadside post. Some (like me) thought the remark ought to be classified with that of Manchester United footballer Eric Cantona when he said at a press conference: 'When the seagulls follow the trawler, it's because they think sardines will be thrown into the sea.' Both dictums sounded as if they offered profound insights, although discovering quite what those insights might actually mean proved damnably difficult, even if you were a fisherman or a traveller on the *autostrada*.

Anyway, *paracarro* in the vernacular is used to mean someone who is a slow driver and not very good.

In the face of this Latin temperament Button went all English, pointing out that Briatore had in fact tried to sign him during the winter. This was like Miss Marple pointing out the culprit while taking afternoon tea: genteel, and all the more devastating for that ('Yes, he did it with the meat cleaver. Do have another cucumber sandwich').

Hell hath no fury like a concrete post scorned, however, because Button added: 'He is obviously a very angry man after the diffuser issues and he is obviously very disappointed that they haven't produced a car that is as competitive as ours. The team has worked very, very hard in difficult circumstances and it's very unfair of Flavio to comment as he has, just because he's a little bit bitter. Instead of getting angry, people need to concentrate on improving and catching us up.'

Barrichello commented: 'There are plenty of good people in the paddock and plenty of bad losers.' I don't know if there is a *Senora* Marple in Brazil but, if there is, that is what she would have said.

To those curious people who thought motor racing should be, well, motor racing there was merciful relief from all these machinations because the cars went out for the two Friday practice sessions in China, preparing for the third race of the season. Hamilton (1m 37.3s) was fastest in the first from Button (1m 37.4s), Barrichello third (1m 37.5s). Button went fastest in the second (1m 35.6s) from Rosberg (1m 35.7s), Barrichello again third (1m 35.8s).

However gratifying this had to be, Ross Brawn pointed out that what they'd really been doing was 'a thorough evaluation of the prime and option tyres,' with the emphasis on the super softs. They were trying to find out how best to work with them in qualifying and the race. The balance of the car, he added, wasn't quite ideal, although 'the car worked well in the cooler temperatures that we are experiencing with the race taking place six months earlier than usual.'

Button felt the balance improved over his last two runs 'after we had been struggling a little to find the right set-up early on'. Barrichello felt 'it was very useful to find out what the tyres are capable of. We tried various things but I did struggle for grip with my last set. There are a lot of marbles on the track at the moment.'

In the third practice on Saturday, Rosberg went fastest (1m 36.1s), Button fourth (1m 36.4s), Barrichello tenth (1m 36.6s), which might mean much or not very much at all.

In Q1, Button dominated with 1m 35.5s from Barrichello (1m 35.7s), then Webber (1m 35.7s), and Hamilton (1m 35.7s). The pace of Webber in the Red Bull surprised both Button and Barrichello. Vettel might have surprised them too, but his Red Bull was suffering from a driveshaft problem and the team decided they only dared risk him for one lap in each of the three sessions. He'd just done 1m 36.5s and now had to wait to see if the others would banish him from qualifying. They didn't: he was 13th.

Vettel's one-lap restriction in Q2 meant that he waited until the track was at its fastest (for the session) and went out with four minutes left. The clocks froze at 1m 35.130s. Webber did 1m 35.173s, Button and Barrichello four-tenths of a second away. 'You could see in Q2 that the Red Bulls were very strong in the high-speed corners and we knew then that we would have a fight on our hands,' Button said.

This was, in fact, a glimpse of the future. The Red Bulls would get stronger and stronger as the season developed.

In Q3, and with a minute to go, Webber seemed to have pole (1m 36.4s) from Barrichello and Button. An instant later Button crossed the line (1m 36.5s) then Vettel at the end of his only lap: 1m 36.1s. Barrichello was rounding the final corner as Vettel crossed the line and, as Vettel's time came up, Barrichello was on 1m 32.7s. The quartz timing numerals flickered and froze as he crossed the line: 1m 36.4s. Alonso came up fast (1m 36.3s) – second. This surprised even him. 'We went aggressive but we never expected to be on the first row.'

It left Barrichello fourth and Button fifth.

Barrichello insisted that the session was evidence of how quickly Formula 1 progresses 'and you can see it. Red Bull have no diffusers and they are doing really, really well. It makes for great competition at the front.' He had, incidentally, outqualified Button for the first time in 2009.

Button, diplomatically, said 'It's a pity we are starting behind them because here it's really tough to overtake. Our car feels good but there were a few cars quicker than we expected.'

Ross Brawn's insight: 'We have always said that our competition would catch up quickly and the evidence of that is clear to see. Our car is working well around this circuit although both Jenson and Rubens experienced too much understeer on their final runs.'

In their brief history, Red Bull had not had a pole before and this confirmed that the old order changeth in Formula 1: Hamilton had survived to Q3 but finished it in ninth position; Kovalainen and Massa hadn't survived beyond Q2; Räikkönen had, but finished eighth. It meant that, of the mighty McLaren-Ferrari duopoly – between them they had won every drivers' championship since 1998 except two – Räikkönen would be the most successful as he lined up on the fourth row.

One significant factor, however, appeared to be that the Brawns were fuelled heavier than the Red Bulls, Button carrying enough to go five laps further than them and Barrichello a lap more than that. In the kingdom of fractions that made Barrichello's out-qualifying of Button (albeit by 0.039 of a second over 3.3 miles) a genuine achievement.

Long before the race was due to begin the rain which had chased Formula 1 though Malaysia began to fall, and when the race did begin it was under the Safety Car, which churned dutifully round for lap after lap. On lap 7, as it churned on, Alonso peeled off to take on fuel as well as new tyres. He had been fuelled light in the hope of seizing the race from the red lights and fleeing into the distance but he needed the Safety Car to have come in much sooner. Alonso said it was 'one of those days when you take decisions at the wrong moment and everything seems to turn against you. We thought that the Safety Car would be out for the next ten or fifteen laps so we came in to get fuel and at the same time the Safety Car came in so we found ourselves starting the race last.'

That lifted the Brawns a place, Barrichello to third and Button fourth.

The Safety Car had pulled off after eight laps and within moments the track vanished under great, rolling balls of spray flung high into the air like geysers before they fell in a dense fog. Immediately Vettel led Webber by 0.8s, Barrichello at 1.8s, Button at 2.7s, they and the necklace of cars behind them moving approximately at equidistant one from another. The visibility barely permitted anything else. This was not yet racing in any sense, nor even processional but, rather, an exploration of the possible.

Hamilton announced that phase was ending when he overtook Räikkönen, gently but decisively, on lap 9 to be sixth. Räikkönen's on-board camera showed the problem inherent in these conditions. Into a right-hander Hamilton went wide, suggesting that Räikkönen might steal up the inside. Hamilton kicked in his KERS and the extra 80hp took him clear but he threw up so much spray that, through the camera, you could see *nothing*. The order from Vettel, completing the lap:

Webber	@ 2.4s
Barrichello	@ 4.7s
Button	@ 6.2s
Trulli	@ 9.2s
Hamilton	@ 11.2s

Cars were spearing off because at one point they were in standing water. 'The conditions were pretty crazy with rivers of water all over the circuit which changed every time you encountered them,' Button said. 'The last turn particularly was like a lake and you just couldn't brake for the corner. I struggled with the car aquaplaning and the tyres shuddering because we couldn't get the temperatures high enough to make them work properly. Every lap I thought I was going to throw the car off.'

He got past Barrichello on lap 11. Barrichello would explain that 'I only had three brake discs working on my car for the first 19 laps which made it even more difficult for me to keep the car on the road.'

Webber pitted on lap 14, Vettel a lap later so that Button led from Barrichello. Button did a 1m 55.8s, three seconds faster than Barrichello and creating a gap of 12.9s.

Kubica thundered into the back of Trulli, bringing the Safety Car out – debris everywhere – and both the Brawns in. The team was able to cope with both cars because Button was stationary for 9.9 seconds and there'd been that 12.9-second gap, so that Barrichello arrived after Button had departed. Barrichello was stationary for 10.7 seconds. Barrichello's brake problem resolved itself because they heated during the pit stop and as he emerged he was back on the pace.

Out on the track Vettel saw a car ahead and knew he was not allowed to overtake under the Safety Car, then saw it was the wrecked, limping Toyota of Trulli, so he could overtake and moved fractionally to do so. He was then struck from behind by Sébastien Buemi sister team's Toro Rosso.

Vettel explained that he'd assumed the car ahead was Barrichello, not the Toyota, because 'I knew he was in front of me. I was just going off throttle to check if everything was allright, I passed him and I really didn't see that Sébastien was coming. I am very sorry for what happened. Obviously it is impossible to see anything in the mirrors – there is a lot of spray.'

The Safety Car came in after lap 23 and Hamilton ran fourth, Barrichello seventh. Vettel pulled decisively away from Button, Webber attacking from close quarters. Vettel set a new fastest lap, 1m 54.6s, and was 3.6 seconds faster than Button on the lap. In the kingdom of fractions this was another big one.

There was standing water at turn 5, sending back-markers spearing off. Webber got past Button who – briefly – went directly ahead at the end of the start-finish straight instead of turning. Webber immediately fashioned a gap of 2.4 seconds.

Vettel led Webber by 11.0 seconds and Button retook Webber who went off at the (by now) notorious final corner and its lake. 'I hit the river there. I had to catch and straighten the car, open the steering and get onto the astroturf [stretching away outside the corner],' Webber said. 'I was worried about that.'

Webber counter-attacked. 'I was totally furious.' In the left-right of turns 7 to 8 he went inside and through, all muscle.

'I didn't have a clue where he was and he was alongside at turn 8,' Button said. 'It was such a shock because you can't see anything when it is raining. Then he just cut across the front and made the move stick. For me it was impossible to do anything about it. As soon as these guys get near you or alongside you, you cannot challenge them and it would have been silly to have tried. We had had a good fight for a few laps but I just couldn't stay with him.'

A gap flashed up, 0.9 of a second, and you could sense momentarily that the power lay with Webber. Vettel was some 16 seconds up the road, however, or 16 seconds across the water if you prefer. Webber pulled a fraction back, to 0.7 of a second, but Vettell, out of sight of them, was going faster and faster. So actually was Webber.

'I didn't have a clue where Jenson was,' Webber said. 'I only looked at my pit board every few laps so I knew he was somewhere there, but I didn't know how close.'

Vettel pitted with 19 laps left, Webber two laps later. As Webber pitted Vettel set a new fastest lap and that built the pressure on Button, who found Vettel behind him. Clearly Vettel knew that Button would have to pit again and, disciplining himself against dramatic gestures, would follow until that happened – unless something presented itself. He followed close enough to put a little psychological pressure on Button: *here I am behind you but a pit stop in front.* Then, on the straight and when he judged he had enough width and distance, he popped out from behind and sailed pleasantly by. Button stayed good and clear of him.

The race was essentially over. Button pitted and Vettel set a new fastest lap. Barrichello set a fast lap, too.

Button was stationary for 7.8 seconds. Vettel led Webber by 15.4 seconds. Barrichello pitted (6.7 seconds stationary), and it settled Vettel, Webber, Button, Barrichello. That's how it finished and they'd made it within the two-hour limit: Vettel 1h 57m 43.4s.

Red Bull had their first victory (Vettel won Monza the season before in a Toro Rosso) and, of course, their first 1-2. In starkest contrast, Räikkönen finished tenth and Massa suffered an electrical failure. Ferrari had yet to win their first point of the season.

Ross Brawn's insight: 'Another dramatic race to continue what is turning out to be a very exciting season. Jenson and Rubens did an excellent job to bring the cars home in the difficult conditions which, combined with a solid team performance over the whole weekend, enabled us to score as many points as possible. We had a good strategy with both drivers fuelled long for their first stints which allowed us to bridge the gap to the leaders. However, on similar fuel, Vettel and Webber were able to pull away.'

PREVIOUS PAGE: *Interlagos, 18 October 2009* (LAT).

OPPOSITE TOP: *The moment – Jenson Button crosses the line after one hour 32 minutes 52 seconds. The world belongs to him and Brawn* (LAT).

OPPOSITE BOTTOM: *The long, agonising wait for the moment – Nick Fry watches and hopes* (LAT).

ABOVE RIGHT: *The emotional release after the moment – Button, dad John and the big squeeze* (LAT).

BELOW: *Embracing the moment – Button and Ross Brawn* (LAT).

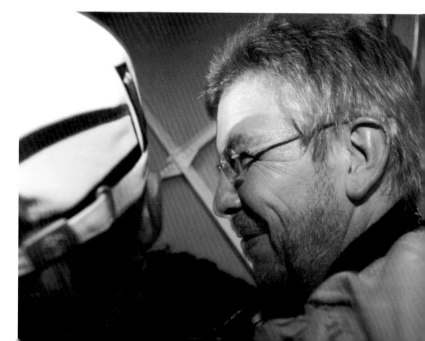

Cooper Oldsmobile by nine year old Ross Brawn (Ashton). Classic gf. body shell, K Mk. 1 motor, 3:1 bevels, 20 s.w.g. wire frame chass s. Airfix steering.

ABOVE: *This was printed in 'Model Cars' as part of a report on the third Newport Open Meeting in 1964* (courtesy Russell Sheldon).

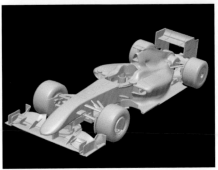

ABOVE: *His own youthful work, and if you want to be technical it's HB Products Formula 32 chassis* (courtesy Stanley Kirk).

LEFT: *The Brawn GP Scalextric F1 car awaiting livery* (courtesy Hornby).

ABOVE: *Flower power meets atomic power. Brawn and colleagues at the Harwell Research Establishment* (courtesy the UK Atomic Energy Authority).

BELOW LEFT: *Brawn received his Honorary Degree from the Chancellor of Brunel University, Lord Wakeham* (courtesy Sally Trussler/Brunel University).

BELOW RIGHT: *Brawn and his wife Jean at the 2008 Formula One Party in the Bloomsbury Ballroom in aid of Great Ormond Street children's hospital* (LAT).

ABOVE: *The Williams team on the grid at Brands Hatch in 1978, Alan Jones in the car and Brawn manhandling bodywork on the right* (LAT).

LEFT: *The Jaguar days. Alastair Macqueen, Brawn and driver Alain Ferté at Silverstone in 1991* (courtesy Alastair Macqueen).

The life of Brawn before Brawn GP . . .

RIGHT: *Rory Byrne (left) and Brawn at Donington in 1993 for the European Grand Prix. Between them they'd redefine the possibilities of Formula 1* (LAT).

RIGHT: *Brawn and Michael Schumacher reunited, however briefly, on the grid in Australia, 2009. Just social because, obviously, they were never going to work together again, were they?* (LAT).

BELOW: *The world before Brawn GP: as Honda they walk the Valencia circuit in 2008* (LAT).

The life of Brawn with Brawn GP . . .

ABOVE: *The start of the astonishing 2009 season. Jenson Button leads Sebastian Vettel, Felipe Massa and Robert Kubica as the Australian Grand Prix unfolds* (LAT).

BELOW: *Button has just won the Australian Grand Prix by 0.8 of a second from team-mate Rubens Barrichello* (LAT).

ABOVE: *Button wins the Malaysian Grand Prix standing still and closely surrounded. He 'beat' Nick Heidfeld by 22 seconds* (LAT).

RIGHT: *The surreal climax in Malaysia after 31 laps* (LAT).

RIGHT: *Brawn (returning from the Chinese Grand Prix) and Maurizio Ferrari (returning from Hong Kong) with his slot car in Dubai* (courtesy Russell Sheldon).

ABOVE: *Reasons to be cheerful in Bahrain: Brawn GP lead the Constructors' Championship by 32.5 points from Red Bull, Button leads the Driver's title by 12 points from ... Barrichello* (LAT).

LEFT: *Magical Monaco as Button wins and Barrichello – here rounding the Loews hairpin – comes a strong second* (LAT).

ABOVE: *A battle in Champagne at Monaco – and Kimi Räikkönen seems to be losing this as well* (LAT).

RIGHT: *Everybody goes home when the sun goes down – except the mechanics. This is Hungary* (LAT).

BELOW: *Face to face: Brawn, Button and Barrichello taking care of public relations at Silverstone* (LAT).

LEFT: *Stirling Moss, the grand old man of Grand Prix racing, surveys the mechanics preparing Barrichello's car on the grid at the British Grand Prix. Moss was never World Champion and, after Silverstone, people wondered if either Brawn GP driver would be either* (LAT).

BELOW: *Button's championship seemed to be going up in smoke round the Hungaroring where he was only seventh* (LAT).

ABOVE: *Bear hug for Barrichello after a superb tactical victory from Lewis Hamilton at the European Grand Prix* (LAT).

RIGHT: *Barrichello reaches for the stars at Valencia* (LAT).

LEFT: *The race that got completely away. Button's Brawn after his crash at Spa, parked beside Lewis Hamilton's McLaren* (LAT).

LEFT: *One for the family photo album. Barrichello bestrides Monza, the championship still very much open* (LAT).

BELOW: *Every point was precious by Singapore. Here Barrichello runs sixth with Heikki Kovalainen's McLaren behind* (LAT).

ABOVE: *Technology dominates the pit lane wall. This is the Japanese Grand Prix* (LAT).

BELOW: *Button and race engineer Andrew Shovlin (centre, wearing headphones) on the grid just before the long slog to a single point at Suzuka* (LAT).

ABOVE: *The beginning of the next era. The team is now Mercedes and Ross Brawn welcomes the 2010 drivers, Nico Rosberg and Michael Schumacher* (LAT).

LEFT: *Crowning glory: Brawn receives the Order of the British Empire from The Queen at Buckingham Palace for services to motor racing, just days before the start of the 2010 season* (Press Association).

Button, meanwhile, explained something almost bizarre. 'The scary thing was that normally when you follow a car you see the two lines in the water and you know exactly where they've been. You can follow that line because there's less water there – but I never saw any lines on the circuit. That was amazing. The water doesn't seem to clear and that was the worst thing about it, I think.'

Constructors': Brawn 36, Red Bull 19.5, Toyota 18.5, McLaren 8, BMW 4, Renault 4. Toro Rosso 4.

Drivers': Button 21, Barrichello 15, Vettel and Glock 10, Webber 9.5, Trulli 8.5.

From an overall perspective, the half points in Malaysia had prevented Button. Barrichello and Brawn from getting their hands round the throat of the season already and now Red Bull were threatening to prise their grip open while everyone waited confidently for the big teams to close the performance gap by weight of expertise, personnel and sheer money. A one-sided season may be endlessly fulfilling if you dominate it – Ferrari never did look bored while Schumacher was winning five championships, one by mid-August, another by mid-July – but March to November can be a long, long haul when you constantly know what's going to happen next.

There was a week between China and the next race, Bahrain, and thereby hangs a tale recounted by Russell Sheldon, long-time friend, slot-car expert and Emirates executive based in Dubai. It centres on Maurizio Ferrari who, working at Ferrari, met Brawn once to say he was leaving. Sheldon gives the background.

'Maurizio was a brilliant electronics engineer, a brilliant computer scientist, wrote his university thesis based on the Life Formula 1 team. They surfaced in 1990 with a (unique) W12 engine that they had designed. They had no money – they had one chassis, two engines and very few spare parts. They had David Brabham and Bruno Giacomelli as the drivers. Maurizio did a thesis on the W12 engine, he was hired and spent his time behind a tow truck going to get the racing car wherever it had broken down. He was then offered a job at Ferrari in 1991–1992, where he worked in the electronics division. Ross joined and Maurizio distinctly remembers saying to his parents "This man is going to make Ferrari great."

'Maurizio, however, was becoming very frustrated with the Formula 1 lifestyle. He wanted to get married, he wanted to do some more ski-ing, because he was a downhill champion, and he said "I can't take this any more, I'm going to resign." His boss said "I'm not going to let you go," and he marched Maurizio off to see Ross Brawn. Ross asked him what he was going to do with himself and he said "Well, I'm going to start a company that manufactures slot cars." They didn't once discuss his resignation – they discussed slot cars.

'Maurizio eventually started a company which makes some of the best commercially available slot cars.

'Ross was on his way from the Chinese Grand Prix but instead of going back to the UK and then on to Bahrain he'd stop over in Dubai. He called his wife Jean and said "Why don't you come and join me?" and I arranged accommodation for them. Coincidentally, Maurizio was coming from Hong Kong, where his cars are manufactured, on his way to Milan. He said he'd like to stop over in Dubai so we could meet for a lunch. We organised a breakfast with Ross, Jean, Maurizio, his business partner and myself. Maurizio had brought with him a 1:32nd scale model of the Jaguar XJR12 – the prototype model. "Well, Maurizio," Ross would say, "I think that perhaps the air intake should be one 16th of a micron further to the right." Here we have a fascinating story of the slot racer becoming the greatest racing car electronics engineer becoming the greatest slot car maker, and still getting lessons from Ross Brawn...'

Maurizio Ferrari adds a postscript. 'Ross showed tremendous interest in the model because he worked on that car for Tom Walkinshaw at Jaguar. Then he moved on to completely designing the XJR 14, which we will make in the future. I don't think there are many people who know exactly how a racing car works but Ross Brawn is certainly one of those who does.'

Approaching Bahrain, nobody knew any more, or, more

accurately, they couldn't be sure they knew. As if to emphasise that, the three practice sessions and then the qualifying all produced different fastest men – and none of them was in a Brawn. The top three in each of the practice sessions turned out to be eight different drivers – and none of them in a Brawn, either.

In fact, Button would have a highest place of fourth (in qualifying) and Barrichello fifth (also in qualifying). Was this the beginning of the end of the dream – a favourite Button word, especially in Australia – already? Were the *rest* of Formula 1 beginning to get their hands round the Brawn team's throat?

Anyone trekking to arid, hot and dusty Bahrain finally had some question marks to exercise themselves with. They might also have kept an eye on that most interesting of all sporting relationships, the one between team-mates. Your best friend is your biggest enemy. Button wanted to be World Champion after a monstrously long apprenticeship, and so did Rubens Barrichello. Continuing harmony? That was another question mark.

Friday practice 1		Friday practice 2	
Hamilton	1m 33.6s	Rosberg	1m 33.3s
Heidfeld	1m 33.9s	Alonso	1m 33.5s
Kubica	1m 33.9s	Trulli	1m 33.6s
5 Button	1m 34.4s	6 Button	1m 33.6s
7 Barrichello	1m 34.5s	9 Barrichello	1m 33.8s

Ross Brawn explained that although the team was now familiar with the medium and super soft tyres the 'unique conditions found at this circuit mean that they are working in a very different range. The track is always very dusty at the start of each session and the track temperatures are by far the highest that we have experienced this year. We have therefore focused our efforts on understanding the behaviour of the tyres and we are happy with the progress made through the two practice sessions.'

Other teams, of course, had been at the Bahrain pre-season testing.

Button described the day as 'pretty standard' but 'our long-run pace with heavy fuel was really competitive.' Barrichello explained that the two cars were set up in different ways to 'gather as much information as possible and compensate for our lack of testing before the season began.'

Saturday practice 3

Glock	1m 32.6s
Massa	1m 32.7s
Rosberg	1m 32.9s
15 Button	1m 33.5s
16 Barrichello	1m 33.6s

Brawn now confronted a problem. To accommodate the Mercedes engines in a car already designed and built, they could not have a cooling package able to cope with temperatures like the 38°C for qualifying. It cost them an estimated 20bhp.

In Q1, Vettel (1m 32.6s) went fastest, Button (1m 32.9s) fourth and Barrichello (1m 33.1s) fifth. In Q2, Vettel (1m 32.4s) went quickest again while Button and Barrichello found themselves locked into one of those statistical freaks which really can't happen. They both did 1m 32.842s.

In Q3, button would say, 'I didn't have a great lap on my final run. We were struggling for grip on the corner exits and locking tyres throughout the session.'

Barrichello had traffic on his final run. 'I was in the middle of a group who were taking it slowly on their out laps. That was different to my approach and meant that I couldn't get enough temperature into the tyres, which compromised my quick lap.'

Trulli (1m 33.4s) had pole from Glock (1m 33.7s), Button (1m 34.0s) fourth and Barrichello (1m 34.2s) sixth.

Button said 'We don't have the pace we did in the first three races so it's going to be a tough race. It won't be a walk in the park' – or a camel ride in the desert, either. 'We were aiming for pole but it wasn't our best qualifying session of the season and the pace just wasn't there. We were surprised.'

Ross Brawn's insight: 'The track and ambient temperatures were incredibly high and we are learning all the time how to make the tyres and chassis work in such extreme conditions.

The track evolved since morning practice and neither driver was completely happy with the balance of their car. However, we were able to make progress through the sessions and we have secured decent grid positions. The forecast is for slightly cooler weather which should be beneficial.'

'At least,' Button reflected with some irony, 'we can look forward to a dry race'.

From the lights he 'got a poor start. I did a practice start coming into the pits and I was struggling with clutch slip. Off the line I had exactly the same thing so it was very lucky that I didn't lose more places.' He had an adventurous run down to the first corner, a right-hander: initially over to the right, hemmed, moving to the left with four cars in front, going almost to the rim of the track on the left, going round the outside of the corner and emerging fourth but ahead of Vettel.

Barrichello stayed to the right from the lights and wet into the corner holding this tight inside line, but as he moved through he was engulfed.

Button ran fourth, Barrichello sixth, soon to be seventh. The initial order: Glock, Hamilton, Trulli, Button, Vettel, Räikkönen, Barrichello. Button jousted with Hamilton while Barrichello stole inside Räikkönen and then went defensive. Glock leading, they crossed the line:

Trulli	@ 1.6s
Hamilton	@ 3.3s
Button	@ 3.4s
Vettel	@ 4.0s
Barrichello	@ 4.8s

Button swarmed Hamilton and at the end of the pit lane straight went decisively inside. Across 2007 and 2008 he may have dreamed of such moments but they could have been no more than dreams. This was the reality of 2009. 'I was not able to keep third place. Jenson was just so fast through the corners,' Hamilton would say. In retrospect it was a pivotal moment because it released Button to run his own race against the Toyotas rather than have to accommodate himself to life behind Hamilton.

'I was really happy with my first lap,' Button said. 'I knew that I had to overtake Sebastian [Vettel] quickly and got him round the outside on turn 1. Lewis is very difficult to overtake anyway, but on the first lap he made a few mistakes and I dived down the inside of him at many different places. On the straight I thought I could get alongside him and I did out of the last corner and then he pushed his button and pulled back in front. I had to tuck back in behind again, get the tow off him and I was able to get him into turn one. That move really made the race for us. I knew I had to make it stick and I did. I'd certainly say it was the finest first lap of my career.'

Completing lap 2 Button was at 4.3 seconds from Glock, Barrichello at 7.9.

The order settled to the first pit stops, which began with Glock on lap 11. He rejoined ninth and one lap later Trulli pitted, giving Button the lead. Trulli emerged sixth – but both Toyotas had moved to a two-stop stategy, were now heavily fuelled and on medium tyres which weren't giving much grip. Button was in full attack mode as the Toyotas prepared to pit. Now the team radioed 'Give it everything you've got.' Button led Hamilton by eight seconds but could only summon a 1m 35.1s lap – he'd gone wide in turn 11.

Button pitted on lap 15, was stationary for 9.4 seconds, and rejoined fourth. Both the Toyotas were behind him...

Barrichello pitted for his second stop on lap 26, taking on the super soft tyres.

Button did a 1m 35.3s, making him more than ten seconds ahead of Trulli, Vettel third, Barrichello rejoining eighth. Button found another fast lap extending his lead to 11 seconds, then 13. A gap flicked up, 12.8 seconds. Here was all Button's smoothness as if driving at these speeds through rearing corner after rearing corner was as natural as water flowing along as a stream.

Button made his second stop on lap 37 and the team fitted medium tyres. He was stationary for 9.2 seconds and led again. The order from Button, completing lap 43:

Räikkönen	@ 8.2s (and yet to stop)
Vettel	@ 12.6s
Trulli	@ 13.7s
Barrichello	@ 14.5s

On lap 47 Barrichello made his third stop, allowing Hamilton into fourth. Barrichello now ran fifth.

Across the last 15 laps Button 'had to conserve it a little bit because this is a lot hotter than we expected. It is not just the engine but everything on the car including the driver and, with the way the regulations are, these engines have to do a lot more running than normal.'

Button led Vettel by 13 seconds, then, with six laps to go:

Vettel	@ 11.1s
Trulli	@ 11.9s
Hamilton	@ 21.7s
Barrichello	@ 39.5s

Vettel closed the gap to 9.5 seconds but that didn't matter because Button was stroking the car home and now there were only three laps left. He'd quip that it felt strange not having a Safety Car or a red stop light ahead.

Barrichello came in fifth. 'I lost a lot of time behind Piquet after my first stop which was a real shame because it compromised my race plan. We went for a three-stop strategy and then took the decision to come in slightly early for my second stop because I was being held up behind Hamilton. It was so hot out there this afternoon and the car was burning my waist on the right-hand side, which made it very difficult for me.'

In the *parc ferme* Button clambered out, stood on the bodywork (the bonnet to you and I), raised his arms and extended them, the index finger of each forming the figure 1. He still had his helmet on but nodded it back and forth, *yes, yes, yes*.

More quietly, and later, he'd say: 'The whole team should be very proud of themselves. They have worked so hard. As you probably know, we are much smaller than we used to be and they are having to work doubly hard to get the job done so I am very proud of all of them and they should be also.' He added 'I am sorry if my radio was played live because I might have said a few words that weren't good for TV, but the traffic was terrible out there.'

Ross Brawn's insight: 'All credit is due to Jenson for an outstanding opening lap, which made victory possible. We have had a challenging weekend in dealing with the extreme temperature conditions, which was made more difficult by our lack of hot-weather testing prior to the season. I am very proud of the way that the team here in Bahrain has worked together to overcome the issues that we faced and how they performed in the race.' Brawn conceded that Barrichello's three-stop strategy wasn't 'great' but it was done because Barrichello preferred light fuel loads.

Constructors': Brawn 50, Red Bull 27.5, Toyota 26.5, McLaren 13, Renault 5 (Ferrari 3).

Drivers': Button 31, Barrichello 19, Vettel 18, Trulli 14.5, Glock 12, Webber 9.5.

Four races were gone and the season had assumed its shape. I put it to Louise Goodman that in the barren years, Button must have known that, given the car, he could do it. That has to have been more frustrating than anything.

'He's the same driver this year. When I say that, I mean largely the same driver this year that he has been for the last couple of years. Am I surprised how gracefully he's handled himself? No, absolutely not. He's been storing away all the different experiences, the good and the bad. He's not a stupid bloke, he's bright and I guess he has learnt, as every racing driver learns, that being a Formula 1 driver is not just about driving a car as quickly as you can. There's a lot more involved. He's been growing and maturing over the years. He's always been noted for his fine touch on the wheel and you can see his style. He's got himself into a position where he's got a car – the designers know him now, too, so maybe he's got what he wanted for his style.'

Leaving hot, dry Bahrain there was another of those questions. How long could it go on?

CHAPTER 7

MONARCH OF MONACO

The Spanish Grand Prix might be pivotal to the whole season because, by tradition, teams upgraded their cars for the first European race, and here it was. In the kingdom of fractions a small upgrade might have large gains and, as Ross Brawn pointed out, the difference between the teams had been 'compressing' since Australia. The Chinese and Bahrain Grands Prix were back-to-back but now the team had two weeks before assembling at Barcelona.

Button dismissed as irrelevant the fact that the team had only tested at the circuit for four days. Every Formula 1 driver of any pedigree had, over long years, been round so many times in testing that the circuit had yielded every one of its mysteries, if it had any in the first place. Button was so familiar with it that he equated the race to a home match and termed the track 'interesting', which is not the most electrifying description.

In the week up to the race he visited the Brawn factory for what he termed 'a small celebration', not the most electrifying description either. He wanted to see what the team had been doing.

Brawn himself said he was thankful for the mini-break after Bahrain because it allowed the team to regroup and reflect, although he pointed out that, while the race team was away, work went on at the factory on upgrades and he was looking forward to seeing what effect they had.

He, and the rest of Formula 1, would get indications in the first Friday practice:

Button	1m 21.7s
Trulli	1m 22.1s
Kubica	1m 22.2s

Heidfeld	1m 22.6s
9 Massa	1m 22.8s
10 Barrichello	1m 22.8s
11 Räikkönen	1m 22.8s
13 Vettel	1m 22.9s
14 Hamilton	1m 23.0s

The explanation for Barrichello's time was simple enough. He ran the 'current package for baseline data', meaning they'd have a direct comparison when they fitted the new developments. Second practice:

Rosberg	1m 21.5s
Nakajima	1m 21.7s
Alonso	1m 21.7s
Barrichello	1m 21.8s
Webber	1m 22.0s
Button	1m 22.0s
Vettel	1m 22.0s
10 Räikkönen	1m 22.5s
13 Hamilton	1m 22.8s
15 Massa	1m 22.8s

Button explained that the balance of the car wasn't quite right with the 'new aero upgrade fitted' and, frustratingly, he lacked grip. Button also explained that he was not convinced some of the other teams had shown their hand. They might, he concluded, have been 'playing games. We've done it before. We will wait and see.'

Barrichello struck an optimistic tone, speaking about focusing 'our attention on evaluating the new aero package. My initial feedback is positive and the car felt good and well-balanced. We ran a fairly conservative programme which has given us valuable data to study overnight.'

Ross Brawn's insight: 'A mixed day: Rubens very happy with the performance but some issues with the performance of the package on Jenson's. We are investigating the cause at the moment and we have plenty of data to study overnight to resolve it.'

The Saturday practice suggested Button's Friday hunch had been accurate. The Ferraris were quickest, then Button and Barrichello, Vettel 16th. If you'll allow me to follow an earlier theme, or rather lightly adapt it, the dreaming, scheming and claiming would stop the moment Q1 began on a dry afternoon at the familiar circuit – regardless of what had, and had not, been revealed in practice.

It did.

In Q1, Massa went fastest (1m 20.4s), then Webber (1m 20.6s), Button (1m 20.7s), Vettel (1m 20.7s), Barrichello (1m 20.8s). Räikkönen did one run and the team felt it would be enough to guarantee passage to Q2, but it wasn't.

Brawn explained that 'after some hard work from the team overnight we were able to resolve Jenson's problems with our upgrade package and we were greatly helped in that process by the input from Rubens.'

In Q2, Barrichello produced a 'great' lap (his description) and became the only driver to get below 1m 20s during the whole qualifying (1m 19.9s), Webber next (1m 20.0s) then Glock (1m 20.1s), Massa (1m 20.1s), Button (1m 20.1s), and Vettel (1m 20.2s) – Hamilton (1m 20.8s) failing to make the cut. He was 14th.

In Q3, Barrichello did a good – not great, please note – lap but felt he may have gone a little bit early. He was disappointed to finish third, and more disappointed that Vettel got ahead. Button had no such concerns. He was fuelled for a three-stop race strategy 'because we thought that would be quicker.' He did have a concern with his final lap because he crossed the line to begin it with *one second* of the session remaining: tight but entirely legal. When it was done Brawn, sitting monitoring the monitors on the pit wall, jerked his arm in a reflex motion of triumph then did it again. In the pit Button's father danced wildly and jerked his arm. In the cockpit Button was jerking his arm while, on the radio, an intoxicated voice bayed 'Awesome lap, awesome lap.'

Button	1m 20.5s
Vettel	1m 20.6s
Barrichello	1m 20.7s

Button confessed he didn't really expect pole because he'd been struggling with finding a balance and he hadn't done 'as much long-run pace as I would have liked'. He felt the pole-winning lap was arguably the most satisfying thus far and 'by far the best I've had this weekend'. He paid tribute to Barrichello, whose set-up helped in overcoming his Friday problems. He noted that Massa was on the second row; he had KERS on his Ferrari and the start-finish straight stretched long and inviting to anyone who had that...

Ross Brawn's insight: 'The developments on the car have enabled us to make good progress and, whilst we are still to fully maximise their impact on performance, the signs are encouraging. Rubens was very quick in the first two sessions on low fuel with Jenson having the edge on the heavier fuel loads in Q3.'

Both were on a three-stop strategy.

When the red lights went out, the cars all weaved – entirely legal – and Button placed himself in mid-track in the charge to turn 1, Barrichello behind him then dancing out to the left, drawing alongside, drawing fractionally in front. Their wheels almost touched and Barrichello went through.

'I had a good start from pole but Rubens had an absolute flier and I couldn't hold him off,' Button said.

The immediate order: Barrichello, Button, Massa, Vettel.

They threaded through turn 1, a right-hander, but in the next – a left – bodywork was being flung from the midst of the pack like an explosion. It involved Trulli, the Force India of Sutil and both Toro Rossos.

The Safety Car came out and circled for four laps. When it pulled off Barrichello led the column back to racing speed and none of the top four found an advantage. The order from Barrichello, completing lap 6:

Button	@ 0.9s
Massa	@ 2.4s
Vettel	@ 3.0s
Webber	@ 3.8s
Alonso	@ 4.7s

Barrichello set fastest lap (1m 24.5s) and they settled to running to the first pit stops, although the Brawn team were exhorting both drivers to go fast enough to pull away from Massa and Vettel.

'After I had the start that I had,' Barrichello said, 'I told myself *everything is coming up again* [coming up roses!], *so use your best knowledge and experience and speed.* Everything was alive.'

Of the leaders, Button would begin the pit stop sequence on lap 18, but Ross Brawn now confronted a delicate tactical situation. Barrichello's car felt, as Barrichello said himself, 'really good', and he was travelling fast enough to pit and emerge in front of Nico Rosberg's Williams. Button, however, was projected to emerge behind it. The Williams, of course, was slower but could easily hold Button captive for five or six laps – Rosberg was fuelled long and wouldn't pit until lap 25. To make the three-stop strategy function properly Button needed to come out with a clear track in front of him so he could sprint to his second stop.

Ross Brawn's insight: 'As we approached the window for the first pit stops it became apparent that Jenson would come out directly behind Rosberg if we went with his planned three-stop strategy. We therefore made the decision to switch Jenson onto a two-stop strategy to ensure that he could run in clean air. Rubens was going extremely quickly at the front at that time and his three-stop strategy was clearly the quickest option for him.'

It sounds simple, sensible and logical. It would carry the weight of enormous consequences.

Barrichello led Button by 1.4 seconds, a more or less constant gap, and then Button pitted. Button was stationary for 9.3 seconds, translating to 88 litres and 29 laps, in turn translating to lap 47 of the 66. Button was now on a classic two-stop strategy.

Barrichello pitted on lap 19 and was stationary for 6.7 seconds. That translated to 52 litres of fuel, translating to 18 laps. Barrichello remained on a classic three-stop strategy, of course. He emerged just ahead of Rosberg.

The on-board radio crackled, informing him of Button's

change, and informing him too that he had to put the hammer down. 'Getting out ahead of Nico set the race up nicely for me. I was quite surprised when Jenson's strategy was switched and from then I knew that I had to go flat out to make my strategy work,' Barrichello said.

With all that fuel, Button said, 'the car felt so heavy. I wasn't sure about going to a two-stop. I didn't think I would come out in front of Massa and Vettel – but I did. When I first drove the car with a lot of fuel it was moving around quite a bit at the back and it took a while to find my feet, which I had to do as soon as possible. Shov [race engineer Andrew Shovlin] was on the radio shouting "You've got to put the laps in now, you've got to put the laps in now." Then, closer and closer to Rubens' second stop, "Rubens has a three-second advantage over you, you've got to keep pushing." Every lap was flat out. I've never driven in that style before and I'm sure it looked pretty messy but it was the best way to get the lap time out of the car. I got every tenth and everything I could.'

Barrichello was averaging 0.9s a lap quicker but needed a second and a half. The race was between them.

The Brawn pit crew were out preparing for Barrichello's second stop on lap 31 and a gap flashed up to Button, 13.6s. It didn't look anything like enough. He was stationary for 6.7 seconds, Button gone by into the lead. He emerged fourth with a great deal to do. 'I suffered on my third set of tyres and was not able to get the lap times which would have kept me ahead of Jenson.'

Button 'had to push so hard on a heavy fuel load that I damaged the tyres quite a bit, but I could get the lap times out of the car being aggressive with it. That's the good thing about this car. You can be aggressive and it doesn't seem to eat up the tyres. It's not normally my style but it's a style I had to take for this race, it made the difference and Rubens had his problems with understeer on his third set of tyres.'

With 35 laps left Button led Massa by 4.6 seconds, Vettel 0.5 behind Massa, Barrichello struggling at 9.6 from Button. The threat to Button was now from Massa and Vettel, both travelling faster than he was, Barrichello out to 11.5 seconds.

On lap 44 Massa pitted and Vettel followed him. They emerged in the same order. Barrichello now ran second but on that lap was actually a fraction slower than Button, who pitted on lap 48. He was away in 8.7 seconds on his hard tyres – like every one of the top ten except Barrichello. Button emerged third and the race turned on how fast Barrichello could go before his third, brief, stop when he'd have to move to the hard tyres. The gap from Barrichello to Button was 15.4 seconds.

Barrichello pitted, was stationary for 6.1 seconds – Button passing into the lead again – and emerged a comfortable second. Webber also pitted and emerged third.

Button led Barrichello by 7.1 seconds and the race was settled. On the way to the end Button lapped Hamilton…

Ross Brawn's insight: 'Unfortunately Rubens' tyres did not perform well after his second stop which compromised his pace and ultimately cost him the race. Rubens has performed extremely well throughout this weekend and it has been largely thanks to his input that we have been able to maximise our pace and achieve the successes of today.'

Barrichello explained that 'my third set of tyres was not good. I don't know if there was something broken on the car or anything. I could not keep my pace up as well as the last set, so I guess it wasn't the tyre, it must be something to do with the car. I was locking wheels all over the place and from there on it was a struggle. I had a big struggle to keep the car on the track and [it was] a relief to come second.'

Barrichello pointed out: 'As Jenson said, we were both on three stops and they changed the strategy for him. Good for him, good for the team as we both covered first and second positions but I would like to understand why we changed that.' He was asked who did the strategy. 'It's a group. Ross is involved. We are together and this morning we decided that three stops was the way to go. This evening we are going to have a meeting again and then we have some answers.'

He was asked about the Austrian Grand Prix in 2002 when Ferrari ordered him to move over on the last lap and gift the race to Michael Schumacher, as we saw in Chapter 4. 'Well, I'm very experienced with that, and if that happens, I won't follow any team orders any more. I'm making it clear now, so everybody knows.' He added: 'It's true it's much different here than it used to be at Ferrari, a much more friendly situation, so I'm not blaming this or that. There's no way I'm going to be crying and saying *I should have done this or done that*. It's in the best interests of myself to learn what went wrong because I had the ability to win the race but I didn't, full stop.

'Jenson is on a flyer and he's doing very well. There's a bit more pressure on my side, obviously, because he's won four races and I've won nothing but I'm there, I'm working and I won't stop working. I'm definitely raising my hands to the sky to give thanks because this is a great car. It was not long ago that people were putting flowers on my grave and saying "so much for your job" and so on. I'm here, very much alive and happy and I'm going to make it work.'

Constructors': Brawn 68, Red Bull 38.5, Toyota 26.5, McLaren 13 (Ferrari 6)

Drivers': Button 41, Barrichello 27, Vettel 23, Webber 15.5, Trulli 14.5, Glock 12 (Hamilton 9).

Ross Brawn described Monaco, a place prey to every manner of cliché, as requiring a 'very controlled approach' to the racing weekend. 'The pit lane and paddock is an intense environment to work in due to the location at the heart of the city and it is therefore more stressful than any other race.'

Button knew Monaco, not least because he lived there. 'My usual driving style is very smooth but I will have to change that a little bit to get the best out of the car. You have to be aggressive around Monaco and not let the barriers intimidate you whilst obviously paying them due respect.'

Monaco, the slowest of the Grands Prix, felt the fastest.

The first two practice sessions were, as tradition demanded, on the Thursday, leaving Friday free for its annual festival of promotional activities and good living. Barrichello (1m 17.1s) went fastest in the first session from Massa (1m 17.4s) and Hamilton (1m 17.5s) – Button (1m 18.0s) eighth, Vettel (1m 19.2s) 13th.

The session 'proved quite challenging' for Button. 'I had rear locking in the low-speed corners and understeer in the high-speed corners and I didn't feel quite comfortable in the car.'

In between sessions the team worked on the set-up.

Rosberg (1m 15.2s) went quickest in the second session from Hamilton (1m 15.4s), then Barrichello (1m 15.5s) and Button (1m 15.7s), Vettel sixth (1m 15.8s).

Barrichello suffered understeer but 'it was controllable', and he was content with the balance of the car – so crucial here where the kingdom of fractions becomes that of milliseconds and, simultaneously, the kingdom of millimetres. Button's balance was better, and 'my last runs on the softer tyres were much better' too. He showed aggression and left tyre marks on the Armco but couldn't find fast times.

Ross Brawn's insight: 'The biggest challenge was finding sufficient free air to allow the cars to have clean runs and achieve a clear read on our set-up evaluations. Jenson had a little unscheduled work in the garage after brushing a wall, a frequent hazard here in Monaco, and we made some precautionary changes to the steering components.'

Alonso (1m 15.1s) went fastest in Saturday's third practice from Button (1m 15.2s), Barrichello (1m 15.2s) fourth, Vettel eighth (1m 15.7s). Barrichello did everything necessary in the morning, 'setting the car up, so I was extremely happy'. And, perhaps, justifiably confident.

That took them to qualifying, always described as crucial because, at a circuit where overtaking is problematical – if in fact it's not simply a state of mind – and poor grid positions (meaning from the second row of the grid backwards) can be prison sentences. In Q1:

Rosberg	1m 15.0s
Button	1m 15.2s
Webber	1m 15.2s
Massa	1m 15.3s
Barrichello	1m 15.4s

In Q2, Button 'did struggle with a bit of understeer. I was

behind another car on my lap which cost me some time. I was a little bit scared that I wasn't going to make it through.' He finished eighth, Räikkönen (1m 14.5s) fastest, then five cars on 1m 14.8s including Barrichello. Button did 1m 15.0s.

It set up Q3 nicely, Button going into it thinking he wouldn't take pole because, in qualifying, Barrichello 'had the upper hand'. Räikkönen (1m 14.9s) seemed to have that all to himself. Barrichello (1m 15.0s) was agonisingly close. 'I love this place in qualifying and my thought was *don't leave anything, don't leave even a hair's breadth for you to think "oh, I should have done better"*. I tell you, round the swimming pool I almost went flat. It was fantastic.'

Button produced a variation on this. 'Yeah, it was pretty much on the edge. I thought I was going to be in the harbour at one point,' adding naughtily that it occoured to him he would 'end up in Flavio Briatore's boat, which he would not have been very happy with. It was a good lap and I really did get everything out of the car.'

Button did 1m 14.9s, not just pole but a lap which stunned Barrichello, who said: 'My fastest lap throughout the weekend was on a used set of tyres, which is quite amazing, and we need to see why the new tyres are not working so much for me. I did a 1m 14.8s [in Q2] and with fuel in the car I did a 1m 15.0s [in Q3] so I've got to be extremely happy with that. I never thought Jenson could do a 14.9s. As soon as I got out of the car I hugged him, I said "Fantastic" – and I asked him how he did it.'

Button's explanation was that the car felt 'great in Q3 and it was definitely one of the best laps I've ever done. I pushed harder in Q3 than I did in Q2. The fuel effect wasn't anywhere near like I thought it was going to be. I was able to brake in similar places with higher fuel as I was with lower fuel and I don't quite understand that. I have been nowhere near Rubens through the swimming pool but I drove as fast as I could through there.'

Ross Brawn's insight: 'To achieve pole and third position on the grid in the most important qualifying hour of the season is a real achievement and puts us in a strong position for the race.

Jenson had to work quite hard on his set-up because he has been struggling with the balance and a lack of front grip all weekend so he knew that the lap had to be extra special. Rubens, as ever, excels around Monaco and he is very well placed to take the fight to Jenson.'

And so it proved.

The Brawns started on super soft tyres (the prime here was soft), and only three others (Hamilton, Sutil and Vettel) did that. 'I was surprised when the covers came off and most people were on the prime tyres,' Button said. The Brawn team hadn't 'thought twice, really' about doing that.

From the lights Button made a powerful start and so did Barrichello, who was past and directly in front of Räikkönen into Ste Devote. The pack all threaded through, too, and by Casino Square the Brawns were already opening a gap. The order completing lap 1, Button leading in the most assured, commanding way:

Barrichello	@ 0.9s
Räikkönen	@ 2.5s
Vettel	@ 3.2s
Massa	@ 4.3s
Rosberg	@ 4.9s

By lap 5 Barrichello was tracking Button at a gap of 1.5 seconds, Räikkönen out to 3.3s, Vettel out to 6.8s.

Barrichello explained that the team read the tyre situation from what 'many of the others' were doing. 'We had the option tyre and we thought the option was going to be the tyre to use for three-quarters of the race, really. Then, all of a sudden, we saw some of the others using the other tyre.' The super soft, however, was 'the tyre to have to begin with. We pulled away. It was great.'

Button was rapping out fastest laps seemingly at will. Massa frisked and champed, tried a major move on Vettel and got it wrong at the harbourside chicane. He went straight on, slowed to allow Vettel back and Rosberg went through too. Vettel pitted on lap 9, Hamilton a lap later but from 17th.

Button came up to lap him on lap 11 while, some ten seconds behind, Räikkönen attacked Barrichello. It was lively but Barrichello knew Monaco very intimately, so intimately that Räikkönen couldn't even glimpse a chance.

'It is just impossible to overtake at this place, even though he had the KERS. If you brake in the middle of the line, Monaco is really impossible. There's 101 per cent of a chance of not overtaking,' Barrichello said.

Räikkönen pitted.

'Rubens had a great start to get ahead of Räikkönen and he was showing excellent pace before his first set of rear tyres began to grain heavily as a result of following Jenson so closely,' Ross Brawn said. 'Unfortunately that compromised his chance of fighting it out with Jenson.'

Barrichello explained that 'just like Barcelona I had a great start and I was able to have a run on Kimi. I was running at tremendous pace but possibly I was just too close to Jenson because, losing that little bit of aerodynamic, I was struggling without the [clear] air in front and I grained the rear tyres. From one minutes sixteens I started to do one minute twenties and Jenson was gaining like three or four seconds a lap. That defined the race pretty much. The car was perfect the whole way through. It was a shame we had the graining.'

After 15 laps Vettel was gone, the car damaged at Ste Devote after sliding into the barrier. As he clambered out, Barrichello pitted. He took on a set of soft tyres and rejoined, crucially, in front of Räikkönen.

'With the tyre graining I lost four seconds so it was great strategy to recover from that when Kimi stopped. I came in a lap later, much earlier than I expected, and after that it was fine but by then Jenson was 16 seconds ahead.'

Button pitted on lap 16. 'I did start struggling with a little bit of oversteer but not quite as bad as Rubens. My times were not quite good enough. That's why they called me in and I stuck the prime tyres on. They worked really well.' Button emerged behind Rosberg but in front of Massa, who hadn't stopped. Neither had Rosberg. After all these years, Monaco was coming to Button, gift wrapped.

Rosberg pitted, Button leading again. Still Massa clung to Button until his pit stop on lap 19 and the order settled Button, Barrichello at 16.6 seconds, Räikkönen at two and a half seconds from Barrichello, then Massa, Webber and Rosberg.

Barrichello came back a little, cutting the gap to 14.8 seconds. However, 'my seat belts started to get looser and looser and I could hear them going clank, clank. I was getting loose, so I had to start driving differently.' That involved adjusting his braking method because if your body is moving 'you get to the pedal and you lock rear wheels more'.

Button set a new fastest lap (1m 15.1s) , almost a second faster than Barrichello's quickest. That forced the lead to 16.4 seconds as they moved towards the second cluster of pit stops.

Barrichello was the first of the front-runners, on lap 49. He took on a new set of soft tyres, the stop went smoothly and he emerged fifth. Massa set a new fastest lap, 1m 15.1s. Button pitted next lap and emerged just as Räikkönen reached him. Räikkönen had the impetus and cut past up the hill towards Casino Square. Massa sneaked up behind. Räikkönen pitted and emerged fifth. Massa continued to push Button to lap 55 when he pitted. Webber pitted at the same time. Massa moved back towards the track and would run fourth.

With five laps left, Button leading:

Barrichello	@ 10.7s
Räikkönen	@ 16.5s
Massa	@ 18.5s
Webber	@ 22.0s
Rosberg	@ 39.1s

'I had the normal Monaco thing when the walls seem to get closer and closer the further you get into the race,' Button said. 'It is a very strange feeling. You start backing off a little bit and in reality that is the worst thing to do because you begin to think *if I get this to the end I am going to win Monaco.* There was so much going through my mind. It isn't that you are *not* thinking about driving but there is a part of your mind that *is* thinking about something else. I had to really concentrate. The last two laps were very enjoyable because I had a big enough gap and you know nothing can go wrong with the car. I could drive at my steady pace and just enjoy the moment. It is a very special moment. In fact, the last two laps were the most enjoyable laps of my career, I would say. As I crossed the line I shouted on the radio to my engineers, "We've got Monaco!"'

He slowed as he crossed the line, shadows full across the track now. He did his slowing down lap waving his right hand, the index finger cocked.

Then something wonderfully bizarre happened. Andrew Shovlin, the man on the other end of Button's on-board radio, told him to park the car on the grid but, as Button would confess, 'I wasn't listening.' He parked it with the others a long way away, thought *oh no* and, still wearing his helmet, ran back. He'd describe it as the best run ever ('You can hear the crowd,' unlike when you drive to the grid). You could also see the crowd, or rather people from the pit lane saluting him and slapping his upraised hand as he went by at a respectable canter. When he reached the podium Nick Fry was there to embrace him.

Barrichello would say 'I have to get as many points as possible while I'm not winning, so if I do start winning then it's a different matter. It's the championship that matters right now and Jenson is on a flier. He's not making any mistakes which is really good for him, it's really good for the team. I'm pushing him as hard as I can. I wanted to win for myself and for the team, and this couldn't be any better for the team because, to be honest, we're pushing each other, we're fair to each other and we're having a wonderful time. He's having a bit more fun than I am because he takes the trophy home but I am pushing hard and I won't stop until the very final race.'

Ross Brawn's insight: 'It is a special race. It is a challenging weekend and, in such circumstances, first and second is just stunning. We were in trouble at one stage in the first stint' – Barrichello's tyre problem – 'and the guys did a super job of recovery. The guys on the strategy called it perfectly. I think the tyres gave us the start but we didn't expect them to be quite so difficult during the first stint. I'm lost for words with Jenson. He's just exceeding everything I thought possible.

'Jenson gave himself the best possible chance of victory after achieving pole position and he was able to control the race from the front. Bringing the car home in one piece after 78 laps is no easy feat in Monaco but Jenson was calm and assured throughout the race and drove with real finesse.

'Rubens did superbly well to keep Räikkönen at bay and bring home maximum points for the team's championship challenge. To win here means so much to everyone at the track, at the factory in Brackley and at Mercedes-Benz High Performance Engines in Brixworth. Special congratulations to Mercedes-Benz for supplying an engine that has now won three Grands Prix.

'We are obviously doing it with a lot less resources than Ferrari, so it's a different approach. This is a small boutique team as opposed to what Ferrari was. It will probably be more difficult for us to keep it going in some ways, but everyone is achieving more than you might expect. We've got the heart of a big team even if we are only a small one.'

Nick Fry's insight: 'The one that was – at least for me, but perhaps most of the team too – a real sense of pride was Monaco. To bring home two cars in first and second place there was frankly mind-boggling. I shall remember to the end of my days walking into the Sporting Club at the dinner for the winners on the Sunday night with Prince Albert and his partner Charlene, Jenson and Jessica, Kate and I, Ross and Jean – and the whole of the Sporting Club standing up and giving us a round of applause. That was almost a pinch-me, I-can't-be-here type of moment.'

Constructors': Brawn 86, Red Bull 42.5, Toyota 26.5, Ferrari 17, McLaren 13, Renault 11.

Drivers': Button 51, Barrichello 35, Vettel 23, Webber 19.5, Trulli 14.5, Glock 12.

The track at Istanbul ran anti-clockwise with turn 8 a sequence of four interlocking left-handers which Button described as the longest corner he'd ever driven.

In first practice Rosberg (1m 28.9s) went fastest, Barrichello (1m 29.5s) ninth, Button (1m 29.7s) eleventh. Kovalinen was fastest in second practice (1m 28.8s), Barrichello (1m 29.3s) eighth, Button (1m 29.4s) twelfth. What was going on? It was all about set-up and balance, or as Barrichello said, diplomatically, it was a 'slightly different' day. 'We don't look that competitive at the moment but it depends on the programs and fuel levels our competitors are running. There is a lot of work for us to achieve, particularly in the first sector where we seem to be suffering the most.' He added that the team understood what actually was going on and would make the necessary changes.

Button described the day as 'tough' as they sought the right balance. 'We tried many different set-up options over the two sessions but unfortunately we couldn't get the car to where I want it to be and struggled with a lack of grip.'

Ross Brawn's insight: 'We've had a challenging opening day because we faced issues on both sides of the garage. The team worked very hard in both sessions on a number of set-up changes and whilst we made some progress we were not able to find a good enough balance on either car. We also experienced a lack of grip on both the prime and option tyre.'

In third practice, on the Saturday, Massa (1m 27.9s) went fastest, Barrichello (1m 28.3s) sixth, Button (1m 28.3s) seventh.

Qualifying, always a shifting mosaic of fast-moving times, would be unusually hectic.

In Q1, Button ventured out with just over five minutes gone and, while he moved into the lap, Trulli did 1m 28.2s, an immediate benchmark. Vettel lowered that to 1m 27.7s. Barrichello was out now and Button went seventh (1m 28.3s). Nakajima improved on Vettel, Räikkönen improved on all of them – Trulli responded, Barrichello tenth. Then Vettel had it with 1m 27.3s.

With slightly over ten minutes left, Button (1m 27.5s) went third and Barrichello was out too. He went fifth with 1m 27.6s and embarked on a second run. He controlled the car perfectly through the final twists and went second – 1m 27.3s. It finished Vettel, Button, Barrichello, Webber, Rosberg, Trulli, Massa.

In Q2 (which Hamilton didn't make) Massa went out early and set the benchmark at 1m 27.4s. Barrichello attacked and did 1m 27.4s, a fraction quicker. Button attacked that, easing in to his first fast lap. It *was* fast: up at the second timing point, swift and sure through the final twists for 1m 27.3s. It moved Martin Brundle to murmur, slightly lost in awe: 'Button drives like a chauffeur. He's so smooth with the car.'

Vettel slotted in between the Brawns, at 0.011 of a second from Button. Then they waited for the final flurry: Webber went third, Räikkönen took that from him then Trulli hammered in 1m 27.1s and Vettel, an instant later, beat that with 1m 27.0s, leaving it Vettel, Trulli, Button, Massa, Räikkönen, Webber, Barrichello.

'I did have a worrying moment when traffic affected my second run and the times were so close between the top 11 drivers,' Barrichello said. The span from Vettel to Alonso, tenth, was 0.457 of a second, and that over 3.4 miles.

In Q3, Räikkönen was out early. The Ferrari looked nervous, his hands looked busy on the steering wheel. He did 1m 29.4s. Trulli trumped that a moment later, 1m 28.8s. The session (literally) gathered pace as Massa went third and Button, on soft tyres, was out travelling fast in the first sector. The Brawn did not look nervous although you could see Button's hands making incisive movements in the slower corners as he set fastest time in sector two. Button did 1m 28.8s, punished for a little loss of grip in the final, slow section. Webber went third.

Now Vettel, with under five minutes to go, on the soft tyres, and 1m 28.8s. Now Barrichello on the hard tyres, but he was 0.3s down in the first sector, 1.1s on the second, and 1m 29.7s put him eighth. Barrichello tried again but he was 0.1s down in the first sector while behind him ten other cars formed a cavalry charge. Barrichello was 0.7s slower in the second sector and another 1m 29.7s lifted him to seventh. He proceeded into a final lap, the session *so* tight that it demands to be expressed to three decimal places.

Webber went fastest in the first sector, Button slower, and suddenly this was like a *race*. Webber's second sector was 0.058s slower, Button's 0.047s faster. Webber seized pole with 1m

28.613s but Button was coming like a missile: 1m 28.421s. Trulli went third and Vettel was still out. He was up 0.093s in the first sector.

Almost unnoticed, Barrichello went second. 'The main question was trying to understand which tyre performed better. I had a better feeling through the high-speed corners with the prime tyre and it was the best choice for me so I went for just the one run on the primes. I lost my first two flying laps to traffic but the third lap was really good.'

Still Vettel came and the clocks froze at 1m 28.316s.

Button said his car felt much better after changing the set-up overnight. 'It was quite difficult to choose between the tyres because their performance was quite similar. The prime [hard] was a little too twitchy for my liking so for Q3 I continued to run the option tyre, which had a more gradual and rolling feel.'

Ross Brawn's insight: 'Obviously we would like to have been on pole but it depends on what the fuel weights are. Normally we are a little bit behind Red Bull in qualifying and then we come back when we put the fuel on the car. If that's the case, you've got to presume they've less fuel but we can't tell that yet. We had a little bit of trouble in the practice sessions – we weren't in good shape. The engineers did a great job overnight to recover the situation, here and the guys at the factory, who also do all the analysis and wrack their brains as to what we are going to do. Jenson and Rubens had different preferences for the tyres so we adopted two very different strategies for Q3. Both paid off.'

On the grid Button pointed out that there was a lot more rubber down on the surface of the track than usual. He was completely relaxed when the BBC's roving reporters Brundle and David Coulthard hoved into view. He explained that, because of the nature of the circuit, some drivers were wearing padding for their heads. He indulged in banter with Coulthard about the naughty name drivers had for this. The model Naomi Campbell hoved into view now, and gave Button a kiss. He seemed so relaxed you could barely believe that he was minutes away from the start of a Grand Prix. Somehow that reflected the mood of the whole team: everything was in hand, everything was going their way and why get stressed?

Everyone except Alonso and Kovalainen started on the hard tyres. From the lights Button – who'd angled his car towards mid-track while he waited – couldn't get away faster than Vettel while, further back, Barrichello was engulfed by the pack and ran 13th. 'We had a problem with the clutch at the start which caused the car to go into anti-stall so I wasn't able to get off the line.'

On the pit-lane wall Brawn's face was impassive, then he pursued his lips, then he became impassive again.

Vettel led to turn 1, a left-hander.

'My start on the dirty side of the grid was good,' Button said. 'Sebastian covered the inside.'

They wheeled and turned, Vettel seeming to establish a gap, but at the exit of turn 9 he 'nearly lost the car. It was my mistake, it was extremely difficult there.'

Button, however, made no mistake.

Into lap 2 a gap flicked up, Button 0.8s ahead. He was now in a position, as he said himself, to control the whole race. Vettel almost lost the Red Bull in turn 9 again and, completing the lap, Button had forced the gap:

Vettel	@ 1.4s
Webber	@ 3.7s
Trulli	@ 5.4s
Rosberg	@ 6.7s
Massa	@ 7.3s

Barrichello was now running 12th, 11.3 seconds from Button. 'To complicate things further,' Barrichello said, 'I was hitting the limiter on the straights which meant that I couldn't overtake and had to take risks.'

Button set fastest lap and was moving into a different dimension from the rest while Barrichello challenged Kovalainen, darting now this way, now that.

By lap 3 Button led Vettel by 1.7s and a lap later it had become 2.2s. He set a new fastest lap while Barrichello's assault on Kovalainen went on and on. Button now led Vettel by 2.5 seconds.

Vettel wondered about moving the strategy from three stops to two.

Barrichello stole inside Kovalainen, who responded by deploying his KERS, which kicked him back past. Barrichello flirted with the inside in a left-hander then they touched as Barrichello nipped inside. Barrichello rotated and set off again, 17th.

Button was rapping out fastest laps and at lap 8 led Vettel by 3.3s.

Barrichello moved past Hamilton and then Piquet in simple, swift movements born of experience, but he remained a racer: he tapped Sutil's rear wheel, damaging the Brawn's front, and had to pit for repairs.

Button led Vettel by 5.7s.

Vettel pitted on lap 15, a decisive moment because if he was changing strategy it would have to be now. He was stationary for 6.5 seconds, taking on 54 litres of fuel to go another 16 laps. He was staying on the three-stop strategy.

'Once Sebastian pitted I was able to push harder,' Button said.

Webber ran second, 11.5 seconds from Button, who pitted on lap 17. He was stationary for 9.3 seconds, taking on 88 litres for another 26 laps: the two-stop strategy.

'Once we knew that Sebastian was going for a three-stop strategy we filled the car up at my first stop and I just tried to be as consistent as possible to keep him behind me,' Button said. 'It's not nice to see a car catching you so quickly even when you know he is on low fuel.'

Vettel was 5.0s away when Button resumed and on lap 19 had cut that to 3.4s. He loomed into Button's mirrors and had a single aim: to get past. He loomed closer, the gap 2.4 seconds. The gaps from Button, completing lap 21:

Vettel	@ 2.4s
Webber	@ 11.9s
Nakajima	@ 18.1s
Rosberg	@ 22.8s
Trulli	@ 24.6s

Still Vettel came, taking 0.7 of a second from Button on lap 22, 0.5 on lap 23. The pressure centred on Button, Vettel swarming, Button taking the pressure. The gap moved like a concertina.

'One time when I caught him up I wanted to dive down the inside going to the last corner,' Vettel said, 'and he defended so it was not possible and he made a mistake, running a bit wide, which gave me a better exit for turn 1 – but it wasn't enough.'

Each lap favoured Button because Vettel needed to get through and build a gap to compensate for the extra pit stop he'd be making soon.

'I just had to be as consistent as I could. I knew that if Sebastian was behind me it was going to be difficult to overtake so I backed off in the corners to help the exits,' Button said.

Webber ran at 13.8 seconds from Vettel and he'd only be stopping twice.

Vettel pitted and emerged third. 'I got caught behind Jenson who was heavier in the second stint and that allowed Mark to get ahead,' Vettel would say.

They ran to the next pit stops on lap 43, Button retaining the lead, Webber holding second, Vettel third.

Soon enough Barrichello would be gone. 'I was prepared to fight my way up the field but the damage caused to the gearbox by the problems at the start began to get worse so the team had to retire my car,' he said. 'It's difficult to have a day like this when you could see the pace of the car was fantastic.'

Button led Webber by 18 seconds, Vettel 8.3s from Webber. The race was coming to Button, who looked assured, unhurried and unharried. 'I had a smile on my face for pretty much every lap – the car felt that good – and I was able to back off in the last stint to conserve the engine. This is the first time that the car has been absolutely perfect for me and it means so much to the team to see just how good this car is.'

Ross Brawn's insight: 'I'm beginning to run out of superlatives to describe our season. Jenson drove an outstanding race and demonstrated the level of talent and composure that we have come to expect. Once again the team at the track, in Brackley and our close partners at Mercedes-

Benz worked extremely hard to improve the car and achieve the perfect set-up we had for the race. My sincere thanks to them all for their commitment and enthusiasm.

'On Rubens' side, we had a problem with his clutch off the start line which was similar to that we experienced at the opening race in Melbourne. In attempting to recover and get off the grid the transmission was over-torqued. As his race progressed it became increasingly evident that this had caused a serious problem with the gearbox and we retired the car whilst the damage was contained. It's extremely frustrating for all concerned when the car was balanced and working well for Rubens going into the race.'

Nick Fry's insight, responding to the question: *Jenson handled adversity beautifully, and then in 2009 he handled the victories as well as he handled the adversity* –

'He is very much the same man and I think that's a product of several fallow years because the car wasn't any good. The time that really made him was 2007 when he didn't feel that he could say anything without being criticised. If he was a team player he was accused by the Press of not being hard enough, and if he criticised the team he was being disloyal and *wasn't* being a team player. In his own mind he got to a state of "whatever I say it's wrong". I think it did him a power of good, and the remarkable thing about him is that as he has matured, he has become more confident in himself but not showy and over-confident. He's not a flash type of guy, he's very down-to-earth and he trusts the people he works with. He has worked with them for a long time. His dad does a great job supporting him and not interfering. He's obviously worked with me for a long time and we get on very well. I think he does a very good job and hopefully he thinks I do a reasonable job as well.'

Constructors': Brawn 96, Red Bull 56.5, Toyota 32.5, Ferrari 20, McLaren 13, Williams 11.5.

Drivers': Button 61, Barrichello 35, Vettel 29, Webber 27.5, Trulli 19.5, Glock 13.

After Turkey, Brawn reviewed the situation. 'It is premature to reach any conclusions because the season is long. Car unbeatable? No. It has some faults and we know them. I'll add that we have been really lucky and anything can still happen if the car has technical problems or if the drivers make mistakes. We are not unbeatable!'

This chapter – embracing the races in Spain, Monaco and Turkey – may appear as a triumphal progress and, if you glance upwards at the Constructors' and Drivers' totals, the statistics do tend to confirm it. Ross Brawn, however understood, after the long journey to here – which started as a humble machinist at Williams and stretched through Jaguar and Benetton and Ferrari – that Grand Prix racing can be a fickle mistress who may withdraw her favours whenever she chooses. The margins are too tight and the complications too many for it to be anything else. Brawn's phrase 'we are not unbeatable!' might have seemed defensive or an exquisite example of English modesty, but it was something else: rooted in hard experience.

The same hard experience allowed him to range over the Formula 1 current crisis – the FOTA breakaway – to find context, to make judgements and to apply good old-fashioned common sense.

He said, speaking after Turkey, that if the breakaway happened the Brawn team would be part of it 'but that is not what we want. This is a fantastic season, we are defeating Ferrari, McLaren and Renault and it would not be the same if we were beating Lola or Campos, although a team without a history can write big stories – and Brawn Grand Prix is an example.'

He felt that having two similar series – in a phrase, splitting the crowns – wouldn't help and would lead to people being confused. 'It is a tragedy to have arrived at this point. We are all guilty. We are all guilty of not having enough time. To develop Formula 1 we have to cut the starting costs, but for some reason the FIA and FOTA have failed. Without an agreement, no one will win and the alternative scenarios would be terrible. There is negotiation going on and it is fine to leave doors open as the negotiation evolves. Formula 1 needs adjustments, not revolutions.

'It is a disagreement which stems from insufficient communication, but we are all clever people and clever people find solutions in the end. Unity is decisive. In my team I would never ask two groups to undertake one project and then choose the one I prefer. There would be one happy group and one demotivated group. If FOTA and the FIA will pool their efforts they'll find a great solution. It is frustrating that we do not think on this basis.'

CHAPTER 8

WAR GAMES

The British Grand Prix reflected every aspect of Grand Prix racing with great, almost terrible, precision: politics, power plays, rumour-mongering, propaganda, threats and counter-threats, an immense crowd who'd paid an immense amount of money, jingoism, nationalism and eventually a motor race which suggested that Brawn were no longer going to be lords of all they surveyed. Around Silverstone's broad, level acres the team's triumphal progress would suddenly become a nervy, uncertain thing. It is a testimony to Brawn's impact that, in the circumstances, anyone noticed,

And in the midst of it all lay the fate of Silverstone itself as the home of the race – which it had been, except when it alternated with Brands Hatch (1964 to 1986) since 1950. That race was the first round of the first World Championship, giving the circuit a primary historical importance as well as a powerful, timeless nostalgia. Silverstone was in no sense beautiful to behold but it did harbour a treasure of beautiful memories.

The Formula 1 commercial rights holder, Bernie Ecclestone, had long been in dispute with the British Racing Drivers' Club, who ran Silverstone, and was now taking the Grand Prix to Donington on a 17-year contract. Donington was beset with several problems, Silverstone was manifestly a great success – more than 300,000 were there over the three days – and Ecclestone was suddenly saying that the race might be back at Silverstone after all.

Meanwhile, the leading teams had formed FOTA and, with the exception of Williams, were prepared to organise their own series if Max Mosley, the president of the governing body, the FIA, was allowed to continue (as they felt) his autocratic style. Ostensibly it was about Mosley's plan to cap what each team could spend but it developed into a trial of strength (which Mosley eventually lost after Silverstone). A breakaway by all the leading teams bar one would have had fundamental repercussions throughout the sport and it provided an ever-moving backdrop to the racing over the British Grand Prix weekend as the politics, power plays and the rest worked themselves out.

Brawn was FOTA's technical man and, repeatedly questioned about whether the breakaway was a bargaining ploy – in simple language a bluff – he insisted that it was not. Work had already begun on the series and it would move up a gear immediately after Silverstone.

He explained that 'FOTA now has to press ahead with its ideas and plans. We can't wait until January and decide which way it is going to go. As each day passes, and each week passes, the options for reconciliation will reduce.' Meetings to frame the technical regulations for a FOTA series would start the following week. 'We will arrive at a technical specification that we think offers the best racing and is cost-effective.'

Sometimes the politics were so intense that the practice sessions and even qualifying became the background, and that despite the fact that Britain had a new sporting hero – Jenson Button – who suited the role as if to the manner born. He took his career seriously of course but, gloriously, did not seem to be taking himself too seriously this mid-season. That helped, because if you are the epicentre of Silverstone on this weekend you are confronted by unending demands and pressures. Button sailed through with his easy charm and disarming honesty.

Red Bull had reportedly introduced 65 upgrades to their car and Vettel showed their value by going fastest in both Friday sessions – from Webber.

First practice		Second practice	
Vettel	1m 19.4s	Vettel	1m 19.4s
Webber	1m 19.6s	Webber	1m 19.5s
Button	1m 20.2s	Sutil	1m 20.1s
Barrichello	1m 20.2s	Nakajima	1m 20.2s
		Barrichello (6)	1m 20.2s
		Button (14)	1m 20.7s

A strong wind raked Silverstone. Button, who did a total of 55 laps, said that this affected the car. 'We tried a few different evaluations with the aero and initially struggled because I had no grip in either the high or low speed corners. We made improvements towards the end.'

Barrichello, who did 48 laps, described the day as 'reasonable' and added they'd 'made some good progress on the balance particularly in the second session.' He found the Red Bull pace 'impressive', itself a disarmingly honest thing to say.

Ross Brawn's insight: 'The track evolution in the morning and the strong winds have combined to make the cars quite difficult to work with and it has been something of a challenge to achieve our planned programme. However, the afternoon session was more productive with both Jenson and Rubens giving similar feedback on the characteristics of their cars.'

All this suggested qualifying might be difficult, and the third practice on Saturday didn't clarify anything: Rosberg (1m 18.8s) fastest from Nakajima (1m 19.1s), Vettel fourth (1m 19.3s), Webber ninth (1m 19.9s), Barrichello tenth (1m 20.0s) and Button twelfth (1m 20.1s).

Qualifying *was* difficult, although before it began Brawn said the car was a bit better and Button was happier with it 'but we're still struggling a bit with tyre temperatures. I suppose it's a typical English summer.' He, too, was disarmingly honest when he added that the Brawn might not be the best car. Nervy? Uncertain? Here it was.

In Q1, Button was out some four minutes into the session and did 1m 21.2s to be fifth. Button tried again on hard compound tyres and did 1m 19.9s – second. Vettel was out and so was Webber. Vettel went ninth, Webber second, Barrichello fourth. Vettel tried again, hands sawing the steering wheel – Vettel was working hard – and did 1m 19.3s, fourth. That was just before halfway through the session. Webber went fastest (1m 18.7s). Vettel responded with 1m 18.6s. At that moment Barrichello had been bumped down to sixth and Button eighth.

There was no late rush, because Sutil crashed and the session was red-flagged. Hamilton (1m 19.9s) didn't make the cut.

Nakajima	1m 18.5s
Webber	1m 18.6s
Vettel	1m 18.6s
Button (5)	1m 18.9s
Barrichello (11)	1m 19.3s

In Q2, Vettel went early, backed off and moved into a second lap, Webber out now on hard tyres and doing a 1m 18.6s before he, too, moved into a second lap and did 1m 18.2s. Vettel thrust in 1m 18.6s – third. The session seemed to be moving against Brawn, Button (1m 19.1s) tenth. By now Barrichello was sixth on 1m 18.9s.

With seven minutes left Button eased out, let some traffic go and then pitted. He'd been bumped down to 11th. With just over two minutes left he was out again and did 1m 18.8s to be seventh. Barrichello moved to third, bumping Button to eighth and then ninth when Glock did 1m 18.7s. It stayed tight: Button 1m 18.6s – eighth. Heidfeld proved no threat but Alonso was out and stayed ninth. Vettel finished the session with a flourish: 1m 18.1s – fastest.

In Q3, every car except Alonso went out onto the circuit immediately. Barrichello looked neat, composed and quick, his 1m 21.4s more an exploration than anything else. Vettel was hard on him behind: 1m 20.8s. Button surged through: 1m 21.0s. An instant later Webber crossed the line: 1m 23.7s, which was his exploration. Vettel swung wide towards the bridge to the complex, Barrichello travelling fast in front of him. He did 1m 20.5s – provisional pole for seven seconds, until Vettel's 1m 20.4s a moment later. Button attacked that but couldn't improve, then Webber took provisional pole with 1m 20.0s. The order reaching towards the mid-point of the session: Webber, Vettel, Barrichello, Rosberg, Button.

The final rush began with three minutes left, the leaders moving in sequence Barrichello, Vettel, Button and Webber.

Barrichello constructed a fast second sector and wheeled through the complex with visible accuracy. 1m 19.8s.

Vettel was already constructing a faster second section. 1m 19.5s.

Button did 1m 20.2s – fifth.

Webber started his second and final flying lap, Vettel already out at the back. Webber did a fast first sector and Vettel pitted. Webber did 1m 19.8s – third, behind Vettel and Barrichello. Nakajima bumped Button to sixth. The fractions were important, Barrichello at 0.3s from Vettel, Webber at 0.3 but Button at 0.7.

Nervy? Uncertain? Was the season suddenly tilting towards Red Bull?

Barrichello felt at home at Silverstone, said so and did not address this question yet. 'After some hard work overnight we changed the car a little and my engineers did a great job to get the set-up to my liking. I really got everything out of the car and we were able to achieve a little more than we expected.'

Button 'really struggled with low grip especially in the complex. Compared to Rubens I was losing a lot of time with the rear of the car, skating around, struggling quite a bit. Sixth is by no means a bad result, of course, but I'm hugely disappointed not to be starting further up. We knew we would find it difficult here because our car doesn't work so well at low temperatures.'

Ross Brawn's insight: 'An excellent performance from Rubens and second place on the grid puts him in a very strong position for the race. Jenson struggled a little more than Rubens with the tyres at the low temperatures we experienced and he was not happy with the balance of the car throughout qualifying. Unfortunately he was also affected by a misunderstood communication on the pit wall which resulted in us bringing him in a lap earlier than we perhaps should have, and that cost him a place. He didn't get the balance he wanted. He was still complaining on the first set of new tyres that the balance wasn't right. We made an adjustment and I'm not sure it worked.'

From the lights Vettel made a superb start, commanding the middle of the track, Barrichello tucked in behind, Webber close up on Barrichello – Button ninth. 'I had a bad start because Trulli was slow off the line in front of me, which left nowhere to go. I tried the inside and then the outside but everyone shot by me.' Button had Massa immediately in front of him.

They stretched towards Hanger Straight, stretched along it, stretched through the complex.

'I had a good start to maintain second,' Barrichello said, ' but Sebastian disappeared in front of me and we knew that we were competing for third.'

Crossing the line to complete this opening lap, Vettel led; then –

Barrichello	@ 1.5s
Webber	@ 2.2s
Nakajima	@ 3.8s
Räikkönen	@ 4.4s
Rosberg	@ 5.6s
Trulli	@ 6.2s
Massa	@ 6.8s
Button	@ 7.0s

'From ninth place it was never going to be an easy race,' Button would say. Massa held him captive, but not for long. On the second lap Massa ran wide on the exit of Becketts and Button was through. Now he had Trulli ahead, and quickly, urgently drew up to him. Vettel meanwhile was now commanding the whole race. Completing lap 2 he had extended his lead over Barrichello to 3.3s, Button at 10.0s. Vettel set fastest lap, emphasising the extent of the command.

Button could do nothing about Trulli, even though – as Trulli later explained – the Toyota was sliding about. It was 'really frustrating,' Button said, 'because the car felt good on the softer tyre and I was much quicker than him but I couldn't overtake.'

Here, in fact, was a problem for Grand Prix racing as an entity, apart from Button's immediate predicament: from lap 2 to lap 14 (the pit stops began on lap 15) the first 13 cars circled in exactly the same order – which is another way of saying that no car among them overtook any other. The immense crowd at Silverstone, an *historic* crowd in the sense that many of them had been coming for generations and understood what they were watching, would understand how difficult overtaking had become in the modern era. It wouldn't put them off coming back in 2010 (if there was a race for them to come to), but the more esoteric venues – Turkey, the desert races, Singapore, China – might be especially vulnerable to new-found spectators who paid a great deal of money to witness a procession.

By lap 6 Vettel led Barrichello by 6.1s, Webber holding station. Vettel kept extending it, kept thrusting in fastest laps and soon enough – lap 10 – the lead was out to 10.8s, Webber 0.5 of a second behind Barrichello.

Button pitted on lap 18 and lost two places.

Barrichello, now 18 seconds behind Vettel, pitted on lap 19, giving Webber one lap before he came in to gain enough time to emerge ahead. Barrichello was stationary for 9.7 seconds, took on hard tyres and set off, now fifth. Webber came in having done a personal best in the middle sector of the lap. He was stationary for 11.7 seconds, took on soft tyres and slipped out along the pit lane exit that curved so gracefully towards the track and Becketts. Barrichello was round Copse, Webber – at this instant at the end of the pit lane exit – firmly in sight. Webber found Barrichello there behind him as they flicked through Becketts. Down Hanger Straight, Webber maintained the gap – the gap recorded at 0.2 of a second meaningless.

Button ran eighth again.

Webber eased away from Barrichello and the race settled again, or rather the problem recurred: from lap 24 to lap 39, immediately before the second stops began, none of the top 11 exchanged places.

'We had a long middle stint on the harder tyre and both Rubens and I struggled to get the tyres into their working range in the cool conditions with a heavy fuel load,' Button said. He had Räikkönen in front, then Trulli, although the team radioed that Räikkönen would be pitting early.

Barrichello fell away from Webber.

'We knew,' Barrichello said, 'that if the track temperatures didn't increase it would be incredibly difficult to beat the Red Bulls. The car has been well balanced and we certainly haven't lost performance since the last race, it's just that we have suffered badly in the cool conditions with our tyre temperatures. There was very little difference between the two tyre compounds but the softer tyre was definitely better in the race so it was tough for us to do the long middle stint on the harder tyre.' In fact, Barrichello would conclude, the weekend had been tough.

Barrichello pitted on lap 47 and only lost one place.

Button pitted late, on lap 49, the last of the front-runners, by which time he'd risen to third. He emerged sixth, Barrichello holding third although with no prospect of catching Webber, never mind Vettel.

Button now had Rosberg and Massa ahead. 'On the softer rubber I was able to close right up easily – so the pace of the car was actually pretty good – but it is so difficult to overtake that I couldn't improve on sixth,' Button said.

Barrichello was 'proud' to finish third because, he judged realistically, it was the best they could do and they'd known this since the day before.

Ross Brawn described the race as 'challenging.' His insight: 'Rubens drove a very composed race to achieve his second consecutive podium finish at Silverstone whilst Jenson recovered well from a poor start to score valuable points for our Championship challenge. We knew from the outset that our car does not work particularly well with the tyres at lower track temperatures and this was clearly evident at Shanghai earlier in the season. The balance of the car and the pace shown by Jenson in the last few laps of the race are, however, encouraging and we will be taking a close look at the issues that we experienced with the tyres to see what countermeasures can be taken.'

Constructors': Brawn 105, Red Bull 74.5, Toyota 34.5, Ferrari 26, Williams 15.5, McLaren 13.

Drivers': Button 64, Barrichello 41, Vettel 39, Webber 35.5, Trulli 21.5, Massa 16.

Button's defeat produced an astonishing statistic. Silverstone was the eighth Grand Prix of the season and Button had won six of the previous seven (Vettel took China, of course). In terms of World Champions, since 1992 – when Nigel Mansell was completely dominant in the Williams – *only* Michael Schumacher could equal the six out of seven ratio.

1992, Mansell 5/7; 1993 Alain Prost 4/7; 1994 Schumacher 6/7; 1995 Schumacher 4/7; 1996 Damon Hill 4/7; 1997 Jacques Villeneuve 3/7; 1998 Mika Häkkinen 4/7; 1999 Häkkinen 3/7; 2000 Schumacher 4/7; 2001 Schumacher 4/7; 2002 Schumacher 5/7; 2003 Schumacher 3/7; 2004 Schumacher 6/7; 2005 Alonso 4/7; 2006 Alonso 4/7; 2007 Räikkönen 1/7; 2008 Hamilton 2/7.

Such statistics are *not* by their nature conclusive – look at Räikkönen's one win (with five more to come and the championship by a single point) against Schumacher's monuments – but they do give a context of their own. Up to Silverstone, to reuse the word dominant, Button had exploited a superior, winning car as effectively as anyone except Schumacher had done since the Senna era. It was harder and harder to remember that, the season before, he had finished with three points, all taken with a sixth place in Spain while the other 17 races yielded nothing.

The week after Silverstone, the warfare between Mosley, Ecclestone and FOTA abruptly ended in peace – although anyone querying the seriousness of the FOTA alternative series was surely making a mistake. You only had to hear Brawn talking about it – and describing that they would be starting work on it the day after the FIA meeting in Paris on the Wednesday if peace was not found – to know that. Anyway, Ecclestone, Mosley and Luca di Montezemolo locked themselves in a darkened room – you know what I mean – and thrashed out a deal: Mosley not to stand for re-election in the autumn, the controversial budget cap to be abandoned, the teams to commit to 2012, the rules to stay the same and Ecclestone to keep the commercial rights, although what might happen to them when the Concorde Agreement expired in 2012 was not clear.

The peace lasted a few brief, precious hours. Mosley then claimed that FOTA had exhibited triumphalism, de Montezemolo had called him a dictator and he was now reconsidering his decision about re-election. Thereafter, something much more amazing than all this happened: both camps fell publicly silent, no posturing, no threatening, no promising, no accusing, no statements and counter-statements, no Press Conferences, no Press Releases vetted by lawyers, not a single word.

It was more than amazing, it was very, very disturbing. In Formula 1, silence is so unusual it invariably means a great deal is going on but you don't know about it.

The silence did not last long. The week before the German Grand Prix, Ecclestone gave an interview to *The Times* of London during which he said, and I quote: 'In a lot of ways, terrible to say this I suppose, but apart from the fact that Hitler got taken away and persuaded to do things that I have no idea whether he wanted to do or not, he was in the way that he could command a lot of people, able to get things done. In the end he got lost, so he wasn't a very good dictator because either he had all these things and knew what was going on and insisted, or he just went along with it … so either way he wasn't a dictator.'

Leaving aside the incoherent structure of what Ecclestone said, to invoke Hitler – and hammer out the crucial phrase 'able to get things done' – would have been ill-advised at any time, but the context assumed nightmarish proportions. The German Grand Prix would be at the Nürburgring, symbol of Nazi power expressed through Mercedes-Benz and Auto Union (Audi) across the races of the 1930s, and two of the Grands Prix then had been attended by Hitler.

Mercedes-Benz and BMW were both members of FOTA. If you wanted to persuade them that breaking away was an excellent idea, the Hitler invocation would certainly do.

Ecclestone apologised and (amazingly) used a Press Relations company to handle it rather than do it himself with a few clipped, adroit sentiments.

Brawn had already turned Formula 1 upside down and now Formula 1 itself seemed intent on doing somersaults every week.

I am not being flippant in saying that Brawn, Button and Barrichello went to Germany intent on world conquest – in perfect peace – and in 2009 the great German public were delighted to witness it, particularly since their own Sebastian Vettel seemed highly capable of thwarting them. Button, moreover, dismissed notions of percentage finishes because 'that won't work.' He needed wins. 'My lead is not a lot with nine races to go. If I finished third in every race, which sounds OK, I have no chance for the championship.'

In the background there were rumours that the Branson-Virgin sponsorship might be transferred to another team.

On the Friday at the Nürburgring, Lewis Hamilton disturbed everything with a lap of 1m 32.1s in the second session, fastest of the day and suggesting McLaren were now recovering to the point where they might be potential spoilers to Brawn and Red Bull.

In the first session, run after light rain had kept the track virtually empty for more than half an hour, Webber went fastest (1m 33.0s) from Button (1m 33.4s) and Massa (1m 33.7s), Vettel eighth (1m 33.9s), and Barrichello twelfth (1m 34.2s). Both Brawn drivers were on hard tyres: Button covered 18 laps, Barrichello a lap less.

The second session mirrored the first, with more rain at the beginning. The Brawns concentrated on the super soft and medium tyres, searching for tyre temperature in conditions Button described as more fitting for winter testing. Vettel (1m 32.3s) was second to Hamilton, Button third (1m 32.3s), Webber fourth (1m 32.4s), and Barrichello seventh (1m 32.6s). Button added that the low track temperature made life with the hard compound tyres difficult and, ominously, 'we will struggle with that tyre if it stays like this.'

Barrichello confirmed the situation but drew some comfort from the performance of the softer tyre.

Ross Brawn's insight: 'We made some useful progress using our experience at previous events where the cold and damp conditions have proved more difficult for us.'

Later he'd explain that 'people are working hard' to resolve the FOTA-FIA conflict 'but until names are on a piece of paper you never know. Everyone is putting a big effort into it – the teams, the FIA – so we can't fault the effort of people in trying to find a solution.'

Before qualifying, the cold weather persisting and rain threatening, he explained that the team were living through 'a difficult weekend struggling with tyre temperatures again, struggling in particular to get the fronts hot and that means it is challenging to get the set-up of the car sorted.'

And what would Hamilton do? He'd been fastest again (1m 31.1s) in the third practice from Alonso (1m 31.3s), Vettel fourth (1m 31.5s), Webber fifth (1m 31.6s), Button 11th (1m 32.0s), Barrichello 14th (1m 32.1s). Button had actually been weaving down the straights to create friction to heat the front tyre.

Vettel came out immediately, leading a crocodile of four other cars from the pits then, like a sudden migration, the others followed. Most were on super soft tyres, a few on the mediums. The track temperature was 22°, Arctic compared to elsewhere, and not good news for the mediums. The threat of rain had forced them all out to get a time just in case.

Vettel (mediums) went into a fast lap and did 1m 33.4s.

Button, on the soft tyres, did 1m 32.6s and flowed into his second fast lap when the tyres ought to have been up to temperature.

Hamilton went fastest (1m 31.6s) and Barrichello did 1m 32.0s – third – but Hamilton was going even faster: 1m 31.4s. Webber on the harder tyre was moving – 1m 32.2s, but only sixth – while Button went second (1m 31.7s) so that Q1 was slightly frantic, slightly frenetic and still only seven minutes old…

Now Vettel struck (1m 31.4s) and Webber tried again on super softs – 1m 31.2s, fastest. With four minutes left Button moved into sixth place, nice and safe and one place behind Barrichello. Q1 ended Webber, Alonso, Vettel, Hamilton, Barrichello, Button.

Rain threatened again. It brought them all out again at the start of Q2 under a heavy, darkening sky. Rain did fall. On the first, tentative lap Nakajima floated off, Massa floated onto grass and Hamilton floated across the chicane. The cavalcade pitted for intermediate tyres and the session was about to get very, very interesting.

Webber, meanwhile, was on super soft tyres, heaving at the

wheel to keep the Red Bull on an even keel and going very gently, 12 seconds off the pace in the first sector. Along the pit lane the pneumatic hammers were locking intermediates on to the cars. The rain intensified then seemed to ease. With eight minutes left the weather forecast offered a six or seven minute window before heavy rain.

Hamilton went fastest (1m 42.3s) and with seven minutes left Barrichello was having super softs fitted. 'We all went on slicks and we all came back for intermediates because we saw Massa going off in turn 12,' Barrichello said. 'I was on my timed lap when I decided that the intermediate was not the right tyre. I thought *let's gamble a little bit more*. I came in and I had no reply on the radio. It was really chaotic and there was a big confusion but they were ready for me. They put on the right tyres. It was a great decision...'

A gaggle of cars jostled at the top of the leaderboard – Räikkönen from Heidfeld and Alonso, Hamilton forced to fourth then Webber (1m 38.0s) forced them all down a place, Vettel suddenly popping up second. Barrichello was 15th at this moment – six minutes left – but in his second sector did 24.7s which was *three seconds* quicker than all the rest. He came upon Button in the final sector, Button moved swiftly aside but Barrichello was momentarily baulked by Nakajima. He did 1m 34.4s, comfortably fastest by almost *four seconds*. This, he said with the broadest of smiles, 'gave me a much more relaxed end to Q2 than some of the others.'

The rush for super softs was under way all along the pit lane.

Button described Q2 as 'madness but good fun. I thought it was too wet for slicks but Rubens made it work and we were able to switch tyres with just enough time to make my timed lap count.'

Nakajima and Vettel collided in the pit lane but emerged. Three and a half minutes remained and rain spots fell, then rain, and Button was 14th, deep into the guillotine zone. Button went for it and lifted himself to fifth. It finished Barrichello, Piquet, Sutil, Webber, Button, Hamilton, Vettel.

Q3 began quietly and Button – first out – didn't emerge until almost a minute and a half of the ten had gone. He weaved, seeking heat for the tyres. His radio crackled and, very calmly, Shovlin said 'Jenson, maybe people are planning on only doing one flying lap.' Button said something inaudible. 'Jenson, can you just repeat, did you say you want to do an in-out and then a three-time run?' Again Button's reply was inaudible. Barrichello was out – and of all the others, only Massa, at this point – and Barrichello went four-tenths quicker than Button in the first sector. Button pitted, the lap uncompleted.

Barrichello kept on and did a benchmark 1m 32.7s. Webber attacked that and did 1m 33.2s, Vettel attacked *that* and did 1m 33.1s. Button came out with two and a half minutes remaining but was slow in his middle sector and was ninth. All the cars were out, the final charge imminent. Button and Hamilton were travelling fast and both did exactly the same time in the first sector.

Hamilton completed the lap in 1m 32.6 to be fastest.

Four second later Button did 1m 32.7s to be second.

Both moved into their final laps and, as they did, Barrichello went second fastest, bumping Button a place. The final charge was unfolding very, very quickly with Webber and Vettel on the circuit too. Button went fastest in the first sector while Webber muscled and stroked the Red Bull to the line in 1m 32.2s, fastest. Still Vettel came, some 14 seconds away. Button lost two-tenths in the second sector while Vettel muscled and stroked the Red Bull to the line in 1m 32.480s, second.

Button rounded the final corner and the clock froze at 1m 32.473s, and that became second by a fraction so small it remains difficult to imagine.

Five seconds back, Barrichello was coming and now he did 1m 32.3s, taking the second place from Button.

Webber had the first pole of his Grand Prix career and Button was happy to be where he was. 'Just getting into the final qualifying session was an achievement so I'm really pleased to have qualified in third. It was a pretty eventful hour.'

Barrichello was beaming. 'It's nice when you have the right tyres at the right moment.'

Ross Brawn's insight: 'The weather ensured an intense qualifying session for everyone and we are extremely pleased to have come out with Rubens and Jenson in second and third positions. Both drivers were superb. Rubens made an inspired call in Q2 to come in early for dry tyres and his direction was crucial in getting Jenson in and back onto slicks with enough time to complete his timed lap, which he did under great pressure as the rain fell again. Q3 was quite calm in comparison and both drivers were able to take full advantage of their well-balanced cars. Congratulations to Mark for his maiden pole position and congratulations to Mercedes-Benz with five cars in the top seven!'

The race was entirely deceptive because initially it seemed to belong to Barrichello with Button handily placed and the Red Bulls scattered. It ended with Barrichello, sixth, facing a thicket of microphones and saying he didn't want to talk to anybody in the team and he wished he was on the aeroplane home. The championship – or rather both championships – had just got a lot, lot tighter, the season continuing to tilt away from Brawn.

From the lights Webber made a strong start and went right, banging Barrichello's flank. Webber subsequently explained that there was nothing deliberate about it. Hamilton, from the third row and with KERS, came down the middle like a bullet train while Button stayed mid-track but by the time he'd reached the mouth of turn 1 he had four cars ahead – Barrichello, Webber and both McLarens. Into and through turn 1 Massa squeezed through on the inside, Barrichello by now cleanly into the lead from Webber. Button was scrabbling in the pack.

The order, as they moved through the opening lap, was Barrichello, Webber, Kovalainen, Massa, Button, Vettel.

Hamilton had a puncture and pitted, resuming at the back. He'd spend his afternoon getting out of everyone's way as they lapped him, so the question of how much of a spoiler he might be was placed in abeyance, pending further examination in Hungary in two weeks.

Button, on a three-stop strategy, swarmed Massa – Button needing to be past him and gone. Button was quicker but not decisively so. Crossing the line, Barrichello leading –

Webber	@ 0.8s
Kovalainen	@ 4.0s
Massa	@ 4.7s
Button	@ 4.9s
Vettel	@ 5.9s

Barrichello needed to be gone too, because, like Button, he was on a three-stop strategy and Webber two. Into turn 1 to begin the second lap Button slotted tight down the inside so that he now had Massa between him and Vettel while Barrichello, handling the Brawn beautifully, clearly had the whole race at his mercy already. It needs saying, especially in view of what Barrichello would be saying after the race: he was driving with the sureness of touch of a mature man, and rarely made mistakes anyway. His hair had begun to thin and recede (a little) but his appetite hadn't.

Button, however, would be tormented behind Kovalainen because the McLaren had the KERS, so that whenever Button lined up an attack Kovalainen pushed the button and spurted. In the background Vettel went wide, slightly off but didn't lose a place. This is how promising it all looked completing lap 2, Barrichello in control:

Webber	@ 1.0s
Kovalainen	@ 5.3s
Button	@ 5.9s
Massa	@ 6.9s
Vettel	@ 7.9s

The gap from Webber to Kovalainen was assuming serious proportions for Button because, at 4.0s, it translated to 2.0s per lap. Suddenly the race which he said he needed to win was going away from him unless he could deal with Kovalainen soon. The problem was the eternal one. You could get close (the Brawn suffered less than other cars in the turbulent air), you could feint and probe, but if Kovalainen covered the slow corners and chicane, and the KERS covered the straights, Button could do nothing but follow.

'I had a poor start to drop back to fifth after the first turn and I was able to get ahead of Massa at the start of the second lap but just couldn't get past Kovalainen,' Button would say. 'His pace was way off what we could have achieved at that point of the race but there was just no way through.'

At lap 3, the Webber-Kovalainen gap was out to 5.3s, Webber rapping out fastest laps. He could afford to track Barrichello, take no risks and exploit the fact that Barrichello would be pitting one more time than he would.

By lap 5 the Webber-Kovalainen gap had grown to 8.1s, Button four-tenths behind Kovalainen and still in prison there. Worse, Kovalainen was backing Button towards Massa (and his Ferrari with KERS) – and Vettel.

The Red Bull pit were relaying the good news to Webber: Barrichello will be pitting soon, clearing the track for you, and Kovalainen is acting as a road block far behind you. Mark Webber had never won a race. All at once it seemed the easiest, most natural thing in the world to achieve that.

Still Webber tracked Barrichello, waiting, waiting, waiting. It wasn't exciting, it wasn't racing in the orthodox sense, it was just what you do.

On lap 9 Vettel drew up alongside Massa, who was having none of that, thank you. At this moment word filtered through that the Stewards were examining the Webber-Barrichello incident from the lights. Meanwhile, the Webber gap to Kovalainen had grown to 13.1s. Moment by moment Button's chances of winning were lengthening in direct proportion to the gap. The three cars so close behind – Massa, Vettel and Räikkönen – were fuelled longer and almost certainly on two stops.

With 11 laps completed Webber was given a drive-through penalty for causing a collision with Barrichello and that seemed to have destroyed his race. He could not, of course, use the drive-through to take on fuel or change tyres. It was almost the equivalent of putting him on a three-stop strategy like the Brawns.

Button's tyres were graining. He pitted and was stationary for 6.6s during which he fitted the super soft tyres. He took on

55 litres, translating to 17 laps: a three-strop strategy confirmed. He emerged 14th, although none of the others had stopped yet.

Webber served his drive-through on lap 14, Barrichello pitting just in front of him.

Barrichello was stationary for 6.6s, the softer tyres on. He, too, took on 55 litres translating to the 17 laps: a three-stop strategy confirmed. He emerged fourth.

Webber had five laps before his own pit stop while, now, Barrichello was a prisoner behind Massa. Webber was stationary for 8.8s, took on 82 litres (translating to 26 laps: the two-stop strategy confirmed), took on the harder tyres and emerged seventh – ahead of Button. Massa wouldn't pit until lap 25 and if he held Barrichello behind until then the whole shape of the race would be altered.

Vettel pitted on lap 21 from third place and went for the harder tyres. He was stationary for 8.6s (79 litres, 25 laps) and emerged 11th.

Button did his best to attack Webber, Massa leading at lap 22:

Barrichello	@ 0.4s
Räikkönen	@ 2.5s
Sutil	@ 4.0s
Rosberg	@ 5.5s
Kubica	@ 9.7s
Webber	@ 10.3s
Button	@ 10.6s
Vettel (11th)	@ 27.2s

Webber gained two seconds to Barrichello on one lap and was only 8.5s from the leaders. At last Massa pitted, releasing Barrichello, who was told on the radio he had nine laps to pull it all back. Across laps 24 to 27 Webber gained every lap and on lap 28 was only 4.2 seconds away. Barrichello could see him in his mirrors and his rear tyres were going off, as he said on the radio. A few moments later he could see a great deal more of him because Webber was catching him and had the gap down to 1.2s.

Button made his second stop, the strategy amounting to punishment. He was stationary for 6.7s, taking on the harder tyre and emerging seventh. By then Webber was full on to Barrichello, who angled the Brawn into the pits. Webber saw the track, and the race, spread before him.

And Barrichello's pit stop went wrong. The harder tyres went on but he was stationary for 11.4 seconds, which suggested a switch to a two-stop strategy. With 28 laps left...

Webber	2 stops
Vettel	1 stop
Massa	1 stop
Rosberg	1 stop
Barrichello	2 stops
Räikkönen	1 stop
Button	2 stops

Räikkönen, however, had a problem and Button surged past. Barrichello, on the radio, said he assumed he'd been filled to the end. His engineer, Jock Clear, said 'Negative, negative, we had a fuel-rig problem.'

Webber was an immense distance in front of Vettel – at lap 35 some 19.9 seconds – made more immense because Webber, of course, had had the drive-through. The season might be moving against Brawn but, within Red Bull, it might also be moving against Vettel. To emphasise this, Webber set a new fastest lap and forced the gap to 22.1 seconds before Webber eased off *with 20 laps to go...*

Barrichello ran fifth and Button sixth, nothing between them, but Button due to make his third pit stop a lap after Barrichello, a lap that might be precious in gaining enough time. Button was weaving in the search for heat.

Webber made his final stop and continued, imperiously. Vettel made his final stop and continued after Webber while the Brawns circled together, Button asking for Barrichello to be told to cede the place – Massa was coming up 12 seconds away. Barrichello pitted with ten laps left, was stationary for 5.8 seconds (hard tyres), Massa through. Button did 1m 34.4s on the lap when Barrichello came in and now hammered out his best first two sectors before he angled the car into the pit lane. He took on soft tyres, was stationary for 6.2 seconds and emerged just as Barrichello arrived. Button fended him off and all that remained was the run for home. Or did it?

The order was Webber, Vettel, Massa, Rosberg, Button, Barrichello and Alonso, who was travelling fast.

At lap 52 of the 60, Webber far in the distance and out of sight:

Vettel	@ 15.6s
Massa	@ 21.4s
Rosberg	@ 26.7s
Button	@ 30.2s
Barrichello	@ 31.3s
Alonso	@ 32.7s

Two sub-plots seemed to be working themselves out, Button catching Rosberg – overtaking him would be worth an extra point, of course – and Alonso advancing with great strides towards Barrichello and Button, who was still catching Rosberg. Then Button fell away, his tyres graining badly. Alonso was full up to them.

The sub-plots never did work themselves out. They all ran for home and reached it in the same order.

Button consoled himself with points on a hard weekend dominated by the tyre degradation, but Barrichello, emotional and looking as if he was suppressing great anger, launched himself.

'I'm terribly upset with the way things have gone because it is a very good show of how to lose a race. I did everything I had to do. I had to go first into the first corner and that's what I did. Then they [the team] made me lose the race. If we keep going on like this we'll end up losing both championships and that would be terrible. To be honest I wish I could just get on a plane and go home. I don't want to talk to anyone in the team because it would be a lot of *blah, blah, blah* and I don't want to hear that. I'm just terribly upset.'

Ross Brawn calmed everything by pointing out, correctly, that the three-stop strategy was flawed and the Barrichello fuel-rig problem made that worse. 'And his radio wasn't great in the race, he was struggling with that. He wasn't getting the briefings and he didn't really have a clear idea of what was going on. Once he calms down and looks at all the numbers he will realise we were too slow. Mark had a drive-through and was still back in front of us after a few laps. When you're cocooned inside the car and your radio isn't working you don't have a clear idea what's going on. I think that's a frustrated racing driver. When you put so much into a race and it doesn't work out that's what you get sometimes.'

Barrichello, calming, then said: 'After leading on the first lap it is of course hugely disappointing to have finished in sixth position. It was a combination of things really which are now very clear to me having spoken to the team. We didn't have enough pace compared to the Red Bulls to win but the fuel-rig problem at my second stop where we had to switch rigs probably cost me a place on the podium.'

Brawn agreed and felt that without the fuel-rig problem Barrichello might have finished third. 'Without doubt it was a very disappointing race for the team, although we were able to score some points to minimise the damage to our championship challenge. Quite simply, we didn't have the pace to match the Red Bulls.'

Paul Stewart, watching and remembering, says of Rubens: 'He's good company but he is emotional, and I see that in some of the difficulties he is having now. It's a shame in a way – and I don't mean this in a bad way about him because he is a great, great guy – but I am not entirely surprised. It makes me laugh: I feel I know him (and I am quite sure he knows my limitations, too, by the way). He will have had his reasons. Ross would know exactly how to calm him down and do all that.'

Ross did.

Constructor's: Brawn 112, Red Bull 92.5, Toyota 34.5, Ferrari 32, Williams 20.5, McLaren 14.

Driver's: Button 68, Vettel 47, Webber 45.5, Barrichello 44, Massa 22, Trulli 21.5.

During the first half of the season Eddie Jordan coined a glorious, and utterly Irish, description of Button. 'He's better in a good car than he was bad in a bad car.' I asked Jordan for his half-time report (Germany was round nine of the 17).

'I think Jenson will go on to win the championship this year. He has a nice, tidy car and it's very reliable, which is particularly the way Ross likes it. Ross is not stupid. He'd rather sacrifice a fraction of performance to make sure the car finishes every race. He and Adrian Newey are, at this moment, a class above the rest, as they have been for years.

'On a slightly negative side I am concerned about the team's commercial application. There seems to be a failing. We hear of all sorts of different stories about a gambling or booze company, or something like that, sponsoring them then we hear about investments from the Middle Eastern people but we are well and truly halfway through the season so it's about time we heard some good news on the commercial side.

'The thing for me at the moment is that Rubens has probably been battered after being used at Ferrari with the Michael Schumacher thing, and then he comes and he sees Ross Brawn, who of course was at Ferrari at the same time – but to be fair Button came out of the box quicker [whatever Barrichello's feelings]. Button has a different driving style that suited this car, these tyres and various other items. Button got the jump on him. Button was that bit quicker than him. Hence, the flow has gone towards Button. Rubens has been a good team-mate but not quite able to pull off the wins that we'd hoped – at least a couple of them.'

If there's any ill luck going, he seems to get it.

'There are a number of people who have fallen into that attitude, and, you know, that's part of something. I think people who are aggressive at the start are inclined to get away with more than those who aren't – you've got Hamilton and if you remember Michael, he tore up the rule book at the start. Then you get kind of a mental thing: *Christ, I'm going to keep away from him.* For sure when you're driving and in a position at the front and you've got a Ferrari behind, what's going to happen is you'll be looking which helmet it is – because they're not going to get out of the way for Räikkönen but they will panic when they see it's Schumacher – just like the yellow helmet of Ayrton. It didn't matter whether it was Prost or Berger or whoever, but if it was Ayrton...'

Barrichello was aggressive in an ordinary sense at the starts, and the same during the races, because all Formula 1 drivers are (or they won't be Formula 1 drivers for long). What Jordan is discussing is the very essence of Grand Prix racing: the ultra-aggressive ones get away with more (and get into more trouble), or to put it another way, between 1988 and 2008 we had two decades of World Championships, and Senna and Schumacher won exactly half of them.

The meek do not inherit this part of the earth.

Barrichello himself says 'I have always considered myself to be a lucky person and in life you have to work around luck, you have to be positive.'

On the Tuesday after the German Grand Prix, Brawn rang Barrichello and suggested it might be a good idea for him to send an email to the team saying that he really didn't have a problem. Barrichello was happy to do this and the outburst could be forgotten, although, inevitably, it would have to remain somewhere in the background – it was the second outburst, after all – because now eight races remained and who knew if, among them, there might not be cases of *perceived* injustice?

Approaching the Hungaroring there was much else to contemplate, not least getting the car back on the pace. Hungary offered warmer temperatures, which ought to have solved the tyre problems but would it?

Button said, predictably enough: 'Hungary is always one of my favourite races and even more so this year because it should finally be a return to some real summer temperatures. I know that the guys at the factory and at Mercedes-Benz have been working really hard on our latest upgrade package and I just can't wait to get back in the car.' He added that there could be no excuses if the team didn't do well.

Barrichello said, predictably enough: 'The feedback from the factory is that our upgrades should be a step forward so we're feeling positive going into the weekend.'

The Friday held out promise, not least because it *was* hot. Between them, Button and Barrichello covered 129 laps, working through their programme.

Kovalainen (1m 22.2s) was quickest in the first session from Rosberg (1m 22.3s), Webber fourth (1m 22.6s), Button tenth (1m 23.1s), Barrichello 13th (1m 23.2s), Vettel 15th (1m 23.2s).

Significantly, Hamilton went quickest in the second session (1m 22.0s) from Kovalainen (1m 22.1s) and that was an indication the judgement held in abeyance since the Nürburgring puncture could now be made. McLaren had worked hard to haul their car back to the pace and Hamilton hadn't lost the ability to capitalise on that – no sane person doubted that he had – but Kovalainen's time was much more revealing. The *car* was fast.

Webber (1m 22.3s) finished fourth, which strongly suggested he was maintaining his impetus, Vettel sixth (1m 22.5s), Barrichello seventh (1m 22.6s) and Button 13th (1m 22.8s).

These Brawn times were deceptive, as Friday times so often can be, but with a single caveat. The McLarens could not have done what they had if they were *not* back on or near the pace.

Barrichello explained that their aim was 'to work with the two tyre compounds to fully understand their working range and the impact on the set-up and balance of the car. Most of my day was focused on evaluating the prime tyre, which proved not to have a great deal of grip so it was important to establish some set-up assumptions. We then tried the option tyre which seemed to be quicker.'

Button insisted it was a better Friday than during the last couple of races. The higher temperature made him happy and 'we have some good aerodynamic updates to the car for this race.'

Ross Brawn's insight: 'A productive day for us and we're pleased with the amount of set-up work we have been able to achieve over the two sessions. The initial feedback from the performance improvements that we've brought to this race looks positive and both Rubens and Jenson were happy with the progress made. The temperatures were pretty much as we expected, with the hot and sunny conditions enabling us to make reasonable use of the tyres and develop our understanding of their performance characteristics.'

In the Saturday morning session Hamilton (1m 21.0s) went fastest again, from Heidfeld, Webber ninth (1m 21.9s), Vettel a place behind (1m 21.9s), Barrichello 13th (1m 22.1s) and Button 17th (1m 22.3s).

Qualifying swept away all memory of this because, in Q2, Barrichello's car shed a spring weighing about 2lb and Felipe Massa, some four seconds behind, was struck on the head by it. The Ferrari went straight on and buried its nose deep in the tyre wall. Massa was stabilised at the scene before being flown to hospital in Budapest, where he was operated on. There were rumours, which Ferrari denied, that his life was in danger.

Before Q1, Ross Brawn said that 'the wind is going to be tricky for people and you might see a few cars off the track because they get caught out by it, but the temperature is up.' Perhaps the wind explained why few cars ventured out early – only three after almost five minutes.

Vettel emerged with 12 minutes left and did 1m 22.2s to go fourth. Webber followed, working hard, and was no higher than 17th. That somehow set the scene for the scramble.

Button and Barrichello emerged within 30 seconds of each other.

Hamilton went second fastest but seemed to have more to come.

Vettel (1m 21.5s) went fastest.

Barrichello did a 1m 21.9s to be seventh and then he pitted. Like Barrichello, Button was on a three-sprint and climaxed at 1m 22.0s, up from 14th to seventh.

He made a second run, had yellow flags in the final sector and got down to 1m 21.4s. Barrichello responded with 1m 21.5s after finding himself in traffic. That left him 13th and Button tenth.

Rosberg (1m 20.7s) was fastest from Hamilton (1m 20.8s), Webber third and Vettel fourth. Kovalainen did 1m 21.6s.

Q2 began in the most ordinary way, Räikkönen setting an early marker (1m 24.5s) that was soon under attack from Webber and Glock. Button went fifth then Barrichello third – though in traffic again – as Button was bumped down. A dozen cars were so evenly matched that you could be bumped from safety to a clear view of the guillotine very, very quickly.

Button conjured 1m 21.1s, the first time during the weekend that the Brawns had been near the pace. That restored him to fifth. Now think about where the McLarens had been, and were.

Barrichello made his second run, Massa – ninth – behind him. Barrichello explained that 'we had used tyres for the first part of the qualifying and it went quite OK, I was seventh [slight shrug of shoulders]. It wasn't perfect but I was pretty sure we could have made it through and I was really hopeful, because the car felt good this morning. Something broke on the back of the car because on the first lap' – 1m 28.7s – 'it felt strange and I completely lost control of the rear end. I couldn't control it even on the straights. I lost something on the back end of the car because I couldn't complete [the second] lap.'

Q3 was delayed until Massa had been taken from the Ferrari.

Barrichello, 13th, had missed the cut. In view of what happened to his car the Brawn team carried out a thorough precautionary examination of Button's, which meant that he could not venture out until just under three and a half minutes of Q3 remained. 'I thought we would be competitive but unfortunately the work required on the car meant that I was only able to get one run and that was on a heavy fuel load with four more laps of fuel than we had planned.' He managed 1m 22.5s, worth eighth place and, here, a crippling disadvantage.

Alonso (1m 21.5s) had pole from Vettel, Webber third but Hamilton fourth and Kovalainen sixth. The KERS on the McLarens might well take them clean past the Red Bulls into turn 1, which might offer scant consolation for the Brawns – but Formula 1 was thinking about Massa, not hypothetical moves from the grid.

Ross Brawn's insight: 'A very difficult day for the team. Qualifying was going well for both drivers in Q1 and Q2 before Rubens' car had a problem at turn 3 on his final run of the session. We changed the same part on Jenson's car as a precaution just before the start of the final qualifying session. The process was completed as quickly as possible but left

Jenson with only one chance of a flying lap. Having already fuelled the car at the start of Q3, he was therefore considerably heavier than we planned and didn't have a particularly good balance. It is of course frustrating to have qualified in these positions after a good start to the weekend but we have two good strategies and will take advantage of any opportunities which arise to score as many points as possible.'

There was nothing else to do.

The chances of a tried, trusted and tested piece coming off were remote. The chances of it striking another driver who was a long way away from it when it came off were more remote still. The chances that the piece was on the car of one driver from São Paulo and struck the only other from São Paulo were surely beyond any chance you could compute. The whole atmosphere was sharpened and darkened because, only the week before, Henry Surtees – the son of 1964 World Champion John in a Ferrari – had been killed when a wheel came off another car and struck him a fatal blow.

Ross Brawn explained that the spring was 'a fairly heavy object, probably one and a half to two pounds, and obviously at the speed you're doing it's a serious impact. The spring is in the middle of the gearbox and it's connected to the rear suspension. We've had a problem there and we are still understanding exactly what happened. Rubens' car collapsed on to the track and obviously the spring came out of the back of the car. We are investigating what the cause was. The spring is part of a complete assembly. We have raced it all season and it gets subjected to a lot of testing. It's a pretty hard track here but that's not an excuse because it is designed to race at all tracks and we are not seeing any unusual suspension loads. We have been studying the data and there are no reasons for any concerns so we need to understand what happened.'

A Ferrari statement said Massa had had an operation and was stable.

Button was as relaxed as he usually is just before the start, happy to give a television interview when other drivers actively fear distraction and shy away.

From the lights Button moved to mid-track while the cars in

front spread and, reaching towards turn 1, compressed: Alonso cleanly away, Hamilton inside Webber, Button ninth. Räikkönen, feisty, bumped Vettel. Webber retook Hamilton in the exit to turn 1 and they strung out into the procession for the first lap *but* Button had Nakajima directly ahead and needed, absolutely needed, to be past him. He probed and into turn 1 the second time round nosed down the inside, the classical way to do it.

Barrichello was running 18th. 'I had some contact from another car when I turned into the second corner which dropped me to the back of the field. It was always going to be difficult to make progress from there,' he said.

Vettel was told by his pit crew that he might have damage to the front of his car, and he said 'Understood.' He could see Button behind. Completing the lap, Alonso leading:

Webber	@ 1.8s
Hamilton	@ 2.4s
Räikkönen	@ 3.4s
Rosberg	@ 4.5s
Kovalainen	@ 6.4s
Vettel	@ 7.1s
Button	@ 7.6s

That gap from Vettel to Button went out to 1.2 seconds next lap but the real comparison was with Webber who, feisty himself, looked a possible winner. By lap 6 he was into the 1m 23s and, apart from lap 10, would stay in the 1m 23s to lap 18 and his first pit stop. Throughout this span Button stayed consistently in the high 1m 24s. The cumulative difference is enormous in the world of fractions.

Button faced damage limitation and, as further scant consolation, he might anticipate attrition up ahead as the Hungaroring took its toll.

Hamilton forced his way past Webber and set off after Alonso.

'I was heavily fuelled after qualifying and our plan was to get a good start, stay with the cars in front and then I was going longer at the first stop,' Button said. 'After four laps my tyres were destroyed. I just couldn't keep with the cars in front. I'd hoped to stay behind them and when they pitted I could go a lot longer. I don't know what it is that was graining the rear tyres. I don't think you can blame the weather.'

At lap 5, Alonso leading:

Hamilton	@ 2.9s
Webber	@ 4.3s
7 Vettel	@ 8.0s
8 Button	@ 11.0s

Alonso pitted very early – lap 12 – so he'd been running extremely light. A wheel wasn't fitted properly and, as he toured back to the pits, it came off, bounding onto the grass and into the Armco. A loose wheel is like a runaway bull: heavy, totally unpredictable and highly dangerous. How many, seeing it, thought of Henry Surtees? Martin Brundle, whose own son had been in the same race and stood next to John Surtees, was commentating on the BBC and made no mention of any of that but explained how the wheel restraints, designed to prevent a loose wheel from breaking free, didn't work when the wheel nut wasn't attached properly.

Hamilton led from Webber, Vettel up to sixth and Button seventh but only 0.5 of a second from Nakajima. Barrichello toiled in 16th and Alonso toiled round to retirement, cars flooding past him. Hamilton was commanding the race as if it was 2008, and suddenly the comparison to Button was embarrassing *in the other direction.*

On lap 15 Hamilton set a new fastest lap (1m 22.7s). That same lap Button did 1m 24.8s. In the kingdom of fractions…

Nakajima drew up and for a moment or two Button looked vulnerable. The gap which flicked up, 0.1s, only emphasised that.

Webber and Räikkönen pitted on lap 19, the Ferrari crew were slightly quicker and as Räikkönen passed Webber's pit Webber emerged. They almost touched and Webber could not prevent Räikkönen going ahead of him – a significant moment for the championship because if it finished like this it would cost Webber 2 points.

Hamilton and Rosberg pitted the following lap, then Kovalainen and Vettel. Hamilton retained the lead but Button now ran an artificial second to his own pit stop on lap 25, and on the way to it was asked by the team whether he wanted prime or option tyres. He replied 'We know the car doesn't work on prime' – meaning give me another set of the softer tyres for the second stint. Button was stationary for 8.7 seconds and emerged behind Barrichello, who, of course, hadn't stopped. As Button worked through turn 1 he drifted wide and Fisichella thrust his Force India through.

On lap 26 Vettel radioed that something had broken on the car and he couldn't control it any more. He pitted, his race all but over, and Button ran tenth, which became ninth when Fisichella made his first stop.

Button said into the radio 'Guys, I'm already getting oversteer. How can this be so at the moment?' (Later he'd phrase it this way: 'The car just doesn't feel like it did a few races ago.')

Barrichello, who'd started on the prime tyre, pitted on lap 33 and took primes again because Button was struggling with the softer tyre. Barrichello would spend the latter part of the race battling from 13th to tenth with Nakajima and Trulli directly in front and the team urging him to get past for eighth. The single point for that might be valuable in the constructor's as well as his own championship hopes. Both were very much alive.

Barrichello did all he could but lacked the straight-line speed to set up attacks into turn 1 and was held captive by the rest of the circuit's infernal corners. 'There were flashes of pace, particularly during the last stint,' he'd say. At the Hungaroring it was never going to be enough.

Button made his second stop on lap 55 and settled to seventh as they ran to the end. 'It's disappointing because we had high hopes for this race but we were fortunate to come away with two points. We've had two different updates on the car and they shouldn't unbalance it in any way. You can say the others have stepped up their game but' – and he repeated it – 'our car is not what it was to drive a few races ago.'

Ross Brawn's insight: 'Hungary has proved to be a very challenging weekend for the team which has left us with a number of questions to answer regarding the performance of the car. After a positive start on Friday, where we felt that we had a good understanding of the tyres, they proved to be our main area of concern in the race. Both drivers tried different strategies with their tyre choices but we were unable to prevent the graining which affected their pace at crucial stages of the race. We have four weeks until the next race and after our factory shutdown we will be working extremely hard to identify the cause of our recent issues and make the improvements required to return to our early season form.'

Constructor's: Brawn 114, Red Bull 98.5, Ferrari 40, McLaren 28, Williams 25.5, Renault 13.

Driver's: Button 70, Webber 51.5, Vettel 47, Barrichello 44, Rosberg 25.5, Trulli 22.5.

There's another context to consider – the tyres; because we've already heard how Brawn were wrestling with them.

'Tyres are very funny things,' Gary Anderson says, 'because what's important is the energy you put into the tyre – I'm not talking about the tread, I'm talking about the tyre itself. The energy frees up the structure of the tyre. In other words, instead of it seeming like you're driving on a cold and frosty day and the tyres feel hard, it gets to be supple like on a nice summer's day. In putting that energy into the tyre, you make the tyre compliant, allow the tread to grip and the rim of the wheel to be able to move around without breaking that grip. If you just put the energy into the surface of the tyre – the tread – by sliding the car or spinning the wheels or any of that sort of stuff, you actually generate too much surface temperature, which leads to graining.

'The Brawn, in its own way, was very gentle on the tyres at the beginning of this year and the tyres lasted very well during the races – but the bad side of that was that it was always difficult to get the tyres working quickly for a qualifying lap *and* it didn't generate enough temperature.

'Take the example of Toyota. They went from the front of the grid to the back just simply by not getting the tyres working – the tyre is everything you have – so it wasn't just Brawn, there were other teams on the fine line of making it work. What happened to Brawn was they stood back and said "Oh, it's the Silverstone temperature, it's too cold," and then in the Nürburgring the same thing, but in Hungary they got a bit of a shock. They made an excuse to themselves, albeit because they were at tracks which were cold. If they had been at a place where it was hot they would have scratched their heads and probably found a solution.'

But they hadn't.

CHAPTER 9

THE GREAT ESCAPE

There was a month between Hungary and the next race, the European at Valencia, with each team obliged to close for two weeks' holiday – they chose which two weeks. They worked at the factory for the other two weeks, of course, and that gave Brawn time to scratch their heads and find a solution to their problems. (Brawn himself divided his holiday between England and Forte dei Marmi resort in Tuscany.)

After Hungary, Button had 'a long conversation' with race engineer Andrew Shovlin and 'we think we found a few things'.

Meanwhile, Brawn enforced the two-week break by closing down the email system and closing the factory – although, as he pointed out, 'you can't stop people thinking; and clearly that was what happened, because the first meeting we had on Monday after the break everyone was full of ideas.'

When Button reached Valencia for the European Grand Prix he said 'in the time available to them, despite the holiday, the engineers now say they know what the issues are. I trust them. I think we understand the car much better than we did one or two races ago. We have made some steps forward since the last race and I think we have also looked at a few of the areas that we thought we had improved in over the last couple of races. We have looked at the possibility of going back on those changes. It does make it very difficult during the season if you take slightly the wrong direction, because you can't test and you can't do comparisons.

'I think, going through the data, we understand the car – which is the most important thing – and we have made some improvements which should help us a little bit. I know everyone is making improvements. We have got to be on the podium as often as possible, but it is very, very competitive now. You haven't just got the Red Bulls who are strong. You've got the McLarens, the Ferraris, the Renaults, and even the Williams has been competitive. Nico Rosberg has finished in front of me the last three races.'

Ross Brawn, welcoming the hot weather, said 'We are back to dealing with a normal car again. We are just setting the car up around the normal parameters rather than trying to generate tyre heat.' Significantly, he added that 'the programme we have here will be repeated at Spa' – the Belgian Grand Prix a week later and not guaranteed to be hot, let us say. They'd know then if the tyre problem had been cured. The race after that, Monza, was guaranteed to be hot and shouldn't be a problem, he said. Singapore at night might be anything.

In this period – from 23 August in Valencia to Singapore on 27 September – the Brawn team did something deeply astonishing, almost surreal. While the competition caught and overtook them in a great onrush, they contrived – by tactics, determination, self-control, common sense and luck which defied belief – to leave Singapore for Japan with the Constructors' Championship all but won and the Drivers' Championship *still* between Button and Barrichello, only Vettel trailing along behind them.

The first year of the Brawn team proved unique in one aspect: no team before had dominated to such an extent, then fallen so far behind and yet contrived to be *still* in there as if nothing had happened.

At Ferrari, Brawn and Schumacher conjured races.

In 2009, Brawn seemed to be conjuring a whole season.

Barrichello would set the tone for that in Valencia.

The Friday was hot and dry. The air temperature would reach 30°C and the track 50°C, which ought to have suited the Brawns nicely. Although every minute of the 90 in the session was precious – no testing of the changes, remember, no proving whether new ideas were good or bad until now – Button and Barrichello only did installation laps and retreated to the pits. The track was too dirty for serious evaluations: let others go out and clean it, put some rubber down for grip.

Button sat at the rear of the pit wearing a special jacket, full of iced liquid, to prevent him from over-heating. 'The focus of our programme,' he'd say, was to check the car's set up and do back-to-back evaluations 'to confirm that the work done back at the factory after our shutdown was in the right direction.'

Barrichello's car had been set up as it was for the Spanish Grand Prix in May, when it was still dominant, and deployed as a marker: Button's car would be changed according to what Barrichello's was doing. It meant both drivers were following very similar programmes on soft and super soft tyres.

Ross Brawn amplified the strategy for the session. The similar programmes were to revisit 'some set-ups from previous races as test items to increase our understanding of the car's performance'. Brawn was his best phlegmatic self, murmuring 'hellos' to whoever he came across as he strolled round his fiefdom.

At 10:37 Barrichello went out, Button soon after. In the session they'd both complete 19 laps, with Barrichello fastest of all (1m 42.4s) from Kovalainen (1m 42.6s), Hamilton third (1m 42.6s) and Button fourth (1m 43.0s). Vettel was fifth (1m 43.0s) and Webber eighth (1m 43.2s).

Barrichello said: 'It feels great to be back to what seems to be a competitive level of pace.'

The second session – Barrichello 34 laps, Button one less – confirmed that, because although Alonso went quickest (1m 39.4s) Button was next (1m 40.1s) and Barrichello third (1m 40.2s), with Vettel ninth, Webber 14th and poor Hamilton last after damaging a wing.

Button, retreating to English understatement, described the day as 'reasonably good', but Barrichello was more effusive. The two sessions 'went well, with a lot of work achieved on both sides of the garage. I'm pretty happy with the data that we collected and with the way that the car developed over the course of the day.'

Ross Brawn's insight: 'We've had a good start to the weekend with two strong practice sessions. The track temperatures are very high here, reaching 50°C this afternoon, so we have been able to manage our tyre temperatures well and not encounter the issues which have hampered our pace at the past few races.

The initial feedback is that Jenson and Rubens are broadly in agreement on the direction that we should follow from here. We have been able to get a lot of interesting information.'

Sutil went fastest in Saturday practice, Button seventh, Hamilton eighth, Barrichello 12th, Webber 17th and Vettel 18th. That was no more than a prelude for the afternoon and what might prove the most significant qualifying of the season so far – a lot of the session was re-flagged after Vettel had an engine failure and left oil on the track.

Brawn needed to be at the front of the grid facing a street circuit where brake wear was heavy, overtaking was only less problematical than at Monaco, *and* they needed to prove they could get to the front again.

In Q1 Button made a late run, attacking Hamilton's 1m 38.6s (Barrichello had done 1m 39.0s) and went fourth with 1m 39.0s. He moved into a final lap with 37 seconds remaining – Brawn, of course, impassive before the timing screen on the pit lane wall, arms folded. Button did 1m 38.5s, fastest. Then:

Hamilton	1m 38.6s
with	
7 Webber	1m 38.9s
8 Barrichello	1m 39.0s
13 Vettel	1m 38.2s

In Q2, Vettel attacked early as Button went fastest – from Barrichello – and went third. Barrichello responded by going fastest with more than eight and a half minutes left. Almost immediately Hamilton bumped him to second. It left the late rush. Button did a 1m 40s and kept on, a moment later Barrichello did 1m 38.5s – still second to Hamilton's 1m 38.1s. Barrichello tried again: 1m 38.0s. Then:

2 Hamilton	1m 38.1s
with	
4 Vettel	1m 38.2s
6 Button	1m 38.6s
7 Webber	1m 38.6s

In Q3, Hamilton went fastest but Kovalainen was strong too, although halfway through the session Button did 1m 39.9s to be second. That wasn't going to survive as the session tightened, and Button came in, changed tyres. 'Unfortunately I made a mistake at turn 4 on my quick lap which compromised my position.'

Barrichello was travelling fast and attacking. That brought 1m 39.5s, second fastest. He'd gone 'for a slightly different strategy to Jenson' with, at the end, two flying laps against Button's one. 'The second lap,' Barrichello said, 'was perhaps a bit too much for the tyres, which started overheating, and unfortunately I lost the car in turn 8.' Webber went fourth but was about to be bumped: Kovalainen second, Rosberg fifth, Vettel fourth, giving this grid:

Hamilton
1m 39.4s

Kovalainen
1m 39.5s

Barrichello
1m 39.5s

Vettel
1m 39.7s

Button
1m 38.8s

Webber would start ninth (1m 40.2s).

Barrichello was 'really pleased with third place though, and it's great to have the car back to a competitive pace'. He was even, he ventured, disappointed not to be on pole.

Ross Brawn's insight: 'It was a tricky session with track temperatures escalating fast, which meant we had to think on our feet and adapt our plan for Q3 during the break. This might have compromised our performance a little because Rubens' tyres went off on his second lap whilst Jenson had only the one flying lap on his final run. However, third and fifth places on the grid is a strong position and we are generally happy with the performance of the car.'

The race consisted of Barrichello mastering two pressure points and then, at the end, mastering his own emotions to beat the McLarens; Red Bull having a nightmare; and Button retrieving two precious points from a potential disaster.

On the grid before the start, Brawn told the BBC the story would be 'just tyres. The start will be what it is but thereafter it's making the tyres last. I suspect we're going to have some cars around us on the option tyres, which looks pretty marginal – certainly marginal for us with our fuel load, so they might be cars which decide quite a lot in the first stint.'

He said that Barrichello had to be within a few seconds of the McLarens to punish them at the first pit stops. 'Normally we'd just drop back a couple of seconds to let the car cool and not strain the tyres too much – if you get too close to the back of another car you lose the balance of your own car and you can damage the tyres. So we'll drop back a couple of seconds and, nearer the pit stop, try and pick it up.'

Barrichello and Button were on the harder compounds.

From the lights, both McLarens moved strongly on the long, curving run to turn 1, Hamilton ahead, Kovalainen tucked in behind, Barrichello nicely placed behind him. Turn 1 was a right-hander and Barrichello tried to get inside Kovalainen but couldn't. It gave a predictable running order but no less intriguing for that.

Button, however, had been engulfed. He drew level with Vettel but was squeezed, arrived at turn 1 seventh and emerged eighth, in front of Webber but behind Alonso. In turn 5 he was squeezed again and went across the run-off area emerging – again – in front of Webber. He thrust the Brawn down the inside into turn 12 and was past Alonso, but the impetus took him wide and Alonso was back through. Completing the lap, the order behind Hamilton:

Kovalainen	@ 1.5s
Barrichello	@ 2.4s
Räikkönen	@ 2.9s
Vettel	@ 3.5s
Rosberg	@ 4.2s
Alonso	@ 5.0s
Button	@ 6.1s
Webber	@ 6.6s

Because Barrichello was fuelled three laps longer he needed to stay with Kovalainen, so the gaps between the two became pivotal. At lap 2 it stood at 2.6s, two laps later it had come down to 2.1s. By now Button was 11.0 seconds from Hamilton but, of more relevance, 2.3 behind Alonso and visibly *not* closing. Worse, on lap 6 Button was instructed to let Webber through because, in using the run-off area in turn 5, he'd gained an advantage.

On lap 6 the Kovalainen-Barrichello gap had come down to 1.7s, Button now 15.4 seconds from Hamilton. 'I got caught in traffic and it's really tough to overtake around this circuit,' Button said.

On lap 9 the Kovalainen-Barrichello gap stood at 1.6s, but that suggested stalemate.

The Brawn team were telling Button he was faster than Webber and to attack him.

On lap 10 the Kovalainen-Barrichello gap stood at 2.1s, the stalemate unbroken.

Far from attacking, Button continued to drift back from Webber.

On lap 12 the Kovalainen-Barrichello gap stood at 1.8s while Hamilton set a new fastest lap and commanded the race.

Jock Clear, Barrichello's race engineer, said over the radio 'the evidence is that you will be able to go much quicker once Kovalainen gets out of the way' – at his pit stop, of course. As so often in modern Grand Prix racing, pit stops unlocked stalemates.

Was Hamilton commanding the race? On lap 14 the Kovalainen-Barrichello gap stood ay 2.0s *but* Hamilton ran only 6.7 seconds from Kovalainen. The race stretching to 57 laps, Hamilton might *not* be uncatchable. The order as the first pit stops approached remained Hamilton, Kovalainen, Barrichello, Räikkönen, Vettel, Rosberg, Alonso, Webber and Button.

Hamilton pitted on lap 15 and had a smooth stop (9.4s stationary) and fed back in sixth. Barrichello cut the gap to Kovalainen to 1.4s but, of direct significance to Button, Vettel pitted and had a fuel hose problem: no fuel going in and the lollipop man, not knowing this, signalling him away. He'd have to pit again the following lap. Kovalainen pitted and Barrichello, released, set a new fastest lap.

Button pitted and emerged 11th while Barrichello went faster and faster to his pit stop. He was stationary for 9.0 seconds, stayed on the harder tyres and emerged well ahead of Kovalainen. Better, he could *see* Hamilton. He'd try and do to Hamilton exactly what he'd done to Kovalainen – reel him in, establish a stalemate and, when Hamilton pitted, summon more some fast laps. But could he? It was the question of the race.

Webber pitted and remained in front of Button. At least Vettel was running 16th, far from any points or hope of them.

On lap 21 the Hamilton-Barrichello gap stood at 3.2s; and two laps later Vettel's engine failed.

On lap 24 the Hamilton-Barrichello gap stood at 3.6s, although both were doing 1m 41s. A lap later Barrichello cut the gap to 3.2s but these were only fractions within the stalemate.

Button ran ninth, with Fisichella between him and Webber.

The question of the race was being asked a lot harder now. On lap 27 Hamilton forced the gap to 4.3s and constructed a lap of 1m 39.7s, a pace which McLaren thought would be enough to hold Barrichello at bay; but then Hamilton did 1m 39.9s and Barrichello responded with 1m 39.8s. Hamilton responded to *that* with 1m 39.7s – and the gap flicked up at 4.1s – before Hamilton did 1m 39.8s. Barrichello responded to *that* by holding the gap.

Fisichella pitted on lap 31, releasing Button, who was two and a half seconds behind Webber.

Jock Clear told Barrichello he had eight laps to reduce the gap to a couple of seconds. On lap 32 it stood at 4.5.

Button closed on Webber and got to within 1.8.

The question was being answered. Barrichello set a new fastest lap, the gap was down to 3.9. Hamilton responded to *that* with 1m 39.8s, Barrichello doing 1m 40.0s before he set another fastest lap (1m 39.3s), cutting the gap to 3.6 at the end of lap 36. Hamilton pitted and Jock Clear said 'Hamilton is in. Five qualifying laps. Come on, Rubens!'

The Hamilton stop went wrong. Somehow the McLaren crew didn't have the tyres ready and the stop stretched to 13.4 seconds. He emerged fifth.

Barrichello took the fastest lap down to 1m 39.0s and that made Ross Brawn smile.

'In the middle of the race,' Barrichello said, 'they were telling me "push, push, push," and although you are pushing like hell there are some things that go through your mind. You know that you cannot commit any mistakes and you want to do it for yourself, you want to do it for your country and you want to do it for your family. There was a lot going through my mind.'

Barrichello led Hamilton by more than 22 seconds and a pit stop took about 22 seconds...

'Towards the end of the second stint I was able to catch him a little bit and that gave me some margin for those three or four laps that I pushed after he stopped,' Barrichello said. He took the fastest lap down to 1m 38.9s and pitted with the gap 23.4 seconds, which might be very, very tight. He took on super soft tyres and fed back out decisively ahead: four seconds. Hamilton had 17 laps to reclaim those seconds.

Button pitted and emerged on to a clear track. He seized the moment. Webber pitted but he'd been hemmed by traffic on his in-lap, and, as he came out along the snaking pit lane exit, Button swept by. So did Kubica. Webber was out of the points.

Now Barrichello needed his self-control as the first victory since China 2004 came closer and closer. 'I have learnt in the 17 years of my career how to be *not* emotional. I can freeze all my thoughts and just drive and I have been doing that very well. Some mistakes at the beginning of my career were because of these emotional thoughts and so on.' He concentrated, but during 'the last ten laps everything came up in my mind. You hear all the noises. You hear everything and you can see people in the grandstands.'

He handled those last laps like an old master. You could see the sureness of touch, a certain ease rather than urgency as the Brawn flowed between the concrete walls and round the 25 corners – some like chicanes, some no more then bends in the road. He made no semblance of a mistake. When it was done and he'd beaten Hamilton by 2.3 seconds he became emotional, as he was fully entitled to.

On the radio Ross Brawn paid sincere tribute, and in that softening, deepening voice said 'Just like the old days' at Ferrari.

When Barrichello had parked the car, he said: 'After five

years you don't forget how to do it, but it is tough. Great pit stops. Delightful. I wish this moment could be forever. I want to be here for the whole Monday as well, so please stay there.'

Barrichello's contract had not been extended to 2010 but he spoke of his team-mate with a lovely candour. 'Jenson is always very competitive, he's a hard worker. He drives the car very well, very, very smoothly, so you just have to be on the top of your game all the time. I cannot say that yes, from now on it's one way or the other. During the past three years in some areas of the championship he got better and then I got better and the best thing for the team is that we push each other very, very much.'

Button was 'not too disappointed' with seventh.

Ross Brawn's insight: 'We knew that having a heavier fuel load would give us an advantage over the cars in front but Rubens had to drive at his absolute best to have a chance of victory. He pushed exactly where he needed to. When we got on the radio and told him that he had to put in some quick laps, he delivered. It was a great performance and an extremely well deserved victory. We're all delighted for him. Unfortunately it wasn't such a good afternoon for Jenson, who had a quick car but was caught in traffic which prevented him from achieving the result that he could have done. In hindsight perhaps we should have been more aggressive in qualifying, but his two points are valuable and we have increased our lead in both championships.'

They had.

Constructor's: Brawn 126, Red Bull 98.5, Ferrari 46, McLaren 41, Toyota 38.5, Williams 29.5.

Driver's: Button 72, Barrichello 54, Webber 51.5, Vettel 47, Rosberg 29.5, Hamilton 27.

After Valencia, Virgin were reported as moving their sponsorship to the new Manor Grand Prix team for 2010, but Brawn had several major replacements and Fry suggested they might be unveiled at the same moment as the 2010 car. The team emphasised that they did not face funding concerns.

Before Spa, Button reacted pungently when he was asked if he wanted to be World Champion, made a rare sarcastic remark ('No, I want to come second or third') and promised to drive more aggressively after criticism that that's what he hadn't done at Valencia.

Spa was initially confusing, not least because half an hour into the first Friday session it rained. Trulli (1m 49.6s) went fastest from Button (1m 50.2s), Barrichello sixth (1m 52.3s), Webber and Vettel out in the worst of the weather, doing laps with meaningless times well over two minutes. 'It was a tough session because we weren't able to get much done apart from some wet running at the end,' Button said. 'However, that experience is good here just in case it rains over the weekend, which is always possible at Spa.'

Second practice proved quite different, Hamilton (1m 47.2s) quickest, Webber fourth (1m 47.3s), Vettel tenth (1m 47.6s) *but* Button 17th (1m 48.1s) and Barrichello 18th (1m 48.1s).

Button described this session as 'much more useful. We worked through a few aero and downforce comparisons as well as looking at the tyres. We collected a lot of information, but obviously at the moment we're not as quick as we would like to be.'

Barrichello insisted that 'as always on a Friday the lap times don't tell the whole story. The car doesn't feel as competitive as it did in Valencia but we're going to be in a good position to fight hard in qualifying.'

Ross Brawn's insight: 'A good start to the weekend and we were able to achieve much of our planned testing programme despite the interruptions from the weather. We're not experiencing any issues with tyre temperatures so far which is positive, and it's good to see our hard work in this area starting to pay dividends. There is still some way to go to maximise the set-up of the car to the requirements of both drivers, so it will be a busy hour of morning practice to get ready for qualifying.'

That morning session produced a bizarre leader board – Heidfeld quickest (1m 45.3s) from Trulli (1m 45.4s) with Hamilton ninth (1m 46.3s), Button tenth (1m 46.4s), Vettel 14th (1m 46.7s), Barrichello 16th (1m 46.8s) and Webber no time. He had an engine or fuel supply problem – the team wasn't quite sure.

Button was about to have problems himself.

In Q1, the Ferraris went out immediately followed by Fisichella in the Force India. He looked fast and he was (1m 48.3s), setting out a yardstick for the others. Six minutes into the session that had become 12th, with Barrichello tenth and Button 13th. The Toyotas were fastest and doing 1m 46s. Button came out again and moved into a fast lap (1m 46.5s) which put him second. Barrichello appeared as Button crossed the line and went second with 1m 46.2s but things were happening with such rapidity that by then Button was *fourth*. Alonso made that fifth, Räikkönen made that sixth, all in an eye-blink. Heidfeld went third, Rosberg seventh and that made it eighth. Buemi went fastest, making that ninth while Barrichello understeered off on to the grass. Q1 didn't have a shape, it resembled a shooting gallery.

Button made another run and it was worth fourth, Barrichello now second. These could be swept aside in the final charge: with three minutes left virtually every car was out, the leader board jumping. Fisichella finished fastest (1m 45.1s) but by now in the season everything had tightened down the grid, so that Barrichello's third (1m 45.2s) was a fraction better than Webber's fifth and Vettel's sixth (both 1m 45.3s), while Button's 1m 45.7s left him 14th. He couldn't balance the car and it was beginning to show. To add to the confusion, Hamilton – everyone's idea of the man who'd win the Grand Prix – only did a 1m 45.7s too…

Of the three timed sectors, the second – from the straight just before Les Combes, the thundering through Malmedy, the loop of Rivage, the fantastic curve of Pouhon, the right-left Fagnes towards the corner named after famous Belgian journalist and driver Paul Frere – offered a driver a chance to gain time by his positioning of the car, his braking points and (to any ordinary motorist) his sheer courage.

In Q2, Kubica set the yardstick (1m 45.4s), but a moment later Trulli forced that into the 1m 44s. Button was sixth at this point, Barrichello eighth. With eight minutes left Webber went second. Button was being bumped, ninth now, Barrichello (seemingly) safe in fifth. Then the late rush, the leader board jumping again: two minutes left and Button was trying to smooth the Brawn round, but he was slow in the second sector (1.8s off the pace) and crossed the line at 1m 46.8s. He accelerated into a final lap.

Barrichello went sixth and accelerated into a final lap too, but Button had been bumped to 11th. He was slow in the second sector and Rosberg bumped him to 13th. He did 1m 45.2s – staying 13th. Barrichello went third and Sutil 11th, pushing Button down a further place.

Hamilton and Alonso occupied the places immediately below Button, who said he hadn't expected to qualify so low down. He said he'd 'really struggled with grip levels, particularly on the softer tyre'. He added that on the tyre 'I just couldn't find any grip, so the rear end felt unstable and I had no confidence under braking, particularly in the middle sector. I'm a little bit worried because something's seriously not right.'

This put direct pressure on Button, whose season was falling away just as Barrichello's was coming on so strongly.

In Q3, Barrichello continued that strength, although the session finished with, astonishingly, Fisichella on pole from Trulli, Heidfeld third and Barrichello fourth. He'd describe this as 'one of the biggest surprises of the year and it's great for Giancarlo Fisichella to be up there on pole. It's good to see that the "old-timers" still have it! I took the best out of my car today, particularly in Q2, which was one of my best laps around Spa, but that was only enough for sixth position in that session. We've been quite aggressive on the strategy and the race is wide open.'

Ross Brawn's insight: 'This was a challenging qualifying hour and the result is one of the most mixed-up grids of the season, which is great for the sport and will probably make for a very interesting race. Rubens put in another very strong performance, and fourth place on the grid, with an aggressive strategy, puts him in a good position for the race. It's fair to say that qualifying got away from us a little bit with Jenson. We have been struggling with the car balance on his side and we were not able to get the car to a position which he felt comfortable with.'

The race was a struggle, too. From the lights Barrichello had a clutch problem, the grid engulfing him.

Button forced his way up to 11th after what he'd describe as a 'really good start'. He'd made up places and ran ahead of Hamilton and Barrichello. 'I had a good run going down the straight to turn 5 just after Eau Rouge. I was on the outside of Heikki and turned in for the corner but quite simply Romain [Grosjean, Renault] outbraked himself and hit my back wheel.'

Grosjean did not agree, insisting the accident was not his fault. 'I was keeping a good pace but then Button took me out. He squeezed me on to the grass. I tried to pass on the left and he was too busy fighting with Hamilton, didn't see me and hit my wheel.'

Four cars were involved and the Safety Car came out.

The team reacted quickly and brought Barrichello in at the end of the first lap to fuel him longer – effectively, as Ross Brawn says, putting him on to a one-stop strategy.

It was 'a good move and gave me the chance to get into the points,' Barrichello felt. He embarked on a long slog, although he had a moment of 'fun' when he jinked past Webber at Blanchimont. However, an oil leak towards the end – ominous wisps of smoke seeping – suggested he might stop at any moment. He'd been battling Kovalainen for sixth but was now instructed to 'back off and manage the car to the end,' as Brawn explained.

'I have to be happy with seventh place and the two points really after such an eventful race,' Barrichello said.

Ross Brawn's insight: 'It was a very disappointing race when there was potential for more. Rubens' car went into anti-stall at the start, which left him stranded on the grid, which was very frustrating for the whole team. It was a technical problem on the car and we have to get on top of that quickly – it has caught us out too many times this season.'

In the championship a curious thing was happening. No single driver apart from Barrichello was emerging as a direct challenger to Button, although Vettel – third here – remained very much in contention. Räikkönen won from Fisichella in the

Force India. The season's spoils were being spread evenly, and that continued to favour Button.

Constructor's: Brawn 128, Red Bull 104.5, Ferrari 56, McLaren 44, Toyota 38.5, Williams 30.5.

Driver's: Button 72, Barrichello 56, Vettel 53, Webber 51.5, Räikkönen 34, Rosberg 30.5.

By now, wherever the spoils went and whoever got them, the questions about Button were becoming more insistent. A World Championship invariably involves unforeseen pressure points, a slow tightening towards the end, and it makes a man ask fundamental questions about himself. Was Button *really* a champion, capable of mastering all this? Monza seemed an ideal place to feel for the answer because it was fast, Bridgestone were making noises that the tyre temperatures weren't the problem and – with 50 points still in play over the remaining five races – if Button kept failing and somebody put a strong run together, everything would change.

Button, however, pointed out that as each race went by his lead became more and more difficult to overhaul. Suddenly, he looked and spoke like the man from early season as if he saw everything with a steady eye again. He pointed out that the five remaining races could be treated as an entity and he was taking a 16-point lead in.

Ross Brawn confirmed publicly that both drivers were 'free to race. We feel that is what will take the team forward in a stronger way than having any team orders. They are both free to try and win the championship. I think Jenson has had two races where it hasn't worked for him. The last race he obviously had the incident, and Valencia wasn't great, but the previous races really the car was not working as well as we wanted, so I don't think you can really lay those races at Jenson's door. He has had a couple of average races and I think over the season if a guy has a couple of average races as well as all the good ones he has had a fantastic season. I am pretty optimistic that he is going to have a strong run to the end of the season.'

I do not believe in clairvoyants but after these words, and after Monza, you'd have to wonder...

In first practice Button did 21 laps (Barrichello 24) to be seventh – Barrichello 12th.

Hamilton went quickest (1m 23.9s) in the first, Button seventh (1m 24.7s), Webber ninth (1m 24.7s), Barrichello 12th (1m 24.8s), Vettel 18th (1m 25.9s). Sutil, confirming Force India's progress, went quickest (1m 23.9s) in the second, Webber 14th (1m 24.89s), Barrichello 16th (1m 25.1s), Vettel 18th (1m 25.3s) and Button 19th (1m 25.4s).

Barrichello explained that 'our set-up work was focused on long runs. I'm fairly happy with how the car feels and with the braking stability. We have some work to do on the balance but overall a good start.' He added that the practices did not point to what might happen in qualifying.

Button had a couple of small problems that restricted his running. He added: 'It feels very different running with such low downforce but the car has been performing reasonably well. We need to work on the fine-tuning of the set-up overnight.'

Ross Brawn's insight: 'With Monza being such a unique low-downforce circuit and the fact that we haven't had the opportunity to test here, the practice sessions were particularly important to work on the set-up of the car. Our main focus has been on race preparation to ensure that we understand how the car feels with the low downforce.'

In Saturday third practice Sutil went quickest (1m 23.3s) from Button (1m 23.4s), Barrichello fourth (1m 23.5s), the Red Bulls far away: Webber 17th, Vettel 18th.

Brawn commented that 'we ran the car on low – or lower fuel – and we seem to be there or thereabouts. It's a simple track because there are so few corners but it's also a driver's track. You get one braking wrong and your quick lap's ruined.'

Qualifying held all manner of significance, at the time and subsequently.

In Q1, Räikkönen set an early marker (1m 24.8s), and after five and a half minutes Barrichello went sixth. He moved into a faster lap and while he was doing this Button went third. Barrichello crossed the line at 1m 24.0s to be fastest. Button continued into a faster lap and went quicker than anyone so far in the second sector. He crossed the line at 1m 24.1s, moving in behind Barrichello. Slightly less than 13 minutes remained and, as a constant throughout the season, we have seen how the running order can change like machine-gun fire, *but* the Brawns at the very top suggested they were back on the pace.

As if to demonstrate precisely that, Räikkönen did a 1m 23.6s and Heidfeld sneaked between the Brawns. Barrichello responded to *that* with 1m 23.4s, Button already bumped to seventh, soon to become eighth ... soon to be fastest with a low 1m 23.4s...

Hamilton was doing a 1m 23.3s.

With three and a half minutes remaining all 20 cars were out on the track, Webber vulnerable in 19th although Vettel had managed tenth. Webber went ninth and Räikkönen fastest. The Brawns *were* back on the pace and for this you need three decimal places.

Räikkönen	1m 23.349s
Hamilton	1m 23.375s
Button	1m 23.403s
Barrichello	1m 23.483s

In Q2 Button went out immediately, and here it was again after so long – the smoothness, the economy of movement on the steering wheel. He did a 1m 24.6s with power to add. Barrichello did 1m 24.1s. Button did add, 1m 23.4s, Alonso and Barrichello into the 1m 23s as well. Then Barrichello did 1m 22.9s and near the end Webber did, too. Astonishingly Webber went third, a position Button took from him with 1m 23.1s. Both Brawns were on the track and Button summoned 1m 22.9s to be fastest. Webber finished sixth, Vettel tenth, which suggested *they* were not back on the pace.

Button	1m 22.955s
Hamilton	1m 22.973s
Barrichello	1m 22.976s

In Q3 both cars ran on the prime tyre and with heavy fuel loads. They each put together one run of three flying laps to fill the third row with 15 hundredths of a second between them. Of the four cars ahead – Hamilton, Sutil, Räikkönen and Kovalainen – three had KERS (Sutil didn't), and three were on a two-stop strategy (Kovalainen wasn't).

The Brawns were on one-stop. Ross Brawn felt the one-stop was 'the logical choice, but a number of teams have decided on two stops and there are going to be two races going on. They'll come together towards the end of the race.' This was not clairvoyance but straightforward race reading, although expressed with almost beautiful simplicity. It was how it would happen.

Barrichello felt his lap for fifth on the grid was 'probably one of my best qualifying laps at Monza and I really enjoyed myself out there. We had the ability to be on pole today but strategically we had to consider the pace of the KERS cars off the line, and so we put a lot of fuel in the car and focused on what was right for our race.'

Button, happy to have done his time with the heavy fuel load, quipped that the 15-hundredths must have been because Barrichello literally kept his head down on the straights to minimise wind resistance and 'obviously I didn't do it enough'. He was joking. Wasn't he?

Ross Brawn's insight: 'An excellent performance from Rubens, Jenson and the team put us in a good position for the race. We have the majority of the KERS cars just ahead of us, so provided our drivers get a good start there is everything to play for.'

Vettel qualified ninth and Webber tenth, the impetus gone from Red Bull.

Barrichello started on medium tyres (as did Kovalainen); Button, Hamilton, Räikkönen and Sutil on soft.

The long, wide run from the grid to the dangers of the first chicane is annually a race within a race, cars weaving and jostling, probing, gaining and losing during the seven seconds it takes them to get there after the red lights go off. They threaded though and stretched into the parkland Hamilton,

Räikkönen, Sutil, Barrichello, Kovalainen, Button – Vettel ninth, Webber tenth.

Barrichello enjoyed 'a great start to get ahead of Heikki and from there I had the pace that we needed'.

Button set about Kovalainen on the inside into the second Lesmo corner, stayed firmly on the inside and that set a tone. The timidity was gone and the racing driver was back. Button judged the move 'absolutely crucial for my race'.

Webber was physically gone after an argument with Kubica that ended against the Armco. Hamilton led over the line:

Räikkönen	@ 1.2s
Sutil	@ 1.8s
Barrichello	@ 3.4s
Button	@ 3.9s

Vettel was drifting back and the Red Bull challenge was drifting away.

Hamilton set fastest lap and increased his gap to Räikkönen to 1.8s, Barrichello at 5.1s, Button at 5.8s. Hamilton needed this because he had to gain the equivalent of a pit stop. Hamilton set another fastest lap and, at lap 4, led Räikkönen by 2.8s – Barrichello at 7.6s, Button at 9.2s. A lap later Hamilton forced that to 8.5s over Barrichello and 10.5s over Button. This pace was enough to give Hamilton the race. He reinforced that with another fastest lap (1m 25.3s, which was moving towards qualifying pace).

Button fell away from Barrichello.

Shovlin told Button on the radio: 'We need you and Rubens within about nine-tenths' of Hamilton. Button had done a 1m 26.6s, Hamilton now did a 1m 25.2s, giving a difference of 1.4s. Button *had* to go faster. At lap 7:

Räikkönen	@ 4.0s
Sutil	@ 5.1s
Barrichello	@ 11.0s
Button	@ 13.6s

Barrichello was now 'holding' Hamilton within the nine-tenths but Button wasn't. Might that be tyres? At lap 9, Barrichello held the gap at 12.4s, Button 15.9s. Button did increase his pace, doing 1m 26.1s, but was still seven-tenths from Hamilton. At lap 11:

Räikkönen	@ 5.3s
Sutil	@ 6.7s
Barrichello	@ 13.4s
Button	@ 16.6s

That lap, Barrichello 'held' Hamilton to 0.6 of a second. He adored Monza, and now, like the old master, he would demonstrate the adoration, using all the track and all the Brawn. He wasn't driving against a physical opponent, to be caught and overtaken, he was racing *time*. At lap 12 the gap had extended, but only by 0.7s, and these fleeting fractions might be enough to take the race from Hamilton and give it to Barrichello.

Hamilton set another fastest lap, his sixth, and the gap to Barrichello elongated to 16.1s. Hamilton set a seventh ... the gap 17.0s. He pitted on lap 15, was stationary for 7.8 seconds, and all Monza waited to see where he'd rejoin: fifth, and 4.8 seconds behind Button.

Sutil pitted and Button was on the move, into the mid 1m 25s. This was quicker than Barrichello as Räikkönen pitted. Barrichello was 2.8s ahead of Button, who was 7.6 ahead of Hamilton.

Button would pit on lap 28, Barrichello a lap later. On the way to this Button began to catch Barrichello and shed Hamilton. Shadows from the trees lay across the track like geometrical patterns now, the sun glinted from between the trees and the Brawns, circling imperiously together at 1m 25.2s, were seizing the race. They were even matching each other in sector times.

Hamilton was getting a radio message setting out that he needed another 'three or four tenths' to beat the Brawns. Button shaved fractions from Barrichello's lead in all three sectors of a lap by 0.081, 0.028 and 0.080. A gap flicked up, 1.9s.

Hamilton lay 12 seconds away.

Barrichello set a new fastest lap, Button all but matching it before he pitted. Then Barrichello pitted, and when he fed back in Button was back in the middle distance.

Hamilton had only five laps before he pitted a second time and needed to gain something like ten seconds over Barrichello. Even he couldn't do that, although you could see how hard he was working the McLaren. He pitted and emerged behind both Brawns with 19 laps left – 3.4 seconds from Button. With 16 laps left, nine seconds covered the three leaders. It had become visual: the Brawns down the start-finish straight, Hamilton coming into view. With 15 laps left he cut the gap to Button to three seconds.

Barrichello led by 5.3 seconds. He looked very safe, even if Hamilton found a route past Button. Hamilton got the gap down to 2.4 seconds, then 2.2.

Ross Brawn gazed at the screen in front of him and sipped mineral water from a plastic bottle. He saw Button was 'very tidy' as Hamilton pushed him – and in fact it was Hamilton who looked ragged.

Hamilton got the gap down to 1.8 seconds but Button responded, opened the gap – a little. Hamilton now did the fastest first sector of anybody on lap 44 of the 53, and although Button was travelling faster than Barrichello, Hamilton had the gap down to 1.6.

Button was holding him and doing his own best lap, 1m 24.9s. That gave a gap of 1.9 and Button was slicing fractions from Barrichello, so that less than six seconds covered the three cars.

'Lewis was pushing hard behind me for the final part of the race but I was confident that I had him covered and it's a very difficult circuit to overtake here, even with KERS,' Button said. It was a confidence shared by Ross Brawn, who felt Button had the situation firmly under control.

Hamilton, 1.7 seconds behind Button, was poised to make a supreme effort. For three laps he gained and, as it would seem, might be in a position to strike at any moment. On the last lap he had the gap down to a second, but he lost the McLaren and thundered the Armco. 'I was pushing incredibly hard on that lap to try to get close to Jenson and use KERS to pass him, then I exited the first Lesmo and the back-end got away from me and I went backwards into the wall.'

Vettel was eighth, his championship very remote at 26 points behind Button.

Barrichello was openly delighted with the circuit, the car, the Mercedes engine, the team, his sons (who had just had birthdays) and the world in general. 'It's going to be a good and healthy fight for the championship over the next few races and I'm really looking forward to that. Two wins in three races is pretty good going and I'll be giving it my all.'

Button was openly delighted to be back on the podium again. 'The car worked very well all weekend and the balance was good throughout the race, which meant I could set consistently quick lap times when it really mattered.'

Both drivers paid tribute to the strategy and how efficient it had proved.

Ross Brawn's insight: 'Refuelling is *still*, after all these years, an opportunity. Everyone is very competent now and they've got all their modelling and their statistics. All of that has become much more refined, and the ability to do something a little bit different or gain an advantage is reduced, but there *are* still opportunities. You saw that at Monza. We took the conservative approach, but in fact the conservative approach was the adventurous approach – it was more nerve-wracking standing out in qualifying with a load of fuel on the car wondering how far up from tenth you could manage. And, when it's five and six, you know you are all right. If we'd fuelled lightly we would, I am sure, have had a good, strong possibility of getting on pole, but that wasn't the objective so it was a game plan for the whole weekend that worked very nicely. I do enjoy that side of my business.

'I am very pleased with how Monza was planned and operated. The car worked well in low-downforce and the Mercedes-Benz engine gave us the power required for such a high-speed circuit.'

Nick Fry's insight: 'In my mind Monza wasn't so much *we're back on it* because I don't think we ever doubted we would come back. People made a little bit too much of it. Remember, we won in Valencia only a couple of races previously.

'Obviously the media have to make a story, but we got very used to ignoring what people were saying over the winter period because there were so many rumours – many of them completely stupid. Most of what was said was rubbish even in some very well respected newspapers. So we got used to ignoring most of it, saying nothing, telling the staff to ignore it, and that stood us in good stead through 2009 - because, you know, when we won a lot it was inevitable that the next story, when we didn't win, would be *their world's come to pieces*. That was never the case. A good car doesn't become a bad car overnight, and good drivers don't become bad drivers overnight.

'Monza was special because it really was a demonstration of how the team has matured, in that even though we won some of the early races some areas weren't perfect. We had little glitches at the pit stops or other little things but we were so superior we got away with it. Monza was operationally an absolutely blemish-free performance. The way the engineers worked on Friday was a wonder to behold, and sitting in the engineering meetings after the practice sessions you really had the feeling of a group of people – the drivers, the engineers, Ross – who were completely and utterly on it. Even when we were right at the back of the grid on Friday afternoon, no one worried about it. We were doing our programme, we were getting on with the job, and we were getting the data that we wanted. I repeat: no one worried about it.'

Ross Brawn would add to that, saying: 'It is always a little bit difficult to hold your nerve. Friday we were running 70 kilos and we were right at the bottom of the order, but the analysis said we still looked OK.'

'You don't worry about what the others are doing and we have been like that right throughout the year,' Fry says. 'We have tried to completely ignore, as best you can, some of the other things that are going on – the ones that were nothing to do with us. Our view was "we don't need to comment, we don't need to talk about it so let's get on and do our job".'

Constructor's: Brawn 146, Red Bull 105.5, Ferrari 62, McLaren 47, Toyota 38.5, Williams 30.5.

Driver's: Button 80, Barrichello 66, Vettel 54, Webber 51.5, Räikkönen 40, Rosberg 30.5.

Without in any way tempting fortune, you could say that the Brawn team were going to be very, very difficult to beat in the constructor's, and that – barring the totally unforeseen – either Button or Barrichello would win the World Championship in the remaining four races: Singapore, Japan, Brazil and Abu Dhabi. It seemed a good moment to ask for Ross Brawn's thoughts, gazing backwards and forwards.

The period off the pace is over.

'What you tend to do is overcompensate, you try too hard. It's a funny thing to say, but you've got the basic fundamentals although you're a *little* bit off, and in trying to make that up you lose a lot more.'

Jenson has come from nowhere to, in 2009, handling it in a most extraordinarily accomplished way.

'I think we do underestimate the ability of the guys in Formula 1, because they have all been exceptional where they have come from. They have all won championships or won loads of races or they wouldn't be there. Very few have not had stellar careers before they got into Formula 1, so it's kind of reigniting what's within them anyway, and which they have proven is within them, but they've never had the equipment to display it again.'

You've got to let him find it for himself again.

'Yes, you have.'

You can't find it for him.

'No, but you can create the best environment to allow him to do that.'

Rubens has driven beautifully this season.

'Yes. Very good, as good as I've ever seen, to be honest. The thing that is impressing me with him is his ability to push during the races. I know we didn't have the equipment last year but there were several occasions when you'd get on the radio and you'd say,

"Look, Rubens, this is the crucial bit of the race, you've got to find some time," and it never seemed to come. You'd get the "I'm doing everything I can, you guys don't understand what it's like." Now, when you say it, you just get "OK," and his times come down. That's the difference. I know he's got the equipment and he didn't have it before, but I always believe a driver can find that extra when you make it clear to him he needs to. What I see with him is that extra that is coming during the races in particular – because he has always been a quick qualifier. Driving a car quickly for 50 or 60 laps is a bit different, and so is building a race as he did at Valencia and at Monza, where you are working to gaps and strategic targets, not working to the guy in front, trying to stay with him. His ability to do that, certainly in the recent races, has been very impressive.'

How are you going to cope with the two of them?

'It is the perennial problem and I'll just remind them that history is littered with two team-mates destroying each other and the guy who was third walking through and picking up the main prize. I hope they are too sensible for that. The most recent example was Kimi when he won the championship in 2007. It should have been Fernando [Alonso] or Lewis [Hamilton], by a mile but in their squabbles they let Kimi come through.

'You can't have team orders, not while there is still the possibility of either Jenson or Rubens winning. If we reach a stage where one can't win, and we've still got the constructor's open, then you say, "Look, guys, we've got to consolidate and there is absolutely no point in us doing otherwise."'

Button described Singapore as a 'tough' circuit 'with the heat and humidity to contend with.' Its nature and the closeness of the barriers 'demand your total concentration'. Yes.

This needs exploration, because, as Formula 1 went to Singapore, these same barriers were the centrepiece in a scandal at Renault which, by a truly destructive irony, had taken place at the same circuit the year before but was only revealed in mid-summer 2009. The complete details were subject to dispute but the essentials were clear: Flavio Briatore, strategist Pat Symonds and Nelson Piquet Junior conspired in a plan which involved Piquet deliberately crashing to bring the Safety Car out on lap 15 – which favoured team-mate Alonso. He'd qualified 15th, pitted three laps earlier, and when the Safety Car pulled off ran fifth. He won.

The scandal, initially difficult to believe, provoked a media storm with respected journalists asking if it was the worst case of cheating in the *history of sport* because, potentially, it was life-threatening as well as all the other betrayals it embraced.

Formula 1 badly needed a clean race weekend now, but in first practice Piquet's replacement, Grosjean, crashed at the same place. This *was* unbelievable, making even Briatore's successor, Bob Bell, smile.

The first two practices were, to borrow from cricket, a day-night match. The first started in what the Brawn team described as 'relative daylight which darkened over the course of the 90 minutes', and the second in 'full darkness'. Ross Brawn said that 'the whole team are enjoying the unusual hours that we are working and adjusting our race weekend programme to suit the particular demands of the night race.'

In first practice Barrichello went fastest (1m 50.1s) from Button (1m 50.3s), Webber third (1m 50.4s) and Vettel fifth (1m 50.6s), but during the second Barrichello and Button concentrated on evaluating the soft and super soft tyres.

In the second practice Vettel went quickest (1m 48.6s), Button fifth (1m 49.311s), Webber next (1m 49.317s), Barrichello 11th (1m 49.6s). He said: 'It was really busy out there with traffic affecting our programme a little, particularly in the second session, but that was the same for everyone really. We've been focusing on our pace for Sunday and that's the most important consideration.'

Ross Brawn's insight: 'We're pleased with how the two practice sessions went. Both Jenson and Rubens are feeling comfortable with the car and the reliable running throughout both sessions has provided us with a wealth of data to study into the early hours of the morning. This is a circuit which should suit our car provided we get the balance and set-up right for qualifying.'

Then in qualifying it went wrong, bringing the pressure back.

Even Ross Brawn, wiping sweat from his forehead, said 'it was a disastrous session for us'.

In third practice Hamilton, as expected, went fastest (1m 47.6s) from Vettel (1m 47.9s), Barrichello seventh (1m 48.5s) and Button 14th (1m 48.9s). One report described Button's mood as 'angry and frustrated' because he couldn't find the right balance for the car. The fact that he'd had to go to hospital overnight to have a shard of fibreglass removed from an eye can't have helped, nor that Red Bull were running strongly again.

Before qualifying, Ross Brawn explained that the team decided to change Barrichello's gearbox because Singapore was so heavy on them and 'further dyno simulations had shown that keeping the 'box was too risky' – it had already caused concern at Monza, where they saw 'worrying signs'. That meant that Barrichello would drop five grid places, wherever he qualified.

In Q1 and under the floodlights, Fisichella came out early – he was still exploring the Ferrari – and Alonso set the first marker at 1m 50.1s. Button emerged after four minutes and went fastest (1m 48.6s). Barrichello was then seventh, moved into another lap and pitched the car through the circuit's 23 corners. He did 1m 47.9s to go fastest. Hamilton was the real marker, the McLaren smooth, almost sensuous – but Button was out at the same time. Hamilton crossed the line at 1m 47.2s, Button at 1m 47.5s – third, with Vettel in between them.

Hamilton, on the harder tyre, took the marker down to 1m 46.9s and that set up the final rush. Button took it on – he was now seventh – and went second (1m 47.1s), Barrichello on a lap but from 15th. He took the car to sixth (1m 47.3s), Vettel seventh (1m 47.5s).

'The car felt pretty good,' Button said, although he had some understeer. The team changed that before Q2.

Button came out early following Vettel, who did 1m 51.9s. As he crossed the line there was Button, rounding the final corner. He did 1m 47.4s. A moment later Barrichello went fastest, 1m 47.1s. The track was getting faster as rubber went down and the times reflected that, because, in an eye-blink or two, Barrichello was down to third and Button fifth. It didn't look at all ominous but several eye-blinks further on Barrichello was down to eighth and Button tenth, Vettel second. Then Kubica pushed Button to 11th and Heidfeld to 12th.

Button started his final run from 13th, the full pressure on him. He set a personal best in the first sector and his time at the second sector would give him tenth place but the third sector settled it: 1m 47.1s represented 11th. Barrichello was slow and both Brawns moved into a final thrust. Button locked up his wheels and, 12th, was out. Barrichello ran wide and over kerbing at turn 10 but recovered to sixth.

Barrichello explained that 'it was a great lap because we were struggling for pace and I knew that I had to push regardless of any damage'.

Button explained that the changes to try and solve the understeer unfortunately 'made the car very difficult under braking and I locked the front left tyre up into turn 7, which lost me a lot of time. Then, with a flat-spotted front tyre, it's impossible to make the time up around here, so that was my qualifying over.'

Hamilton duly took pole from Vettel, Barrichello a strong fifth, although he felt he must have damaged the floor over the kerbing because 'the car wasn't feeling quite right at the end of the session'. Barrichello needed, of course, to be as high up the grid as possible with the five places drop, and that brought its own pressure. He reached turn 5, a sharp right-hander. 'I was really going for it on my final run and unfortunately the car bottomed out. I lost control and ended up bouncing off the wall.'

Ross Brawn's insight: 'I think we underestimated the competition in Q2 because we used one old set and then one new set of tyres and we didn't get the car balanced while we were on the new set, so we were perilously close to losing both cars in Q2. Rubens put in a good lap at the end to progress.'

Those who enjoy mental arithmetic were calculating that, with overtaking opportunities strictly rationed, Vettel could win it if he made a good start and both Brawns might not reach the points, however lowly. That would put Vettel only two points behind Barrichello and only 14 behind Button with three races, and a maximum 30 points, remaining.

Nick Heidfeld had qualified his BMW eighth but it was found to be underweight. The engine and gearbox were changed and he'd start from the pit lane. That moved the Brawns up one place *and* to the cleaner side of the track.

Ross Brawn described this as making him 'thankful for small mercies'.

Button was fuelled long – almost ten laps further than Barrichello – and by then all the leaders would have made their first stops. That might give Button openings and possibilities to exercise damage limitation. It was about all he could hope for.

From the lights Hamilton started well while Rosberg nosed in behind from the second row, all the cars threading through the initial left-right-left giving an immediate order of Hamilton, Rosberg, Vettel, Alonso, Webber, Glock, Barrichello, Kovalainen, Kubica and Button. It meant Button had found a way past Nakajima. Doing that, Button said, 'really made my race'.

Completing the lap Barrichello was already 7.4 seconds from Hamilton and Button 9.6.

'I had a great start to make up two places and everything was going well in the first stint,' Barrichello said.

By lap 3 Webber had overtaken Glock and both had overtaken Alonso while Barrichello and Button circled, calmly and methodically, on the long, hot journey to the first pit stops. Barrichello was already – this is lap 4 – 12.8 seconds from Hamilton and Button 18.0. Hamilton controlled the race, Rosberg stayed with him and Vettel stayed with Rosberg, the Brawns lost in another, distant world.

Button was held by Kovalainen, which he found 'quite frustrating' especially since he could see Barrichello moving away. At 11 laps Barrichello was 23 seconds from Hamilton and Button 29.

Vettel pitted on lap 17 and emerged behind Barrichello. Rosberg pitted a lap later and emerged fourth, but as he came from the pits he crossed the white boundary line. That would cost him a drive-through penalty. While he waited for that to be confirmed he ran wide into a corner and Barrichello was through.

The order: Hamilton, Glock, Alonso, Barrichello, Rosberg, Vettel, Kubica, Kovalainen, Button.

Glock and Barrichello pitted together and would run ninth and tenth.

Hamilton pitted, and a moment or two later – lap 21 – Sutil in the Force India tried to overtake Jaime Alguersuari (Toro Rosso), spun, and clouted Heidfeld, spreading debris everywhere. The Safety Car came out, wrecking Button's strategy. Nobody knew the great escape had begun.

Button said the Safety Car 'made it very difficult because I still had fuel for a few more laps and should have been able to make up two places at my first stop'. He pitted immediately and emerged eighth, although still behind Kovalainen. The Safety Car pulled off, Rosberg did the drive-through and emerged 14th. Vettel was running just over a second behind Hamilton. At lap 29, Hamilton leading:

Vettel	@ 0.8s
Glock	@ 5.0s
Alonso	@ 7.2s
Barrichello	@ 10.6s
Kovalainen	@ 11.5s
Button	@ 12.5s

The Hamilton-Vettel duel became, naturally, the focal point of the race, one young man pitted against another – and young Glock was gaining on both of them, the gap down to 4.2 seconds. Who noticed Button? 'I had to put in some quick laps before my second stop to close up to Rubens.' Who noticed Barrichello?

Vettel made his second stop with 22 laps left and fed back in seventh, behind Button. Vettel was under investigation for speeding in the pit lane *and* he ran heavily over a kerb, smashing his diffuser. He was given a drive-through and emerged from it ninth.

With 16 laps left Webber had a brake problem and head-butted the barrier, taking any lingering championship hopes with him.

The second pit stops were under way, Barrichello in a lap after Webber crashed but 'unfortunately I had a problem when I couldn't engage neutral and the engine stalled, which lost me the crucial time needed to stay ahead of Jenson.'

McLaren gambled on a Safety Car after the Webber crash

and brought Kovalainen in. Astonishingly that promoted Button to third and Barrichello to seventh. Button, with super soft tyres available, started doing laps of 1m 48.7s. Were they enough to pit and leapfrog Barrichello? Button went even faster, finessing the car to the circuit and did 1m 48.5s.

Button pitted with a 17½-second lead over Vettel, which wasn't enough. He was stationary for 6.4 seconds and fed out fifth, behind Vettel but in front of Räikkönen and Barrichello.

Ten laps remained. Räikkönen made his second stop and now the three championship leaders were together: Vettel fourth, Button fifth, Barrichello sixth.

Button was told on the radio that the Brawn team believed Vettel had brake problems. In fact Button would suffer brake problems himself on the run to the end and backed off to be safe. Ross Brawn came on the radio and told Button just to get the car to the finish, to which Button replied with a chirpy 'Roger!'[1]

Barrichello was complaining about the brakes too. They were 'struggling and I couldn't fight any more'.

And that was the great escape.

Ross Brawn described it as a good recovery from qualifying despite the Safety Car 'not playing into our hands', which was one of his nice understatements.

Hamilton won it imperiously. The story, though, was Button emerging from an understated weekend having lost but one point to Vettel and actually gained one over Barrichello.

Constructor's: Brawn 153, Red Bull 110.5, Ferrari 62, McLaren 59, Toyota 46.5, Williams 30.5.

Driver's: Button 84, Barrichello 69, Vettel 59, Webber 51.5, Räikkönen 40, Hamilton 37.

Notes

1. The traditional use ('Roger, over and out') seems to be of military origin. The letter 'R' was used in Morse code to signify 'I have understood', and expanding the R to 'Roger' would be sensible for vocal communication. It used to be commonly heard in movies, but sounds rather dated now.

CHAPTER 10

AMAZING GRACE

At Suzuka, Jenson Button could become Britain's tenth World Champion, and the whole season resolved itself into a great simplicity. He needed only to finish five points ahead of Barrichello and Vettel. The Brawn team had their own simplicity. They needed four points to win the constructor's.

In the background, rumours circulated that Mercedes were buying into the team and Button hadn't had his contract renewed for 2010. Nor had Barrichello.

Piquet Junior's crash continued to bring fallout because journalists scoured the recent past for comparisons, and in that matter all roads led to Ayrton Senna and his crashes with Alain Prost in 1989 and 1990. Then, of course, there were Michael Schumacher's journeys down similar roads.

Inevitably, Button was asked questions within that framework and said it 'was Schumacher. It's not me.' He set out his creed: *it would be like robbing a bank or taking a short cut in a running race.* 'You would always think "I got this title but I cheated." What is the point of that?'

Both Brawn drivers had been scrupulous down all these years in *not* playing dodgem cars with anybody. Both were *non*-controversial figures in any racing sense (whilst allowing Barrichello a tantrum or two). They raced hard, invariably did *not* complete their weekend explaining their innocence to the Stewards and, in this Grand Prix season of so many sore and running wounds, they were proving you could still do that.

Button also said: 'It sounds silly but it is a bit of a rollercoaster when you're fighting for a championship, and it's been a long time since I've been fighting for a championship, so you do forget, but if it was easy we'd all be doing it. It's part of the challenge, it's a sport that is very emotional for me. I've always loved motor racing since I was very, very young, and being in the position I'm in I'm certainly very privileged and very lucky to be fighting for a championship. I also have some great people around me who keep me grounded and focussed.'

Unfortunately the weather on the Friday grounded just about everybody. The morning session started wet and finished dry, both Brawn drivers working with the intermediate and wet tyres. Kovalainen went fastest (1m 40.3s), Barrichello ninth (1m 41.8s) and Button 18th (1m 43.3s). Heavy rain drowned the afternoon and the Brawns didn't venture out.

Ross Brawn's insight: 'As the weather forecast shows a dry qualifying and race – and with limited wet weather tyres – we felt that there was nothing further to be learnt from running again.'

In third practice Trulli went fastest (1m 31.7s), Vettel fourth (1m 32.414s), Barrichello seventh (1m 32.488s) and Button ninth (1m 32.6s).

Qualifying was chaotic (Ross Brawn's own description) and at times almost surreal, something which continued afterwards and had a direct impact on Button and Barrichello.

Because Friday had been washed out the teams were restricted to the third practice to explore and improve their cars, rather than doing it in careful increments. It wasn't long enough, and as the drivers went to what they thought represented the limit – qualifying now so close this season that hundredths of a second were important – they found themselves beyond it, and found that Suzuka, massively refurbished, had very fast corners and very short, gravel-bedded run-off areas. This was the recipe for the chaos and Webber had already crashed in the morning. He would take no part in the qualifying.

In Q1 Button came out less than two minutes into the session and almost immediately Buemi lost the Toro Rosso in Degner 1, a high-speed sharp right. He backed into the tyre wall but was able to continue. Button moved into a fast lap and did 1m 33.1s, which wouldn't keep him safe. Trulli exposed that with 1m 31.8s to be fastest, but Button stayed out and went second. Barrichello was out as Vettel set a new pace, 1m 31.6s.

Everything was nicely normal.

Trulli increased the pace and Barrichello went third before Kovalainen went through Degner 1 spinning nose-to-tail. Vettel increased the pace again (1m 30.9s), the first driver to get below 1m 31s so far during the weekend and next lap shaved a tenth from that – Barrichello already bumped to fifth, Button to seventh, which became tenth with just over seven minutes left.

With two and a half minutes left Barrichello, now 12th and a place above Button, was on the track and so was Button. Barrichello went fifth as Button approached the line and crossed it third. Vettel remained fastest.

Everything was still nicely normal.

Button ventured into Q2 with the soft tyres but, three minutes in, Jaime Alguersuari lost control of his Toro Rosso at the by now dreaded Degner 1. He ploughed the tyre wall head first, halting the session. That meant Button's lap had to be aborted and *that* meant he'd lose time coming in and lose more time going out again when the session resumed.

He emerged almost immediately and by now everything was anything but nicely normal. With less than nine minutes left only Räikkönen had actually managed a fast lap. An instant later, Glock's Toyota speared the tyre wall at the final corner, halting the session again. Only Trulli and Räikkönen had fast laps.

Glock was helicoptered to hospital with a leg injury.

The Brawns would wait until the very end. They came out together with just over two minutes of the session left, giving them single flying laps. Vettel went quickest (1m 30.3s) as the Brawns began. They were slow in the first sector but the track, as they say, came to them. They reached the exit of the corner called evocatively Spoon and, at the exit, were among debris because Buemi had run along the Armco and his front wing lay in the middle of the track. Yellow flags were waved but both Brawns pressed on, one to the left of the wing and the other to the right.

Button went fourth, Barrichello sixth, Vettel fastest again.

Barrichello attacked Q3 early and Button joined a general

early exodus from the pits before the dreaded Degner 1 claimed Kovalainen, halting the session. On the resumption the Brawn team decided to wait and do a single flying lap again using the option tyres. With less than four minutes left *nobody* had completed a flying lap.

Vettel took a majestic pole and with less than 20 seconds left neither Brawn had begun their flying lap. They set off, Button slower than Barrichello in the first sector. Button explained that, under the weight of the fuel he was carrying, 'I struggled with rear grip through the first sector and that's where I lost the time on my quick lap. The car was working well through the rest of the lap.' Button went seventh – Barrichello fifth, saying 'we didn't have particularly competitive sessions in Q1 and Q2 and it was difficult to predict where we might end up.' He added that the car worked well on race fuel loads.

Ross Brawn's insight: 'I'm pleased with how the team reacted to the changing circumstances and kept calm throughout. We were realistic on our expectations prior to qualifying.'

The Stewards got busy. Button, Brawn, Alonso and Sutil were judged *not* to have lifted off under the yellow flags in Q2 and each dropped five grid places.

Button explained that when he'd come upon the scene of Buemi's crash he'd had about 'a second' to make a decision. 'The yellow flag was just before where the front wing was. I thought it would be unsafe to lift off because there could have been a car behind.' He explained this politely and carefully, accepted that he hadn't lifted off and fully respected the Stewards' decision.

Equally, Ross Brawn acknowledged and respected it.

Buemi dropped five grid places for taking his damaged Toro Rosso all the way back to the pits, baulking other drivers.

Kovalainen and Vitantonio Liuzzi (Force India) would be dropping five places for making gearbox changes, and as darkness fell nobody knew if Glock would be able to race. The FIA announced it would be announcing the grid on race morning.

The grid when it was announced:

Vettel (Red Bull)

Trulli (Toyota)

Hamilton (McLaren)

Heidfeld (BMW)

Räikkönen (Ferrari)

Barrichello (Brawn)

Rosberg (Williams)

Sutil (Force India)

Kubica (BMW)

Button (Brawn)

Kovalainen (McLaren)

Alguersuari (Toro Rosso)

Buemi (Toro Rosso)

Fisichella (Ferrari)

Nakajima (Williams)

Alonso (Renault)

Grosjean (Renault)

Liuzzi (Force India)

Webber (Red Bull)

Ross Brawn felt that, in an attempt to find the right balance for their cars, the drivers were pushing too hard and that explained the number of accidents.

The Brawn drivers were operating two-stop strategies and on the grid Shovlin insisted Button was pretty 'chilled out' as usual on race day.

From the lights Vettel settled the race, moving to mid-track and travelling so fast that nobody could catch him before turn 1. Button, however, was lost in the middle of the pack and emerged 11th, Fisichella past him. Barrichello ran sixth.

Vettel completed the opening lap 1.1 seconds in front of Hamilton, Barrichello at 4.3, Button at 7.5. Unless something dramatic happened to Vettel, the Drivers' Championship would go to Brazil. Button was already into damage limitation – or perhaps the great escape was just going on and on.

Button had Kubica in front and tried a move into turn 1 as

the second lap began while Vettel moved away from Hamilton. Barrichello finished the lap 6.1 seconds behind and Button 11.4. At least Button got past Kubica, on the inside into the right-handed 130R corner. Sutil was a second ahead and Button began to reduce it.

On lap 6 Vettel led Hamilton by 2.6 seconds, Barrichello at 11.4, and Button at 19.3 – Sutil now slightly *less* than a second away and tracking Kovalainen.

On lap 13 Sutil tried down the inside into the chicane – Kovalainen left him space – and drifted across, clouting Kovalainen. Sutil rotated and Kovalainen worked a passage round him, but Button sailed imperiously through to take eighth place. With Barrichello still sixth, Brawn would take the constructor's.

Button pitted on lap 17, replacing one set of prime tyres with another. He emerged into clear air 14th, cars ahead still to make their first stops. Barrichello pitted and emerged ninth. The order: Vettel, Rosberg, Hamilton, Trulli, Heidfeld, Kovalainen, Kubica, Räikkönen, Barrichello, Alguersuari, Nakajima, Liuzzi, Alonso, Button, Grosjean, Fisichella, Sutil, Webber.

As the pit stops developed Button ran only seven seconds behind Barrichello, and when the pit stops were done the order had become Vettel – lording it – Hamilton, Trulli, Heidfeld, Räikkönen, Barrichello, Rosberg, Button.

'I was able to follow Kimi when we were both running on primes in the first stint,' Barrichello said, 'but once he switched to options he gained a lot of time on me.'

Button ran just over five seconds from Barrichello but Kubica was catching Button. Rosberg, Button and Kubica moved in tandem. This was lap 35, the second pit stops imminent. These went to lap 45 of the 53, Button actually sixth when he made his. Barrichello had a smooth stop (6.1 seconds stationary) and emerged just in front of Button. Rosberg had yet to make his stop and there was a chance the Brawns could leap-frog him when he did. This was not an academic matter of lowly points because, as the season tightened and tightened, every point had a currency and a value of its own.

Just then, in an instant or two of shocking visual violence,

Alguersuari lost control of his Red Bull in 130R. It pulverised an advertising hoarding and savaged the tyre barrier. The Safety Car came out, Rosberg could now pit under it and luck favoured him because he emerged fourth, restricting Barrichello to seventh and Button to eighth.

Four laps remained when the Safety Car pulled off and Kubica attacked Button, Button tried to attack Barrichello and they ran to the end like that. Vettel won it cleanly, showing throughout the maturity of a master.

Barrichello said he 'struggled with the set-up' but felt the 'most important' thing was the point he'd gained on Button.

'I was pulling massive amounts of time out of the guys in front me but they were on heavier fuel loads which held me up because it's difficult to overtake here,' Button said. 'I did the best I could in the car that we had and we got the maximum performance out of it with a points-scoring finish. I only lost one point to Rubens, which is my main priority. Obviously we lost a few points to Sebastian but we were expecting them to be strong here.'

Ross Brawn's insight: 'We recovered well in the race from a problematical qualifying session and both drivers brought home valuable points in the fight for the Constructors' Championship. Whilst we were aware that this track would favour our competitors I am pleased with the performance of the team and drivers to extract the maximum from the car. The next two races, at Interlagos and Abu Dhabi, should suit the characteristics of our car much better.'

There was a bizarre postscript to the race. Rosberg appeared in front of the Stewards for allegedly speeding under the Safety Car and, if he'd been demoted, Brawn would have had the constructor's. The Stewards didn't do that and mercifully it would be settled on the track.

Constructor's: Brawn 156, Red Bull 120.5, Ferrari 67, McLaren 65, Toyota 54.5, Williams 34.5.

Driver's: Button 85, Barrichello 71, Vettel 69, Webber 51.5, Räikkönen 45, Hamilton 43.

Button took some time off in the sun before he flew to São Paulo on the Tuesday to 'get used to the time zone' and found the weather 'really strange'. Tuesday was cold, Wednesday was hot and Thursday it rained. No Englishman could be disconcerted by a weather pattern he'd known all his life (until he'd gone to Monaco, anyway).

Barrichello returned to Brazil on the Tuesday immediately after Japan and spent his time 'booking *churrascarias* for friends of mine'. This sent the world's media (well, me) back to the dictionary, because *churrascarias* seemed to be in there with Button's *paracarro* and Cantona's seagulls. Actually it means Brazilian steakhouses. Barrichello was leading 'just my normal life: picking up the kids from school and just being at home exercising nicely.'

By now the British media were going heavy on Button's chances with extensive coverage and, inevitably, many words setting the scene, although there was very little left to say because a podium finish would win it for Button and all anybody could do was wait and see. Vettel had to win or come second to remain a contender, Barrichello had to think of winning.

On the Friday, Webber (1m 12.4s) went quickest in first practice from Barrichello (1m 12.8s), Vettel third (1m 12.9s) and Button seventh (1m 13.1s). Light rain deepened into something heavier about half an hour in and briefly kept the cars off the track.

Second practice – dry – offered confusion. Alonso now went quickest (1m 12.3s) from Buemi, Barrichello third (1m 12.4s), Button fifth (1m 12.5s) and Vettel seventh (1m 12.6s). Barrichello moved to the softer tyre towards the end of the session and was able to do what he described as a 'good lap'.

The Brawn team concentrated on set-up, Barrichello covering 70 laps and Button 74. This allowed Barrichello to insist that while 'the times may not have always looked competitive' that wasn't the point.

Button was optimistic. 'The car seems to be working well on the prime tyre, which is encouraging, and the pace was good.' However, he was 'struggling a little with the balance on the option tyre over one timed lap so hopefully we can resolve that to be ready for qualifying.'

Ross Brawn's insight: 'Two good practice sessions and we are reasonably happy.'

Bad weather all but destroyed the Saturday practice session. For more than 40 minutes the medical helicopter couldn't be used and consequently no car ran. When Grosjean battered a barrier, halting the session, Rosberg had gone fastest (1m 23.1s), Button third (1m 24.1s), Barrichello 14th (1m 26.5s), Vettel just behind him (1m 27.0s). In the conditions these times carried little or no meaning.

And now, as this extraordinary season moved towards its possible climax, Interlagos drowned when the third storm of the day attacked it. The Gods, it seemed, were determined on torment for Button: Barrichello was an expert in the wet here and Vettel was an expert in the wet everywhere.

Mist shrouded distant skyscrapers. The crowd huddled under umbrellas or had their hoods up. Raindrops stabbed insistently at the standing water on the track. The Safety Car and the Medical Car went round, their wheels cutting watery furrows. Button's father John, walking down the paddock to find shelter, grinned and proclaimed 'We're in England.' Later he'd be more specific and liken it to Snetterton during winter races long ago. Interlagos felt just like that and the whole qualifying would be etched into shades of grey.

Vettel tried early, Button a moment later because the imperative was to get a time in case the rain washed the whole thing away. Vettel moved into his fast lap and, in the first sector, the car was visibly wobbling. He crossed the line at 1m 39.6s and all but two cars were on the circuit. Lightning streaked, the Gods seemingly not placated by floods. Grosjean skated here and there and Fisichella parked his Ferrari across the track after skimming sideways. This was not driving but aquaplaning. The session was red-flagged after just over four minutes with Vettel fastest, then Fisichella, Alguersuari, Rosberg, Grosjean, Nakajima and Buemi. Neither Brawn had a time.

The medical car circled and the session resumed at 2:18 local time. Hamilton was waiting at the pit lane exit to be first out, followed by a rush of the others, although Vettel stayed in.

Hamilton crossed the line at 1m 27.4s, which translated to 12.2 seconds quicker than Vettel. The conditions had improved and Button went seventh although three full seconds slower than Barrichello. Vettel was on track and crossed the line at 1m 29.2s to be eighth. Rosberg travelled very, very fast for 1m 24.3s, Barrichello now in second place behind him.

Just after halfway through the session Button went third (1m 24.9s), leapfrogging Barrichello. Vettel was 15th and slipped to 17th. He pressed doggedly on but could do no more than 1m 25.0s to be 16th. Some four minutes remained. Still Vettel pressed doggedly and just then Hamilton went off. He was 18th. The Gods seemed intent on sacrifices.

Barrichello was comfortably into fifth 1.2s from Rosberg, and Button comfortably into sixth, 1.4s from Rosberg. Comfortably? Button's father confessed how fearful he was in these conditions and his mood wasn't helped by the fact that Jenson was reporting aquaplaning on the straights.

Hamilton came into the pits and said he'd had virtually no grip at all.

Vettel's first sector time was 22.0s, 0.1 down. The rain hardened and his second sector was 1.4s down. The Red Bull was quivering and wobbling again and Vettel abandoned the lap. The Gods had their second sacrifice because Vettel's championship had gone. He brought the car in, took the steering wheel off and hurled it away in disgust. Later, struggling to mask his disappointment, he said he had the impression he's spent the afternoon at a swimming pool, not a motor racing circuit. He wasn't smiling when he said that.

'The first session went well and our pace was reasonably good in the wet, which was encouraging,' Button said, downplaying everything.

Q2 began with the track still sodden. Rosberg set an early marker with 26.5s in the first sector and Liuzzi lost control of his Force India at the end of the pit lane straight. The session was red-flagged, thunder echoing and the rain falling even harder.

The Medical Car circled occasionally, monitoring conditions, and the session did not resume until 4:10, which was more than two hours after Q1 began.

The Gods demanded one more sacrifice, and it was to be Button. He was 15th when the session resumed and the shades of grey which were Interlagos engulfed him.

Barrichello came out early but Rosberg was setting the benchmark with 1m 21.8s, Barrichello going fourth (1m 22.7s). Just over eight minutes remained and Button was eighth, soon bumped to 11th. He was on a lap and did 1m 22.9s to lift himself to tenth.

With just over six minutes left Williams were fitting intermediate tyres to Rosberg's car, the sun out, the track changing. Was this the right decision? Nobody truly knew. Barrichello had been bumped to tenth, Button back to 11th. Rosberg moved into his fast lap while Button, now 12th, continued on the full wets. He did 1m 22.5s and found himself 13th.

At this moment Barrichello lay fifth.

Button's sector times told a terrible story, and he battled into another lap but the times told the same story. He remained 13th until Grosjean bumped him and he tried a final time, but 1m 22.5s would be worth only 14th.

By then Barrichello had been bumped to ninth, and Alonso with a late thrust bumped him to the edge of the precipice.

'The track had dried out a little,' Button said, 'so we made some small set-up changes, but the balance of the car just felt transformed. I had massive understeer for the first two laps' – something he reported despairingly over the on-board radio – 'and tried everything that I could to set a time but the pace just wasn't there. By the third lap the rear tyres started to go away leaving me with no rear grip, and I just couldn't improve my time. I think it was a mistake not putting the intermediates on at the end.' If the championship had become all but impossible for Vettel it might now be becoming problematical for Button.

Ross Brawn said that the 'lack of balance which Jenson experienced on his set of wet tyres was unexpected and proved costly because we believed it was possible to get through without using intermediates, which proved with hindsight to be the wrong strategy'.

'We were lucky to make it through – we should have gone for intermediates,' Barrichello said.

The track continued to dry into Q3 and seven of the ten cars left came out at once. Buemi set an early marker (1m 21.7s), Barrichello circumspect (1m 25.7s) and, because the track was drying, provisional pole became a transient, fleeting thing shared among many. With just over five minutes left Barrichello went quickest (1m 21.1s), bringing the crowd to their feet.

Kubica beat that and Webber got close to Kubica. Räikkönen put the Ferrari third but Trulli seized provisional pole. An instant later Rosberg had that off him, Barrichello down to sixth.

With just over three minutes left all ten cars were on the track.

Barrichello got into a fast lap, two tramlines of dry track appearing at strategic points round the circuit. Trulli did 1m 20.3s to seize provisional pole back from Rosberg. He held it for four seconds. Barrichello crossed the line at 1m 20.2s and the crowd were back on their feet. Barrichello continued and set a new fastest first sector into the next lap. Webber was fast now, so fast he shaved Barrichello by doing 1m 20.1s.

Barrichello backed off and prepared for his final assault. He was fastest through the first sector again, fastest through the second, and as the rooster of spray pursued him to the line the timing froze at 1m 19.5s, convulsing Interlagos.

He waited and waited on his slowing down lap for Jock Clear, his pit race engineer, to tell him on the radio he had pole. Clear couldn't because several cars were still on track. Barrichello couldn't hear the crowd – a Formula 1 engine prohibits anything like that – but he could see the immense crowd and sensed something good was happening. Suddenly, as he reached turn 10, Clear bayed 'You beauty! That is P1 – in Brazil! Jenson Button P 14, Sebastian Vettel P 16! Where are you now?!?!' *Barrichello* thought that Clear should 'cool it' a bit

– in context, a statement of epic proportions and the equal of pole itself. Barrichello added that sometimes in life you have to let your emotions out and, quite rightly, that was what Clear had just done.

The longest qualifying session in Formula 1 history had finally ended.

Barrichello was hugely delighted and his family, a whole throng of them, made their little part of the circuit into carnival. He'd describe the qualifying as 'unusual', a piece of understatement Button and Brawn would have been proud of. 'I love these conditions,' he said. 'Qualifying is a great time when you go out and the car feels nice.' The problem he suffered was maintaining concentration over such a long period and with so many breaks. It was so long he had to go and relieve himself twice, which he pointed out was something he'd never done in his whole career before.

'There were plenty of strategies regarding which tyres to choose, how many laps to do and how wet the track would be. You never knew what was going to happen next. It's a good situation to be starting from the front and have your own race pace rather than be in the pack. However, the job is only half done and I'm keeping my feet firmly on the ground. I'm not going to watch what's going on anywhere else. I'll go as hard as I can and then get on the radio at the end to see where Jenson and Sebastian have finished.'

Button reflected ruefully that 'it was a crazy session' which would make the race 'very tough. I will be right in the middle of the pack but I'll make the most of it.' Ross Brawn's insight: 'A day of mixed fortunes with Rubens achieving a quite superb pole position and Jenson unfortunately not progressing from Q2. It was a chaotic and delayed qualifying with the heavy rain causing havoc and requiring the team and drivers to stay focused through the long delays. We were lucky in Q2 with Rubens. He did a fantastic job to get the pole position. The car has been working well all weekend and the potential was evident from the result that he achieved in Q3.'

The grid might be all-important.

	Barrichello (Brawn)
Webber (Red Bull)	
	Sutil (Force India)
Trulli (Toyota)	
	Räikkönen (Ferrari)
Buemi (Toro Rosso)	
	Rosberg (Williams)
Kubica (BMW)	
	Nakajima (Williams)
Alonso (Renault)	
	Kobayashi (Toyota)
Alguersuari (Toro Rosso)	
	Grosjean (Renault)
Button (Brawn)	
	Vettel (Red Bull)
Kovalainen (McLaren)	
	Hamilton (McLaren)
Heidfeld (BMW)	
	Fisichella (Ferrari)
Liuzzi (Force India)	

Liuzzi had a gearbox change, relegating him five places and putting Vettel immediately behind Button. That did not disturb the essential question: how would Button approach the race? He had the precious 14-point lead which brought its own strength but now he must consider that Barrichello could win and he get ten points, cutting his lead to four at Abu Dhabi. He had to consider this against a background of many murmurings that he wasn't driving like a champion but an accumulator and, consequently, he wasn't a champion at all. He was not, as someone observed, a man for the great gesture anyway.

Well…

Father John said that on the race morning the mechanics had told Jenson he could finish fifth but Button replied, 'No, I am going for the podium.'

John added: 'I knew the mood he was in. I said to the mechanics, "You can fit a rubber bumper on the front because I think he might need it."'

Jenson Button prepared to show the world he *was* a man for the great gesture.

Barrichello thought pragmatically, speaking about qualifying as 'the first phase in achieving a dream'. He'd competed all these years in the Brazilian Grand Prix and not won it. He wanted to very badly. He also felt that 'playing catch-up' was better because you weren't afraid of taking risks. He added graciously that he and Button were friendly rivals, they'd remained friends even when Button won the six races at the start of the season, and if it was anything to do with him – Barrichello – they would be remaining friends.

Button knew several drivers would be fighting their way up the field. Without specifying it, or having to specify it, he included himself. He meant Vettel and Hamilton. 'You can win from 14th, you can win from 16th and that's my aim,' Button said.

On the grid Barrichello was relaxed, repeated that his feet were firmly on the ground and he intended to push as hard as he could.

The crowd gave Jenson Button the bird and he waved back. They appreciated that. The crowd gave *John* Button the bird and he waved back. They appreciated that, too.

The five red lights blinked off and Barrichello was away fast and clean, already positioning the Brawn for the first corner, a corkscrew of a thing called the Senna S – downhill hard left into a hard right – which had claimed its many victims over the years because it was a terrible compression at the start of a race and a favoured overtaking place during it. He went round and the snake of cars behind *snaked* as they threaded through, Button still 14th. He might have hoped to snaffle a couple of places on acceleration from the grid. The crowd were making animal noises at the sight of Barrichello forcing a small gap to Webber, Räikkönen third and Sutil fourth.

Between the left and the right Vettel touched Kovalainen and darted across, forcing Fisichella deep on to the grass. Webber blocked Räikkönen and they touched, leaving Räikkönen with a broken front wing. As they stretched out into the country Räikkönen limped, cars moving easily past him. Sutil and Trulli collided heavily, Alonso involved, and that brought the Safety Car into play. When Sutil and Trulli were out of their cars they remonstrated and grappled.

Button was ninth.

Kovalainen pitted immediately and sett off before the fuel hose was completely out. He dragged the hose like a monstrous reptilian tail and Räikkönen, moving from his own stop, caused a flash fire when his exhaust ran over the fuel spilling from the hose. Kovalainen halted at the Brawn pit and the mechanics there heaved the hose from the McLaren before waving him away, itself a gracious gesture.

Shovlin warned Button that 'the guys ahead are not going to be experienced at restarts and they may not know how much they've got to warm the tyres.' They were Grosjean, debutant Kamui Kobayashi, Nakajima and Buemi.

The Safety Car held them until lap 5 of the 71, released them for Button to attack Grosjean. At that lap 5, Barrichello leading:

Webber	@ 0.4s
Rosberg	@ 0.9s
Kubica	@ 0.9s
Buemi	@ 1.9s
Kobayashi	@ 2.4s
Grosjean	@ 2.6s
Button	@ 2.8s

On the back straight to turn 4 Button moved to Grosjean's outside, but as they approached the left-hander at the end Grosjean stayed inside and on the power. He ran wide and Button twisted the Brawn to the gap that had opened inside. They ran to the next left-hander, a curve, and Button stayed in front. Button knew he had to 'dive through' because the cars ahead were fuelled longer and he needed to be in front of them.

John Button had his hands clasped into a screen so he couldn't see what was happening but watched through his fingers...

Button was eighth.

If the race finished in this order Barrichello would go to Abu Dhabi with 81 points and Button 86.

Grosjean counter-attacked and Button held him. Grosjean went wide again, allowing Vettel through. Button had Nakajima ahead. At lap 6, Barrichello leading:

Webber	@ 1.0s
Kubica	@ 1.6s
Rosberg	@ 2.6s
Buemi	@ 3.5s
Kobayashi	@ 4.6s
Nakajima	@ 4.8s
Button	@ 4.9s

Nakajima and Button fled across the bays of the grid towards the Senna S and Button slotted the Brawn inside, the pit lane wall running at his elbow. The two cars went in abreast but Button emerged decisively in front and Nakajima followed.

John Button had his hands clasped into a screen so he couldn't see what was happening but watched through his fingers…

If the race finished in this order Button would be taking 87 points to Abu Dhabi.

There was a problem, however, and the problem was young Kobayashi. He'd started in karting in 1996, when he was nine, and graduated to single-seaters. He'd been a Toyota test driver but, by definition, lacked actual Formula 1 race experience. In the next few laps it didn't look like that, as he resolutely defended whatever Button could pitch at him. Button initially tried on the inside but he was taking a constant risk that any of the drivers he overtook might touch him, send him spinning away.

Barrichello rapped out fastest lap, 1m 14.6s, lowered it to 1m 14.4s. Kubica was closing on Webber and Button tried on the inside into the Senna S, thought better of it, backed off and hunted him again. At lap 8 Barrichello led Webber by 1.7 seconds, Kobayashi at 7.7 and Button at 8.0.

Button tried again down the inside at the Senna S, backed off and hunted again.

Webber set fastest lap and Kobayashi moved three-tenths of a second further away from Button.

The race was assuming its running pace, its shape and a certain continuity, however infuriating that was for Button, who had cars behind which might trouble him if he couldn't free himself of the Kobayashi obstacle.

Barrichello needed to be three or four seconds in front of Webber when he made his first pit stop because Webber would be going a couple of laps further. Barrichello presented a familiar sight, at ease in the car and at ease with the circuit as he prepared to summon faster laps from himself.

Button did his fastest lap (1m 15.4s), a full second slower than Barrichello was doing and, within a moment, slower than that because Barrichello moved into the 1m 14.2s and next lap 1m 14.1s before dipping into the 1m 13s, the pressure on him to gain before he pitted: he led Webber by 2.7 seconds. Barrichello did pit on lap 21, the pressure transferring to Webber.

Barrichello emerged eighth, just ahead of Vettel who promptly drove round the outside to make Barrichello ninth. Button was fully on to Kobayashi while Hamilton attacked Barrichello. The shape and continuity were breaking up.

And Button attacked Kobayashi into the Senna S, went classically inside and through but the impetus pitched him wide, just wide enough to let Kobayashi back.

Significantly Kubica pitted and emerged in front of Barrichello.

Button complained that Kobayashi was 'moving around' in the braking zones and Shovlin said they'd 'get on to Charlie [Whiting]'. Kobayashi, Button would say, was 'absolutely crazy'. Now Button feinted outside into the Senna S, Kobayashi instinctively moved to cover that and Button did another dive on the inside.

John Button had his hands clasped into a screen so he couldn't see what was happening – but watched through his fingers...

Shovlin would describe it as 'a massive turning point in our race' and judged that once Button found himself in 'clear air' he would win the championship.

Button, released, knew he could disappear into the distance. He also knew Barrichello wasn't leading...

Webber pitted on lap 26 so that, however briefly, Button actually led the Grand Prix. He hadn't done that since Turkey on 7 June. Webber was stationary for 8.3 seconds and emerged clearly in front of Button, who'd gained 3.6 seconds on Kobayashi in the lap and a half since he'd overtaken him. The order: Webber, Button (yet to stop), Kobayashi (yet to stop), Vettel (yet to stop), Kubica, Barrichello, Hamilton, Kovalainen.

In practical terms, with the non-stoppers stripped out of the equation, Barrichello would be running third, giving give him 77 points to take to Abu Dhabi. Seventh place gave Button the championship because, *if* Barrichello won Abu Dhabi and *if* Button scored no points there, they'd both have 87 but, crucially, Button would win the championship on the most-wins tiebreaker.

Around the loops, the descents and the ascents which threaded round the bowl of Interlagos, the championship might be coming to Button with a third-distance gone. It could turn on his pit stop and where that pitched him back out. It could turn on Vettel, feisty, brim-full of racing vigour and a mere four seconds behind Button.

Button pitted on lap 28 and was stationary for 7.5 seconds. He emerged tenth and with enough fuel to run a further 25 laps. Then he'd stop again and take on the softer tyres for the final push. Kobayashi pitted, making Button ninth. He hunted Buemi, caught him and, with an astonishing surge of speed – foot firmly off the brakes – rammed the Brawn down the inside at the Senna S. Button slithered to mid-track and Buemi almost – helplessly – tapped his rear wheel.

John Button had his hands clasped into a screen so he couldn't see what was happening but watched through his fingers...

Button was eighth. A lap later Grosjean pitted, making Button seventh.

Webber commanded the race and Vettel had still yet to stop. Completing lap 35:

Vettel	@ 4.7s
Kubica	@ 7.5s
Barrichello	@ 11.2s
Hamilton	@ 11.7s

| Räikkönen | @ 24.9s |
| Button | @ 26.3s |

Vettel pitted on lap 37, was stationary for 9.2 seconds – a problem with the left front wheel coming off – and took another set of the harder tyres. He emerged just behind Button, who was now sixth. The championship might have turned on that awkward wheel because it cost Vettel the place and gave Button one more point.

If the race finished in this order Button would have 88 points and Barrichello 77.

Kubica circled seven seconds from Webber and Barrichello eleven. Webber was like Barrichello in his ease of movement, looking unhurried, lap melting into lap with a sort of inevitability. The shame for Webber would always be that so many eyes were looking elsewhere, to Barrichello trying to reach towards Kubica, to Button so physically far away yet psychologically *in front*.

Hamilton harried Barrichello, who was falling away from Webber and Kubica, but pitted for his second stop – the first had been behind the Safety Car – and emerged after almost clouting the barrier in the pit lane exit. He was ninth and easily fast enough to be a spoiler.

Räikkönen pitted on lap 44, making Button fourth. Completing lap 44, Webber still leading:

Kubica	@ 5.5s
Barrichello	@ 14.5s
Button	@ 29.1s
Vettel	@ 30.0s

The second pit stops were yet to come. Shovlin informed Button that Hamilton, fiuelled to the end, was 15 seconds away and 'we need [1m] 14.4s to beat him'.

Kubica pitted and emerged ahead of the Button-Vettel duo, or duet if you prefer. That made Kubica third, Barrichello up to second some 15 seconds behind Webber. Barrichello pitted on lap 50, took on the softer tyres and emerged sixth.

Hamilton went faster than he'd gone before with a 1m 14.5s and was coming at Barrichello.

Webber made his second stop unchallenged.

Hamilton, meanwhile, was tightening up to Barrichello, offering the prospect of a struggle for third place which, if Hamilton won it, would have a direct bearing on the championship.

The Brawn team carried out the tyres from the bowels of their pit and on lap 56 Button came in. Ross Brawn, face impassive, swivelled on the pit lane wall and watched as if it was an academic exercise and not, potentially, the most famous pit stop in the world. Button was stationary for six seconds, but when he emerged, Kovalainen, on track, carried more impetus and went by, making Button seventh. It was still enough.

Vettel pitted and emerged fifth, Kovalainen holding Button away from him.

John Button was simply watching now, no hands evident.

Kovalainen had to pit again, opening sixth to Button *but* Räikkönen was only just over three seconds behind him. The situation completing lap 59, Webber still leading:

Kubica	@ 5.1s
Barrichello	@ 17.9s
Hamilton	@ 19.0s
Vettel	@ 26.3s
Kovalainen	@ 30.3s
Button	@ 30.6s
Räikkönen	@ 34.4s

Kovalainen peeled off into the pits, freeing Button, while Vettel advanced towards the Barrichello-Hamilton duo so that, with 11 laps to run, the whole situation remained fluid but, as each lap went by, favoured Button. Might Vettel be the spoiler?

Barrichello radioed that he was 'having a lot of vibration' from a tyre.

'You have to look after it – ten laps to go,' Clear said.

Hamilton came up, predatory, almost like a hunter sensing

weakness in its prey, and flowed by towards the Senna S. Barrichello left him just enough room on the inside and, in a milli-second, realised he might not have left him enough. He flicked the Brawn away. Barrichello was now fourth. He clung to Hamilton as they moved out into the depths of the circuit but he couldn't get close enough to mount a counter-attack.

Button was controlling the gap to Räikkönen.

With nine laps to go Clear said plaintively, 'You have a puncture, you have a puncture, Rubens.' It was the left rear – caused, evidently, when Hamilton struck it, slightly damaging the McLaren in the process – and Barrichello had no choice but to pit, a championship ruined by something so simple and so familiar to every motorist. It took nine seconds to change the wheels and Barrichello ebbed out in eighth place.

Button ran for home, seven laps to go, and still he controlled Räikkönen.

John Button was 'watching it with the lads and we were all crying'.

Button was 33 seconds from Webber and seven seconds from Vettel, immediately in front, but that didn't matter any more. Räikkönen was three seconds behind and that didn't matter any more either. Fifth was ample. Fifth was all your dreams come true. Fifth was golden.

Still Ross Brawn's face remained impassive as his eyes scanned the screens in front of him. If you hadn't known what was going on you could not, looking at him, have deduced it or indeed deduced *anything*.

Button circled alone with four laps to go and Shovlin warned about the possibility of a 'few drops of rain' which would come in 'around turn 12. We don't think it will be much.'

They might not have been raindrops but tears for Barrichello.

John Button clamped headphones on to listen in on the radio.

That was with two laps to run.

Vettel hadn't had time to worry about finishing first or second because 'when you're driving you're quite busy. Obviously I am smart enough to see that if Jenson is ahead or just behind me I will not score massively more points than he does, and finishing fourth is not enough. The last couple of laps I had time to realise because before that you never know what can still happen. I was praying for rain. There was the smell of rain in the air but it didn't come down.'

Perhaps, as Button flowed into the final lap, he allowed himself to reflect that for a *paracarro* he hadn't done badly, and where was Flavio Briatore, anyway? Banned for life, not at Interlagos and never to be seen at Interlagos again. Perhaps, as he flowed into those final 2.6 miles, he thought back across a career which, in sum, had been a long journey to exactly here. Perhaps he reflected on what he and the team owed to Norbert Haug and the Mercedes-Benz High Performance Engines for getting them here. Watching him you didn't wonder about any of that. You were watching a professional who'd hold the emotion until he crossed the line, and you were watching the diffident, softly-spoken Englishman who had fashioned a whole race into his great gesture.

Webber crossed the line after an hour and 32 minutes, Massa waving the chequered flag. Kubica crossed it 7.6 seconds later, then Hamilton at 18.9, Vettel at 19.6 and Button himself at 29.0. As *he* crossed the line he was making tight, pummelling-the-air gestures with both fists. He kept his right forearm out stabbing the air. He clenched his fist and began stabbing the air again.

Two men embraced John Button so copiously that he vanished within them. 'We were crying and he was crying on the radio,' John Button said.

Ross Brawn still gazed at the screens although, as Button crossed the line, his team took the Constructors' Championship – something precious because it is a measure of the communal effort to create a better car than everybody else. The world watches the Drivers' Championship, the teams watch the constructor's *and* the driver's.

Button kept stabbing the air as he slowed and toured what was no in a literal sense his world.

In the pit John Button kept stabbing the air too.

Button's voice, like a tremendously drunken wail – the distortion due to the radio being on a highly-stressed missile – belted out, with an exquisitely timed small pause between each word for emphasis 'WE ... ARE ... THE... CHAMPIONS,' followed by a whooping sound, part ecstatic, part animal, followed by 'WE ... ARE ... WORLD ... CHAMPIONS.'

On that slowing-down lap Barrichello drew alongside, raised his hands from the cockpit and openly applauded Button. It was one gentleman communicating with another, and it was a gesture of great grace. Barrichello accelerated away so that he wouldn't be a distraction as everybody's focus locked on to Button and his gestures.

John Button was holding his emotions back hard.

Button brought the car into the pit lane because, of course, he wasn't in the top three and wouldn't be going to the special enclosure before the podium ceremony. He stood on the car and splayed his arms, the fingers fashioning the number 1. Barrichello hugged him, another gracious gesture. They clasped each other's crash helmets and embraced again. Button took half a dozen urgent paces towards a bank of photographers and then sprinted, towing the photographers with him. His physio, Mike Colliery, seized him and hugged him clean off the ground. When he regained *terra firma* he sprinted on to be weighed and emerged from that with both arms raised again, the fingers making the 1. He sprinted to where some team members stood behind temporary metal railings and sprang into them. He still hadn't had time to take his crash helmet off. When he did he faced the photographers again and bowed – his own gracious gesture.

Within the pit Ross Brawn moved quietly round shaking hands. He resembled a colossus, physically dwarfing those around him. He found gracious words. 'The work the team did over the winter was sensational. I have to say that my thanks go out to all the people who couldn't be with us because we had to re-size the team: they worked all winter and then they had to leave. I hope they have enjoyed what *they* have achieved because they were a part of what we'd done.'

Vettel offered congratulations to Button and the Brawn team. 'I think overall they did the best job this year.'

Button had by now all but lost his voice. In a semi-croak he'd judge the Brazilian Grand Prix 'the best race that I've driven in my career'. He'd describe the season as a 'rollercoaster ride from the elation of the wins at the start to the hard graft in the second half of the season which has seen us grind out the results needed to take the titles'. It was, he added, very much a team effort.

Wonderfully, he explained that the car wasn't fast enough to have won the race 'but I came through and finished sixth'.

Fifth, of course, but that was among so many factors that really didn't matter now.

Barrichello remained gracious. 'We really have a great car and a great team and it has truly been an amazing year when you consider the situation that we were in just before the start of the season. I'm truly pleased for Jenson as a friend and he is a great champion. We have a fantastic relationship working together and that has really shown through this year. Well done to him. It was a true fight and I fought really hard but he won it in the first half of the season. The team have been superb this year and they thoroughly deserve to win both the constructor's and Drivers' Championships today. We're going to have a great night together and I'm pleased to have played my part in securing the constructor's.'

Ross Brawn's insight: 'I am so incredibly proud of the team and our drivers and it's so very special to have won the constructor's and the Drivers' Championships in our first year as Brawn GP. The second half of the year has been tough after such a successful start, but getting the results in the difficult times is what counts in a championship season. It's really going to take a while for what we have achieved to sink in. Jenson knew what he had to do, he did just that and is a very deserving World Champion. Rubens has made a fantastic contribution to this season without which we could not have won the constructor's today. The spirit in which our two drivers have fought for the championship makes me very proud. They have been a credit to the team and our sport.'

Constructor's: Brawn 161, Red Bull 135.5, McLaren 71, Ferrari 70, Toyota 54.5, Williams 34.5.

Driver's: Button 89, Vettel 74, Barrichello 72, Webber 61.5, Hamilton 49, Räikkönen 48.

As the tears were dried and the partying began it was time to find perspective.

Steve Matchett, who'd worked with Brawn at Benetton, says perceptively: 'For a number of years a lot of people in the paddock always suggested *Ross is very good but only really good because he's got Michael Schumacher driving the car.* You can have pretty much anybody involved with the car and if Michael's driving it he's going to be bloody fast. To an extent I went along with that, because all of Ross's time in the sport had been with Michael driving the car – then you see now what has happened to Honda/Brawn under his leadership. All of a sudden it shows in sharp relief the fact that so much of it is down to *Ross.*'

Tom Walkinshaw, who hired Brawn to design the Jaguar sports car, says equally perceptively: 'I am not surprised at what has happened this season, not in the least. The drivers trust Ross's decisions, which they should do. He's been making the right calls for so long, why shouldn't they? Ross gets the best out of them and he trusts the drivers as well, so when he calls the strategy he knows the driver is capable of delivering – important, because you can't call a strategy if you don't think the driver is capable of it. With Schumacher, Ross worked out that he could deliver it and Jenson seems to be the same.'

Derek Warwick says that since the Jaguar sports car triumphs 'I have had a particular interest in whatever Ross is doing because of my involvement with him and my feeling for him, not just as an engineer but as a man, as a gentleman, as a family man. His principles are not questionable. He is a fantastic person in every respect but having said that he is hard. When you are a at race track he expects you to give 100% and anything less will lose his respect. For me he is the champion of champions, the Schumacher of engineers.'

Frank Dernie, who goes back to the early Williams days, says: 'We go fishing together and we are family friends as well. My wife is friends with Jean and what have you. My wife actually sang at their daughter's wedding so we are quite close. He plays chess. He's good, a bloody sight better than I am – he's better at fishing, too. You have to look multiple moves ahead in chess to be on top of it and I think Ross is very good at that. He's ahead of most people in Formula 1 in terms of having worked out what's likely to happen, not only next but into the long term. If you take the calmness, and the way he goes about his fishing and his chess, that's a very strong indicator of the sort of man he is. He's a normal guy who's a born engineer, who's a chess player and fisherman, and in terms of long-term car planning, and he's very quietly determined.'

The determination reached a natural climax at Interlagos on 18 October 2009. Small wonder, just this once, he shed a tear. He was entitled to.

In direct contrast, Abu Dhabi would have to be anti-climactic although the circuit – not only new but resembling a futuristic base on Mars – suggested a climax all on its own whatever happened there.

Hamilton went fastest in first practice (1m 43.9s) from Button (1m 44.0s), Vettel third and Barrichello (1m 44.2s) fourth. Kovalainen went fastest in second practice (1m 41.3s), Button third (1m 41.5s), Vettel fourth and Barrichello (1m 41.8s) eighth. Button went fastest in third practice (1m 40.6s) from Hamilton, with Barrichello third (1m 40.9s).

It all looked promising for the day-night qualifying and there Barrichello was content with fourth (1m 41.7s), Hamilton on pole (1m 40.9s) from Vettel, Webber third and Button (1m 41.8s) fifth. Barrichello had his eye on a strong finish to the season, taking second place from Vettel in the Championship, of course. In Q3 Button suffered 'massive vibrations' under braking, creating understeer 'which made the car quite a handful to drive.'

Barrichello was tapped by Webber at the start of the race and Button went by into fourth place. Hamilton, leading, had a brake problem, giving the race to Vettel. In the closing laps Button caught and duelled with Webber – and here was another racer's gesture, late braking, probing, forcing, trying to get alongside. By now, this first day of November, the critics had fallen very silent.

Button looked completely relaxed, as if many layers of pressure had finally fallen away from him. 'After the second stop I found I had very good grip with the option tyre. I had very good initial turn-in, which meant I could carry a lot of speed through and that's why I was able to close down Mark. The last couple of laps were a lot of fun for me.'

He added that the car had been reliable throughout. 'I need to thank everyone at Brawn and Mercedes-Benz for all their hard work. We've come away with a podium, which is a nice way to end the year and everyone should be very, very proud of themselves.'

Final insight from Nick Fry. 'It's a genuinely happy team. It's got happier partly because it's got smaller. At 450 people we are probably the smallest team that makes everything for itself – as opposed to those who buy someone else's chassis – and at 450 people you can know everybody, and everybody just gets on very well. There are no politics. Ross is totally non-political in that sense and obviously it stood him in good stead at Ferrari. I think it's worked very well here.'

Final insight from Ross Brawn, emotions firmly under control and that soft smile back as he surveyed the astonishing season: 'It's all much more than any of us expected and I think we made the best of what we had. The pit crew did a fantastic job – you can just rely on them – and everyone back at the factory.'

Already he was looking forward. 'If you pursue a musical analogy, we're going to have a difficult second album next year.'

CHAPTER ELEVEN:

'BEST OF BOTH WORLDS'

It took your breath away. No. It took everybody's breath away. The chequered flag fell at Abu Dhabi on 1 November 2009 but long, long before the lights went off to start the 2010 season at Bahrain on 14 March, Brawn GP had become the first Mercedes works team for 55 years, Button had become a McLaren driver, Barrichello a Williams driver and Nico Rosberg a Mercedes driver. Also, Ross Brawn had found that a social beer or two was entirely the right way to lubricate – gently – Michael Schumacher's desire to resume his conquest of the world.

Brawn himself had no need for histrionics over Schumacher and of course he wasn't the man for histrionics anyway. The specialist motor sport magazines would take care of that, calling it The Comeback of the Century.

Even Formula 1, an activity rendered essentially shock proof by a daily diet of dreams, dramas and disasters, was (slightly) shocked.

Brawn explains it all step by step, his voice perfectly quiet, his reasoning perfectly clear. 'Obviously being partners with Mercedes-Benz and having a long-standing relationship with some of the Mercedes personnel, particularly Norbert Haug [their top man in motor sport], we had some clauses in our agreement with Mercedes as an engine supplier to advise them if there was going to be any change in the majority shareholding of the company.

'We advised them in the summer that we were looking towards investment and really the discussions developed from there. We didn't approach them with a view to Mercedes becoming a partner but they certainly indicated they'd like to investigate the possibility. At that time there was another partner who was interested in coming in but, in turn, when Mercedes showed an interest they bowed out with understanding on both sides, and eventually we did the deal with Mercedes. Actually it's Mercedes and Aabar [the Abu Dhabi investment fund] – we mustn't forget Aabar in this equation. Mercedes have a large shareholding, Aabar have a large shareholding and then Nick [Fry], myself and the rest of the Brawn GP shareholders have a minority holding but still an interest in the company. It made perfect sense for us.'

You get the security of Mercedes, you get the name of Mercedes and you don't have to go round the world trying to find sponsorship – and if you don't get sponsorship then you've a lot of people out of a job.

'Yes, and I think stability and security are very important. Almost immediately we managed to close the deal with Petronas, who we'd been talking to for some time, and Mercedes's involvement made that happen. It's just one example of the stability and security that Mercedes, as the majority shareholder, brought to the company.'

Did you feel a personal twinge that your name was coming off the team?

'I felt both emotions, really: one was a bit of relief after the journey we had been through and the fact that the company now had security for the forseeable future and it had been such a wonderful adventure that it would have been nice to think it could have carried on, but I am primarily involved in motor racing to try and win races. That's a tough battle, and when you're fighting people with the resources of McLaren, Ferrari and Red Bull you have got to be realistic.

'We had an exceptional year, partly due to some unusual circumstances with the regulations and one or two other things.'

Many people would find it difficult to give up power, particularly supreme power in the sense that what you said went.

'I think it was important to me – in my view of how the team would continue to be successful – but that remains, so I have authority to run the team. I do have to answer to the Mercedes board now but I still have that power and authority to do what we need to do within the team. Once that's diluted, in the sense of becoming a committee or a group decision, then it's not for the best and not what I would be interested in.'

We know from experience that very often the small teams that react fast might be in a better position.

'The epitome of that is the pit wall. It spreads all the way through the company that you need to be fast-responsive but of course you need experienced people to make those decisions. Otherwise you can get yourself into trouble. So hopefully I've got the best of both worlds: security, and the authority and flexibility to run the company as we see fit.'

The situation with Jenson Button was inevitably complicated because, as we saw in Chapter 4, 'Men in waiting', he had been waiting a long time and, in the aftermath of Honda's withdrawal, volunteered a pay cut to help the Brawn team survive. How much drivers earn is a more closely guarded secret than, say, how to make atomic weapons. You can, however, postulate that by taking the pay cut Button was not condemning himself to spending the season in a secondhand caravan at Yarmouth but, if the rumoured figures are approximately accurate, he was making much more than a gesture. Clearly if Button won the World Championship he would be in a position to reclaim that sum and negotiate for more. World Champions may come from different continents and different cultures but one language unites them: what they believe they are worth. They all speak it, adding 000s to whatever sum they or their management first thought of.

All this is standard fare for the real negotiation, when the team owner tries to knock as many 0s off the 000s as he can.

There's something else in the background, which is a paradox familiar in motor sport and football. You can have the strongest, most personalised bond with your team – and they with you – but leave and this ceases immediately, as if it had never been. The footballer may spend sincerely happy years playing for Manchester United until he signs for Manchester City, where he may spend sincerely happy years trying to *beat* Manchester United, and if Manchester United sign him back …

It is just as ruthless in Grand Prix racing. The driver is a solitary creature, alone in the cockpit except, these days, for a voice from the pit wall for solace, instruction and admonition. The driver needs the team to get him the car but *he* has to maximise it. He believes he is the best driver in the world and is constantly scanning the near horizon for a car which will enable him to prove this. It has led to generations of drivers behaving like mercenaries, impelled to that because they won't be winning the title by staying loyal and finding themselves in the wrong car. Juan Manuel Fangio was a master of this and early in his career Button had tried to do the same thing, albeit making the wrong moves.

But if Button had just won the World Championship wasn't he in the best car already? Yes, he was, *last season* – which is what 2009 became the moment the man flaunted the chequered flag at Abu Dhabi. Long before that – in fact throughout the season – all the solitaries were scanning the near horizon trying to work out which would be the best car in 2010 and how to get their hands on it.

This sounds very logical but it is complicated by a host of other factors: whether there is a vacancy, money, potential status within the new team and, frankly, whether the other team and its sponsors fancy him. (Team players are preferred, for example, and these days a taste in lap dancing clubs is not to be put on the CV.)

The final complication is equally logical. The driver is usually convinced he took the car to the championship and the team is usually convinced the car took *him*. All parties know the truth lies somewhere in the middle although, as it seems, in this instance Button felt it was the car. Undeniably, some cars are so good that any one of a number of drivers would have won in them. What did Mario Andretti says about the Lotus and being able to put monkeys in it?

This has led to a startling sequence. Nigel Mansell, Damon Hill, Jacques Villeneuve and Alain Prost all won the championship with Williams and departed immediately, albeit for differing reasons. Williams, legend insists, really did feel their cars won championships. Don't forget, too, that Michael Schumacher left Benetton for Ferrari as reigning World Champion.

The teams have worked so hard to make their man champion and it entitles him to have the coveted number 1 on his car the following season. If he moves to another team he takes the number 1 with him. This alone is not a strong enough factor to influence any team's major decisions but it is perhaps something else to weigh in the balance.

Into all this, in the autumn of 2009, came Jenson Button.

Rubens Barrichello, the team-mate, had gone to Williams and Nico Rosberg had come from Williams in one of those driver exchanges which seem to satisfy everyone's needs. In the long history of F1, seldom can an exchange have created fewer ripples – in fact no ripples at all.

Button was on another level.

'The negotiations were not very easy,' says Brawn, 'and we decided in fact to put them on hold until after the championship was finished, because what I didn't want to do was disturb the championship effort. So I agreed with Jenson that the best thing we could do, rather than have difficult discussions in the middle of a crucial stage of the championship, was to start again as soon as the championship finished. Maybe there is an argument that it was something which should have been closed a long time before but I think he wanted to see what his situation was – especially with the championship open – and we wanted to see where we were commercially because, obviously, that influenced what funding we would have. Anyway, we decided to leave it.

'Negotiations re-started, I would have to say, at both ends of the spectrum: we were low, he was high and we worked to find a position in the middle, as always. I thought we had found that position. We then had the bombshell of his visit to McLaren, which soured the negotiations. We had no inkling of that at all. It was a total shock to us and I think we all know that if you want to visit a facility to look at its capacity and depth and so on, you can do it very discreetly. This was a shock and that didn't help.'

It happened in the same week that the Mercedes purchase of Brawn was officially announced.

This all seemed slightly bewildering to any outsider, and a magazine with the reputation and contacts of *Autosport* described how Button's management felt the negotiations were 'becoming an unrealistic proposition' and speculated that, although Ross Brawn had the say on drivers, Mercedes wanted two Germans. Rosberg, son of Keke from Finland, fluent in English and brought up in the south of France, was in fact a German national. Nick Heidfeld, the magazine intonated, might be the other.

This was contradicted (in the same issue of 19 November) by Dieter Zetsche, Chairman of Daimler AG, who was quoted as saying: 'Ross Brawn is the boss of the team and it would not be smart for us to dictate to him anything like a driver decision, nor would it be smart for him not to tell us the decision he had made. We will talk and we will very much listen to what he wants to do.'

It is time to hear Brawn, who explains that 'a little while' after Button visited McLaren he 'advised us' he was taking the drive there.

Did he tell you personally?

'I heard from other sources that it had happened and then he told me a day or so later.'

How did you feel about that because I had assumed he was simply upping the ante, albeit in a fairly brutal sort of way?

'It was a disappointment, perhaps, in how it had gone and a disappointment in the end result but his logic, and his thinking, was that he wanted the challenge of beating Lewis Hamilton in the same team in the same car. He felt that he had been branded as a lucky driver who just happened to be in the right place at the right time. I think that's unfair but he felt aggrieved by that to the point where he wanted to meet this challenge.'

In all consciousness, it can't have been about money because he's already got more than he can spend.

'From what I understand retrospectively, our offer was the same if not better than he received at McLaren. So we have got to assume his motives were true – and I do have some understanding of that *drive* that he wants to prove himself the best. I mean, it must be in every racing driver, it must be in their DNA to want to do that.'

The bond between you and a driver can be incredibly strong, to the exclusion of almost everything else, up to the moment when they say 'I'm going' and then it just ends.

'It does. In our case, it didn't end in animosity, it ended in a little bit of bewilderment, I have to say, on our side and I wish Jenson all the best, but now he is a competitor to us and along with all the others we have got to beat him. Whilst he was a member of the team I'd defend him and his actions and his driving up to the hilt – but the moment he stepped out of being part of the team he then became a competitor and we will do everything in our power to beat him.'

When Michael Schumacher retired at the end of the 2006 season he had achieved more than any Grand Prix driver before him. He held every major record, most significantly seven World Championships. The hunger he had always felt was surely satiated by this, the thirst slaked, the ambition fulfilled, nothing more to prove, nothing to add. If Button had more money than he could spend, Schumacher had enough to support the budget deficit of a small country like Greece.

Yet there had been something slightly unsatisfactory and slightly unexplained about his decision to retire. The 2006 season, when he was beaten to the championship by Alonso, didn't seem like a natural climax, the point where he felt *enough*. He'd say later he was just plain tired, but a rest – even a season off – would have cured that.

The mystery of the retirement was compounded by the fact that his future seemed unplanned. He now spent his time as a Ferrari race adviser and worked on their road cars as well, but that didn't feel like the rest of his life. As is the way of it, the world moved on and the sight of him at the races (even imparting his wisdom to Massa) or sometimes talking to the people on the pit wall had a certain sadness about it.

After the German Grand Prix at the Nurburgring he and Brawn had a social beer. It must have felt a bit like the old days.

Significantly Schumacher tried motor bikes and it was on one of them – or, more accurately, falling off one of them – that he injured his neck so that when Massa was cruelly injured in Hungary just after the Nurburgring and Ferrari needed a race-winning replacement (not always the easiest thing to find mid season, with all the other drivers locked down by ferocious contracts) he badly wanted to help but physically could not.

Badly wanted to: that alone suggested his retirement had been, at best, The Wrong Thing To Do.

After the Ferrari approach, Schumacher trained hard, although he was already very fit, and found in the car that his body could still do it. The neck injury was irrelevant to that because in time it would heal. If his body had cried *the G-forces are now too much, your reactions are three years off the pace and not coming back, you're never going to regain the stamina, none of* this *will heal,* then the career truly would have been over. His body hadn't said that. His body had whispered *welcome back.*

'I was intrigued,' Brawn says, 'when I realised how much he wanted to get into the Ferrari again. It really hurt him mentally that he couldn't. So that stuck with me and then after the race at Abu Dhabi there were big celebrations. He was there and we shared a beer – and again the subject came up of how disappointed he was that he'd missed the opportunity to drive the Ferrari.'

In fact, of course at that stage Brawn had Rosberg and might reasonably believe that, after the inevitable sparring, Button would re-sign. He was not, that evening, looking for Schumacher or anybody else.

Schumacher's spokesperson and business associate, Sabine Kehm, has even said:[1] 'We wanted to celebrate Ross's title win and that evening they were talking about him driving, and Michael was kind of making fun of it. Ross was saying come on, and Michael wasn't taking it seriously. It wasn't an option, it was a joke – entertaining gossip.'

To understand this delightful little interplay, you have to remember that Brawn and Schumacher worked together to win the two Benetton championships, Schumacher went to Ferrari and said he wanted Brawn and, at Ferrari, they became *rulers* of Formula 1. They surely could read each other as easily as they could read lapcharts, both men have a dry sense of humour and must have known that over the beers, euphoria in the air, the jokes and the entertaining gossip could be translated into a more profound language if that ever became necessary.

It would depend on Jenson Button.

'When things started to go askew with Jenson,' Brawn says,

'I gave Michael a call. I never thought of pairing him with Jenson because of course we had signed up Nico but I wouldn't offer it to Michael until the situation with Jenson was clear. I didn't think it was fair to either party.

'Michael wanted a little while to think about it. He went off for a few days and during that period *we* had to start thinking about what else we would do because obviously Jenson had made his decision. So we had to look at all the alternatives, which were limited, but fortunately he came back and said "it's worth us exploring this to see if it is feasible." It went from there.'

Brawn remembers how Schumacher moved through a penetrating list of questions about the team, what was happening in it, where it was going and so forth – probing, seeking assurance that it was The Right Thing To do. Brawn was not surprised. He knew this was how Schumacher thought and how he worked. Schumacher also wanted an assurance that Brawn would remain captain of the ship for 'a good while' and required assurance that Brawn wouldn't be gone fishin' again...

Brawn had no need. He was just about to reel in the biggest fish in the whole sea.

Kehm watched and couldn't help seeing 'Michael was reacting' to the Brawn offer and 'there were a lot of things suddenly fitting together.'[2] The fact that the Brawn team won both 2009 championships was one. Mercedes was another, because Schumacher had driven for them in sportscars and that had enabled him to establish his reputation outside Germany. Mercedes took him into Formula 1 with Eddie Jordan in 1991 and, immediately after his debut there, took him to Benetton, where he'd meet Brawn. (As Brawn says, 'you must not forget that Mercedes was his home a long time before he went to Ferrari.')

Rejoining Brawn at Mercedes was a variant on the Barrichello-Rosberg exchange: it seemed to satisfy everyone's needs.

Interestingly, Schumacher had a new three-year contract with Ferrari which, by chance, he had not yet signed...

Did you have any doubts about it?

'No, not really, once he'd made his decision,' Brawn says. 'It was a matter of tying up all the commercial loose ends. That took some time, putting everything in place, but I think once it became clear to me he wanted to do it then it was a question, as I say, of tying all the other things up. And then it was done.'

Because of the Formula 1 testing restrictions Schumacher set off for Jerez to drive a GP2 car, playing himself back in, as it were. Guess what? He was quick…

Time is a curious dimension because – at the end of January, beginning of February 2010 – Mercedes would present Rosberg and Schumacher (and the 2009 Brawn car but now liveried in silver) in Stuttgart, where Mercedes are based, and McLaren would launch their new car in their Woking factory and present Button. Was it only just over a year before that Honda withdrew from F1 and Brawn mounted the buy-out? Was it only a year since the Brawn car, adapted to take the Mercedes engine, had not yet turned a wheel? It seemed very close and very far away all in the same moment. Even by the pace Grand Prix racing sets itself, almost *too much* had been distilled into the year.

Major car launches had over the years grown in size (and ambition) until they came to resemble Hollywood epics: scenery, a great quantity of smoke and fire, dramatic music, pop stars, celebrity hosts and a great quantity of girls. They'd likely have got Charlton Heston in a chariot to unveil the cars if they could.

That had changed however because, wonderfully, the world's most extravagant activity wanted to show it had regained control of its spending. Car launches returned from showbusiness to what they had previously been although, by now, the growth of Formula 1 was being reflected in the number and variety of Media covering it (fans running websites were invited to the McLaren launch, for example, because McLaren felt they were entitled to be there).

Mercedes had, as you might imagine, dark suits dignifying the presentation (even Brawn himself) except for Rosberg and Schumacher who, of course, were encased in silver overalls with Petronas emblazoned across the chest. Schumacher spoke in his own way, hinting at what he hoped the team would achieve and simultaneously guarding against any excesses of optimism. Had it really been *three years* since we'd heard this voice saying exactly these kinds of things just about every weekend?

It was as if the natural order had been restored, courtesy of Ross Brawn's intuition.

The McLaren launch centred on the volcanic possibilities of pairing Hamilton and Button, with a ravenous Media (well, nearly) probing, wondering aloud and watching every twitch of body language. In fact both drivers presented themselves so professionally and gave so little away that Charlton Heston would have been proud of them (and probably couldn't teach them much about competitive chariot racing, either).

Something interesting happened, however. John Button was there, moving in the background and happily chatting to anyone who wanted to. He explained that the day after Jenson won at Sao Paulo they both felt an emptiness because they'd invested so much in getting there. Perhaps it's something common to all first-time champions. They never allow themselves to think about afterwards and, when it comes, don't really know how to cope with it. The sense of anti-climax could be overwhelming.

Maybe at such a time the driver has a gut reaction *I have to move on to the next challenge, I have to re-prove I am the best ... I have to take on Lewis Hamilton at McLaren...*

And then, almost from nowhere, late February had come around already and the teams flew to Barcelona for the 2010 pre-season testing. Was it really only a few days short of a calendar year since Button brought the Brawn out of the garage and twisted it hard right into the pit lane, the circuit beckoning and, all unknowing, a sensation on hand?

This Thursday, Nico Rosberg brought the Mercedes gently, smoothly forward and twisted it right into the pit lane. The 2.8 miles of track beckoned, just as it had for Button. The great adventure had ended or, if you prefer, had begun again in a different way. By Bahrain, the first Grand Prix, the new order would be firmly established. Because testing is a ritual far from the public gaze, the great adventure *really* began again at Bahrain.

Formula 1 is like that, restless, constantly reinventing itself, always on the move to somewhere else. I am not just speaking about the movers and shakers because they are *all* movers and shakers. Under Formula 1's eternal impetus, yesterday is a long time ago and nostalgia is *something we won't do until we're old, if we ever bother to do it at all* – and nobody in Formula 1 is ever going to be old, anyway.

Everything which happened between Monday 9 March 2009, when Button brought the Brawn out, and Sunday, 14 March 2010, when Schumacher and Rosberg brought the Mercedes round to the grid, stands in direct contrast to this. It will provide a rich, enduring seam of memories for each of the several hundred people involved, long before they are old.

What happened wasn't just outrageously improbable, it was wonderful, almost wondrous.

We will never see its like again.

Notes
1. *Motor Sport*
2. Ibid

STATISTICS

The Honda timeline to Brawn

1959 Debut at the Isle of Man TT bike races.

1964 Grand Prix car debut at the Nürburgring.

1965 First Grand Prix win, Mexico.

1968 Withdraw from racing.

1980 Return, supplying engines in Formula 2.

1983 Return to Grand Prix racing, supplying engines to Spirit.

1984–6 Supply engines to Williams.

1987 Supply engines to Williams, Lotus.

1988 Supply engines to Lotus, McLaren.

1989–92 Supply engines to McLaren (and Tyrrell 1991).

2000–5 Supply engines to BAR (and Jordan 2001–2).

2006 Honda buy out BAR/Jenson Button, Rubens Barrichello.
36 races/1 pole (Button, Australia)/1 win (Button, Hungary)/86 points.

2007 Button, Barrichello. 34 races/0 poles/0 wins/6 points.

2008 Button, Barrichello. 36 races/0 poles/0 wins/14 points.

2009   Brawn GP (qualifying in brackets):

29 Mar	Australia	Button (P)	1
		Barrichello (2)	2
		Trulli (Toyota)	3
5 Apr	Malaysia	Button (P)	1
		Heidfeld (BMW)	2
		Glock (Toyota)	3
		Barrichello (9)	5
19 Apr	China	Vettel (Red Bull)	1
		Webber (Red Bull)	2
		Button (5)	3
		Barrichello (4)	4
26 Apr	Bahrain	Button (4)	1
		Vettel	2
		Trulli	3
		Barrichello (6)	5
10 May	Spain	Button (P)	1
		Barrichello (3)	2
		Webber	3
24 May	Monaco	Button (P)	1
		Barrichello (3)	2
		Räikkönen (Ferrari)	3

7 June	Turkey	Button (2)	1
		Webber	2
		Vettel	3
		Barrichello (3)	DNF
21 June	Britain	Vettel	1
		Webber	2
		Barrichello (2)	3
		Button (6)	6
12 July	Germany	Webber	1
		Vettel	2
		Massa (Ferrari)	3
		Button (3)	5
		Barrichello (2)	6
26 July	Hungary	Hamilton (McLaren)	1
		Räikkönen	2
		Webber	3
		Button (8)	7
		Barrichello (12)	10
23 Aug	Europe	Barrichello (3)	1
		Hamilton	2
		Räikkönen	3
		Button (5)	7

30 Aug	Belgium	Räikkönen	1
		Fisichella (Force India)	2
		Vettel	3
		Barrichello (4)	7
		Button (14)	DNF
13 Sept	Italy	Barrichello (5)	1
		Button (6)	2
		Räikkönen	3
27 Sept	Singapore	Hamilton	1
		Glock	2
		Alonso (Renault)	3
		Button (12)	5
		Barrichello (5*)	6
4 Oct	Japan	Vettel	1
		Trulli	2
		Hamilton	3
		Button (10**)	7
		Barrichello (6**)	8
18 Oct	Brazil	Webber	1
		Kubica (BMW)	2
		Hamilton	3
		Button (14)	5
		Barrichello (P)	8

1 Nov	Abu Dhabi	Vettel	1
		Webber	2
		Button (5)	3
		Barrichello (4)	4

(DNF = did not finish)

Constructors' Championship: Brawn 172, Red Bull 153.5,
    McLaren 71, Ferrari 70, Toyota 59.5, BMW 36.
Drivers' Championship: Button 95, Vettel 84, Barrichello 77,
    Webber 69.5, Hamilton 49, Räikkönen 48.

* Dropped five places after gearbox change.
** Originally 5 and 7, dropped five places for not respecting yellow,
gained places when others ahead were dropped five places.

THE WHOLE TEAM

Ordinarily, a list of several hundred names arranged in alphabetical order and containing no further information would rank somewhere below the telephone directory as reading material. In this case, the list is both revealing and evocative.

It demonstrates the depth of commitment Ross Brawn and the other directors took on – the several hundred are breadwinners with, for some, families to feed and, for all, bills to be paid. As Brawn says, it's not something you can just walk away from if you get fed up. Before he took over, he had never faced anything like this in his whole career – nor thought of facing it.

The list also demonstrates quite how many people it takes to run a successful Grand Prix team, and remember, the numbers were some 300 *more* before financial necessity forced cuts.

There's something wonderfully egalitarian and democratic about setting down the list without titles or job specifications. A team is, after all, a chain, and every link is important to the function of the whole.

Here it is:

Adams, Alice

Adcock, David

Allnutt, Peter

Alsworth, Andrew

Andrewartha, John

Armitage, Steven

Armstrong, Nicola

Arnaboldi, Philip

Arnold, Andrew

Arrundale, Dave

Arthur, David

Atterbury, Neil

Aust, Richard

Back, Daniel

Baker, John

Baldry, Neil

Barnes, Martin

Barrichello, Rubens

Barson, Graham

Basford, Dean

Bates, Alan

Bates, Christopher

Baxter, Steven

Beacroft, Andrew

Bearne, Nicole

Beason, Martin

Bebb, Charlie

Beck, Colin

Bendy, Alan

Bennett, Mark

Bennett, Paul

Benton, Tom

Berry, Richard

Betts, Nigel

Bidey, Keith

Bigois, Loic

Binnie, Gary

Blanchard, Bob

Boccacci, Nicholas

Bonnington, Peter

Borgeais, Sebastien

Bosak, Michael

Bosson, Nick

Bowen, Bowen

Brawn, Ross

Bretonnier, Hugues

Britton, Anthony

Broadhurst, Chris

Brooker, Warwick

Broomfield, Adam

Brown, Christopher

Brown, Nick

Brown, Robert

Brown, Simon

Bruce, Richard

Buckley, John

Bull, Christopher

Burr, Dale

Burton, Darren

Button, Jenson

Campbell, David

Campbell, Shay

Candler, Clive

Carlisle, Neil

Carter, Robert

Cartlidge, Patrick

Cawley, Brendan

Chalk, David

Chambers, Andrew

Chant, Robert

Chapman, Martin

Charlesworth, James

Cherrill, Mark

Childs, Mark

Clark, Steven

Clarke, Geoffrey

Clarke, Julian

Clatworthy, Ian

Clear, Jock

Clifton, Brian

Cobley, Adam

Cole, Simon

Collett, Steven

Collins, Peter

Conconi, Lucia

Cooke, Ric

Cooley, Russell

Coombs, Roger

Cooper, Daniel

Cooper, Edward

Cooper, Nicholas

Cooper, Phillip

Corbett, Daniel

Corson, Matthew

Cotterill, Stephen

Cotton, Andrew

Court, Trevor

Cousins, Paul

Coysh, Peter

Cranidge, Darran

Davidson, John

Davies, Anthony

Davies, Christopher

Davies, Mark

Davies, Steve

Davis, Douglas

Davis, Luke

Deacon, Peter

Deane, Matthew

Diamant, Henrik

Dickens, John

Diederichs, Valerie

Digman, Nick

Divey, Nathan

Dixon, Adam

Dixon, Peter

Dixon, Tarquin

Doddemeade, Peter

Donovan, Marc

Duc Tiep, Tran

Dumbleton, Louise

Dunford, Russell

Eagles, Richard

Eccles, Jonathan

Edmonds, Lee

Edmonds, Michael

Edmonds, Vincent

Edwards, Christopher

Edwards, Richard

Edwards, Steven

Eldred, Phillip

Elliott, Duncan

England, Neil

Ewin, Michael

Fairey, Jason

Fanson, Karl

Fanthorpe, Thomas

Farren, David

Fasulo, Giuseppe

Featherstone, Stuart

Felix, Paul

Fenemore, Joanne

Field, Paul

Flannery, Mark

Flannigan, Peter

Fleming, Bruce

Fletcher, Christian

Fletcher, Graham

Foote, Gary

Forbes, Jim

Ford, Martin

Ford, Peter

Frith, Steven

Frost, Gary

Fry, Chris

Fry, Nick

Fuller, Michael

Furness, Mark

Gagliardi, Lucy

Galvao, Charles

Garrood, Barnaby

Geekie, Fergus

Gilmore, Mark

Gluyas, Ian

Goff, Will

Goodall, Scott

Gosling, Mark

Grace, Steven

Grace, Stuart

Graham, Joanne

Grant, Dominic

Green, Christopher

Green, Melvin

Green, Richard

Green, Steven

Griffiths. Nathan

Grist, Nigel

Grundy, Ian

Guilfoy, Mark

Gutteridge, Sean

Hale, David
Haley, Nick
Hall, Nathan
Hands, David
Hanna, David
Hanson, Benjamin
Hare, Timothy
Harris, Brian
Harris, Craig
Harris, Matthew
Harris, Paul
Harrison, Jonathan
Harrison, Mark
Harrison, Philip
Harriss, Anthony
Harte, Alex
Harvey, Aden
Hawthorn, David
Hayhurst-France, David
Haynes, Paul
Hazell, Denise
Hennessey, Christopher
Herbert, Derek
Herman, Daniel
Heslop, Mark
Hewitt, Mark
Hibon, Bastien
Hicks, Kevin
Hill, Christopher
Hillier, John

Hilton, David
Hinchcliffe, Shaun
Hodgkinson, Peter
Hodgson, Paul
Hodgson, Stewart
Holbem, Craig
Holder, Tony
Holland, Mark
Holyoak, Chris
Hopkinson, David,
Horn, Michael
Hough, David
Howe, David
Humphrey, Paul
Hunt, Lee
Ingle, John
Ives, Andrew
James, Barry
James, Jamie
Janes, Michael
Jarman, Clare
Jeffrey, David
Johnson, Neal
Johnson, Victoria
Johnstone, Paul
Jones, Heather
Jones, Ian
Jones, Lewis
Jones, Mark
Keen, Simon

Kelly, Rebecca

Kemp, Martin

Kennard, Stephen

Kerr, Nigel

Kerwood, Danny

Kew, Jason

Kilby, Richard

King, Peter

Koren, Peter

Largue, James

Lawson, Mark

Le Fleming, Ralph

Leathcrland, Ben

Leatherland, Daniel

Lee, Jason

Lee, John

Lemmon, James

Lettis, Christopher

Lewis, Nathan

Lockett, James

Long, Stuart

Loosley, Stephen

Macaskill, Ian

Macconnachie, Robin

Macdonald, Marc

Mackenzie, Katherine

Mallock, Ben

Marques, Sergio

Marr, Simon

Marsden, John

Martin, John

Martin, Steven

Martinet, Francois

Mayers, Dean

Maynard, Christopher

McCabe, Andrew

McCracken, Martin

McGee, Michael

McGrory, Caroline

McIlvar, Craig

McLaughlin, Mark

McWilliams, Richard

Meadows, Ron

Melvin, Arron

Middleton, Chris

Middleton, Jon

Middleton, Paul

Millar, Graham

Miller, Graham

Minshull, Samantha

Mitchell, Steven

Miyakawa, Victor

Moody, Andrew

Moore, Kevin

Moreton, Lee

Morgan, Stuart

Morris, Michael

Morris, Nigel

Morse, Stephen

Moulin, Caroline

Muir, Andrew

Muir, Lorraine

Murray, Stuart

Musconi, Riccardo

Myers, Colin

Neal, Mark

Needham, Leon

Nelson, David

Newman, Jonathan

Newman, Paul

Nicholson, Mark

Noon, Scott

Norris, Nicholas

O'Brien, Sam

O'Connor-Boyd, Roger

O'Hare, Ronan

Orton, Simon

Osborne, Mark

Owen, John

Oxley, Alistair

Oxley, Mark

Page, Brett

Pain, Jonothan

Pamphlett, Tim

Papagni, Giuseppe

Parker, Garry

Parker, Mel

Pasanen, Sakari

Pearse, Steven

Perrott, David

Perry, David

Pett, Stuart

Pezzack, Paul

Phillips, Paul

Piddington, Brian

Poelijoe, Owen

Pople, Martin

Poppy, Daniel

Potts, Richard

Prangnell, John

Price, Christopher

Priest, Peter

Prince, Ian

Prinsep, Emma

Prinsep, Ian

Pryce, Graeme

Purslow, Andrew

Purves, Andrew

Rapson, Greg

Read, Gareth

Reeve, Gayle

Rehling, Mark

Reid, Alan

Reilly, Andrew

Richards, Kathryn

Rickatson, David

Rickatson, Michael

Roberts, Michael

Roberts, Tina

Robertson, Scott

Rose, Samantha

Rosling, Mark

Runnacles, Stephen

Rush, Ian

Rush, Kevin

Russell, Marc

Russell, Paul

Sadlet, Jonathan

Sales, Mark

Sanders, Martin

Sanders, Richard

Sargent, Micky

Savage, Gary

Scott, David

Shariff, Irfan

Shepherd, Mark

Short, Evan

Shovlin, Andrew

Shufflebottom, Daniel

Simpson, Scott

Sims, Paul

Sinclair, Matthew

Slator, Martin

Smith, Dominic

Smith, Keith

Smith Paul

Smith, Richard

South, Richard

Southam, David

Spiers, Michael

Spina, Thomas

Starr, Mick

Stokes, Sean

Storry, Matthew

Strudwick, Daniel

Summerhill, Lara

Swain-Fossey, Russell

Takeuchi, Seiichi

Tate Stephen

Thomas, Alex

Thomas, Guy

Thorne, Kevin

Tickner, Mark

Townsend, Mark

Tunnicliffe, Lisa

Turner, Derrick

Turner, Martin

Turner, Stephen

Tynan, Steven

Venables, Dudley

Vowles, James

Waddell, James

Walkling, Colin

Waller, Jason

Walshe, Max

Walton, Tony

Warren, Paul

Wasyliw, Matthew

Wasyliw, Terry

Watson, Ian

Way, Ashley

Webb, Gareth

Webb, Justin

Western, Paul

Weston, Alistair

Westwood, Stephen

Wheeler, Robert

Whitmore, Carl

Wilby, Mick

Wilkin, Matthew

Wilkinson, Lawrence

Williams, Andrew

Williams, Chris

Williams, Graeme

Williams, James

Williams, Julie

Williams, Paul

Williams, Simon

Wilson, Craig

Witham, David

Wood, Jonathan

Woodford, Martin

Wright, Ian

Yates, Mark

Yeowart, Robert

Young, Les

Zanre, Dina

Zerihan, Jonathan

INDEX

McGrory, Carolyn 15, 23
McLachlan, Laura 140
McLaren 6, 12, 14-16, 24, 26, 34,
40-42, 53, 62, 69-71, 73, 76, 106,
112, 117, 119, 126, 130, 132, 137,
142, 157, 174, 177, 184, 192, 199,
206-207, 216, 219, 223-224, 229,
232-234, 239, 242, 246, 248, 250,
255, 261, 264, 267, 270-271, 276,
278, 285, 287, 293, 296, 300-300,
304-305, 309-310
McLaren, Bruce 7, 112
Meadows, Ron 82
Melbourne (Albert Park) 14, 76, 114,
120, 121, 125-126, 131, 132, 138, 206
Mercedes-Benz 8, 17-18, 24-25, 51,
55, 74, 118, 138, 218, 300-301,
304-305, 308-311
C291 50
Mercedes-Benz High Performance
Engines 137, 199, 205-206, 294, 299
Mexico City 56
Michibata, Jessica 98, 199
Minardi 82-83, 106
Model Cars magazine 31, *164*
Monaco 69, 192, 279
Monaco Grand Prix 192, 197, 244;
1997 103; 2005 91; 2008 124;
2009 *170*, 192-193, 195, 197-198,
199, 207
Montermini, Andrea 98
Montoya, Juan Pablo 95, 112
Monza 14, 40, 51-52, 55, 123-124,
160, *174*, 242, 256, 258, 260,
262-263, 265, 267
Mosley, Max 56, 209-210, 217-218
Moss, Stirling 31, 112, *172*
Mugello 114
Musconi, Ricardo 83

Nakajima, Kazuki 117, 119-120, 133,
143, 154, 186, 200, 204, 211-214,
221, 236, 237-238, 269, 276, 280,
285, 287-288
Needell, Tiff 36
Neerpasch, Jochen 55
Newey, Adrian 41, 61, 230
Nielsen, John 48, 52

Nissan 48
Noble, Jonathan 110
Nürburgring 55, 108, 219, 232, 240

Oatley, Neil 28, 37, 39-42
Oliver, Jackie 41-42, 44-45, 127
Oshima, Hiroshi 13, 24
Owen, John 81-82, 122

Pacific Grand Prix 1994 100
Palmer, Jonathan 110
Pantano, Giorgio 83
Peterson, Ronnie 112
Petronas 301
Peugeot 46, 48, 51
905 50
Piquet, Nelson Jr 116-117, 120, 183,
204, 221, 265-266, 272
Pironi, Didier 36
Pollock, Craig 10
Porsche 44-45, 48, 74
Portimão 114
Portuguese Grand Prix 1997 102
Prodrive 18
Prost, Alain 44, 116, 217, 231,
272, 303

Race tactics and strategy 10, 28-29,
49, 57-58, 63-64, 69-70, 73-74, 86,
183-184, 187-190, 191-192,
202-203, 223-224, 227,
228-229, 234, 250, 254,
258, 276, 283-284, 297
Räikkönen, Kimi 76, 112-114,
116-120, 133, 141, 143-144, 146,
148, 151, 157, 160, *171*, 181,
186-187, 194-197, 201, 214,
216-217, 221, 225-227, 231, 233,
236, 246-247, 252, 254-255,
256-260, 264-265, 271, 274,
276-277, 278, 283, 286-287,
291-293, 297
Ratzenberger, Roland 100
Reading Grammar School 32
Reading slot car club 32
Red Bull 76, 113, 117, 122, 132, 136,
149, 156, 160, *170-171*, 184, 192,
199, 202, 206, 210-211, 213, 216,